Consumption and Public Life

Series Editors: **Frank Trentmann** and **Richard Wilk**

Titles include:

Mark Bevir and Frank Trentmann (*editors*)
GOVERNANCE, CITIZENS AND CONSUMERS
Agency and Resistance in Contemporary Politics

Daniel Thomas Cook (*editor*)
LIVED EXPERIENCES OF PUBLIC CONSUMPTION
Encounters with Value *in* Marketplaces on Five Continents

Nick Couldry, Sonia Livingstone and Tim Markham
MEDIA CONSUMPTION AND PUBLIC ENGAGEMENT
Beyond the Presumption of Attention

Forthcoming:

Jacqueline Botterill
CONSUMER CULTURE AND PERSONAL FINANCE
Money Goes to Market

Roberta Sassatelli
FITNESS CULTURE
Gyms and the Commercialisation of Discipline and Fun

Consumption and Public Life
Series Standing Order ISBN 1-4039-9983-X Hardback 1-4039-9984-8 Paperback
(*outside North America only*)

You can receive future titles in this series as they are published by placing a standing order. Please contact your bookseller or, in case of difficulty, write to us at the address below with your name and address, the title of the series and the ISBN quoted above.

Customer Services Department, Macmillan Distribution Ltd, Houndmills, Basingstoke, Hampshire RG21 6XS, England

Also by Daniel Thomas Cook

THE COMMODIFICATION OF CHILDHOOD: The Children's Clothing Industry and the Rise of the Child Consumer

SYMBOLIC CHILDHOOD

Lived Experiences of Public Consumption

Encounters with Value *in* Marketplaces on Five Continents

Edited by

Daniel Thomas Cook
Rutgers University

160201

First published 2008 by
PALGRAVE MACMILLAN
Houndmills, Basingstoke, Hampshire RG21 6XS and
175 Fifth Avenue, New York, N.Y. 10010
Companies and representatives throughout the world

PALGRAVE MACMILLAN is the global academic imprint of the Palgrave Macmillan division of St. Martin's Press, LLC and of Palgrave Macmillan Ltd. Macmillan® is a registered trademark in the United States, United Kingdom and other countries. Palgrave is a registered trademark in the European Union and other countries.

ISBN-13: 978–0–230–51704–2   hardback
ISBN-10: 0–230–51704–8   hardback

This book is printed on paper suitable for recycling and made from fully managed and sustained forest sources. Logging, pulping and manufacturing processes are expected to conform to the environmental regulations of the country of origin.

A catalogue record for this book is available from the British Library.

Library of Congress Cataloging-in-Publication Data

Lived experiences of public consumption : encounters with value in
   marketplaces on five continents / edited by Daniel Thomas Cook.
      p. cm. — (Consumption and public life)
   Includes bibliographical references and index.
   ISBN 0–230–51704–8 (alk. paper)
   1. Markets—Social aspects. 2. Consumers—Social aspects. 3.
   Consumption (Economics)—Social aspects. I. Cook, Daniel Thomas,
   1961–
   HF5470.L58 2007
   306.3—dc22

                                                          2007051164

10   9   8   7   6   5   4   3   2   1
17   16   15   14   13   12   11   10   09   08

Printed and bound in Great Britain by
CPI Antony Rowe, Chippenham and Eastbourne

For my buddy, Gene Michaud (1946–2005). We are all only memories anyway.

Contents

List of Figures

Acknowledgements

I am thankful for the various kinds of support given by Frank Trentmann and Stefanie Nixon of the ESRC Cultures of Consumption Programme, Birkeck College, University College of London, where I was in residence as a Visiting Fellow for a part of this project.

Notes on Contributors

About the editor

Daniel Thomas Cook is Associate Professor of Childhood Studies and Sociology at Rutgers University, Camden, New Jersey, USA. He is editor of *Symbolic Childhood* (2002) and author of *The Commodification of Childhood* (2004) as well as a number of articles and book chapters on consumer society, childhood, leisure and urban culture.

About the contributors

Jonathan Shapiro Anjaria is a doctoral candidate in Anthropology at the University of California, Santa Cruz, USA working on conflicts over open space and visions for the future of Mumbai. His essays on street vending and urban reconfiguration have appeared in *Space and Culture* and *Economic and Political Weekly*.

Anette Baldauf, University of Applied Arts Vienna, Austria. Studied at the University of Vienna educational theory and at the New School University in New York sociology and urban studies. Her research focuses on postindustrial city formations, urban de- and re-territorialization processes, everyday life, feminism and social movements. Her book publications include *Lips. Tits. Hits. Power? Feminismus und Popkultur* (with Katharina Weingartner), *Der Gruen Effekt* (with Dorit Margreiter) and *Entertainment City. Unterhaltungsindustrie und Stadtentwicklung* (forthcoming). In addition, her work involves the continuous cooperation with artists in visual art projects, radio features and video documentaries. She lives in New York and Vienna.

Keith Brown is a doctoral candidate in sociology at the University of Pennsylvania, USA. His dissertation looks at how meanings and moral boundaries are constructed through consumption and is tentatively entitled 'Altruistic Consumption: Fair Trade and Consumer Identity.' His research areas include consumption, culture, work in the service economy, and identity formation.

Winnifred R. Brown-Glaude is currently a Research Analyst at the Institute for Women's Leadership, Rutgers University, New Jersey, USA. She is directing a national study that examines ways in which faculty members in institutions of higher learning are confronting racial and gender inequities on their campuses. Her chapter in this volume forms part of her forthcoming book, *Dis/orderly Women: Bodies, Public Space and Women's Informal Work in Jamaica,* that examines the lived experiences of Jamaican higglers in the informal economy of Kingston.

YuLing Chen serves as a faculty member at National Taiwan College of Physical Education, Taiwan. She received her PhD in Leisure Studies from University of Illinois at Urbana-Champaign. Her dissertation 'A Choice among No choice: Exploring Taiwanese Mother's Agency and Identity along the Blurred Boundaries between Leisure, Work, and Consumption' traces emerging discourses on mothers' everyday lives. She is currently pursuing research on women's agency in leisure and variations in the style and meanings of leisure in an urban setting.

Jenny Huberman is Assistant Professor at the University of Missouri, Kansas City, USA and has published papers on children and consumption in *Childhood* and *Biblio: A Review of Books.* Currently, she is working on a book entitled, 'Ambivalent Encounters: Tourists and Children in Banaras.'

Kim Humphery is Associate Professor of History and Social Theory in the School of Global Studies, Social Science & Planning at RMIT University in Melbourne, Australia and has a long-standing interest in the history, theorization and politics of consumption. In his most recent work Kim is exploring the nature of Western materialism and the renewed politics of overconsumption based on concerns about the social, personal and environmental costs of global commodity capitalism. He is currently working on a book exploring the politics and theory of anti-consumerism (a project funded by the Australian Research Council). Among his previous publications is *Shelf Life: Supermarkets and the Changing Cultures of Consumption,* (1998).

Jan Phillips is a community and educational activist in Maine, and holds an MA in sociology from Brown University and a faculty appointment in social and behavioral sciences at the University of Southern Maine/Lewiston-Auburn College, USA. Her scholarship has focused on issues of family consumption and on constructions of place and placelessness. She chairs a regional education initiative, College for ME – Androscoggin, and teaches courses in family, childhood, place, and consumption.

Giovanni Semi is Assistant Professor in Sociology of Culture at the Dept. of Social and Political Studies, University of Milan, Italy. His areas of interest include ethnographic methods, migrations in West-European cities and the sociology of culture and has published research on urban commercial markets. He is currently working on a book about the history and the making of the field of urban ethnography.

Joel Stillerman is Associate Professor of Sociology and Coordinator of Latin American Studies at Grand Valley State University, USA. His research focuses on labor politics, consumer culture, and urban development in Chile as well as transnational labor activism in North America. His recent articles appear in *City and Community, Qualitative Sociology,* and *Journal of Consumer Culture.*

Frederick F. Wherry received his PhD in Sociology from Princeton University and is currently an Assistant Professor at the University of Michigan at Ann Arbor, USA. His publications have appeared in *The Annals of the Academy of Political and Social Science, Ethnic and Racial Studies,* the *Journal of Consumer Culture* and the *International Review of Sociology.* His writings on authenticity are based on his book *'Global Markets and Local Crafts: Thailand and Costa Rica Compared'* (forthcoming).

Introduction: Dramaturgies of Value in Market Places

Daniel Thomas Cook

Rutgers University

A context

The contemporary dominance of global capitalism rests strongly on the continued ideological vigor of a particular notion of 'the market' as much as it does on the availability of capital, the efficiency of distribution systems and the exploitation of labor. In prevailing conceptions, as many point out, 'the market' arises as a kind of supra-intelligence, even a kind of a deity (Frank 2000), that is said to effectively arrange social and economic life according to an unbending, and ultimately unerring, calculus of value – an idea clearly descendent from Adam Smith (Carrier 1997; Slater and Tonkiss 2001). In its present day manifestation, the neoclassical ideology of the market informs a neoliberal politics that exhorts, in ways that Smith never intended, the absolute right-of-way for commerce to shun governmental regulation or public oversight (Comaroff and Comaroff 2000).

Scholars like Ferdinand Toennies (2001) and Karl Polanyi (1957) in the own ways have grappled with explicating the extent to which economic life and action are antagonistic to notions of civic and social life or whether they can be accommodated to one another (see Bevir and Trentmann 2004; Harris 2004). The view of social–civil life as economic in origin and temperament rests upon the assumption of the existence of an extremely individualized, unencumbered, freely choosing person (usually imagined as a male) who engages in exchange based upon the impulse of self interest. If left unfettered, his actions furthermore are supposed to combine with others' to produce benefits for all (England 1993, 2003; Carrier 1997).

The economic perspective on markets and exchange leaves no space wherein culture, meaning, sentiment and everyday practice can be

1

brought to bear on the study of social life (Zelizer 2005; Hochschild 1993). It is an inherited, conceptual legacy organizing much of the discussion about markets and market society. As Don Slater (2002) notes: 'The division between economic and social-cultural analysis constitutes a kind of deep structure in modern, Western thought' (p. 59). Cultural analysis, he continues, is formed around the idea that culture and economy are macro entities 'operating as externalities' to one another, rather than integrated with one another (p. 59). Indeed, it is common to encounter research that sets up clear divisions between 'culture' and 'economy' or between 'cultural studies' and 'political economy,' often affirming them in the process of arguing for their transcendence (see Miller 2006).

The works comprising *Lived Experiences of Public Consumption* reject such categorical distinctions and dichotomies from the outset in favor of engaging closely with the materiality and sociality of marketplaces – i.e. of public exchanges spatially situated. Eschewing predetermined and overdetermined conceptions of 'the market' in the abstract, the contributors take as points of departure the experiences, practices and embodiments in and of public sites of consumption. They situate themselves and their work in commercial marketplaces – on the streets and in the plazas, grocery stores, coffee shops and malls of five continents – offering the kind of rich description and analysis enabled by ethnographic and interpretive forms of inquiry. In so doing, the authors demonstrate a shared conviction that something irreducible occurs in the public, face-to-face encounters of buyers and sellers, of observers and participants, in the terrestrial market, be it a Borders bookstore, a mall, shop or a flea market. This conviction centers on the idea that whatever overarching dynamics of power, meaning and identity inform markets and consumption – be they global structures of capital or deep structures of thought about economic action – these arise and are made manifest in some discernible, observable manner as people go about their daily rounds of living.

It is widely accepted that since antiquity, the 'market' has continued to be separated from 'place' (Bahktin 1984; Agnew 1986; Zukin 1991; Slater and Tonkiss 2001). Indeed, it may be said that the ability to separate buyers, sellers and products from each other and to abstract the exchange process from any particular place, as in stock and commodity markets, has provided classical and neoclassical economics the foundation upon which to build the powerful figure of rational economic man whose disposition is thought to be above the frenzy. With the rise of internet shopping and electronic trading, it would appear that much of face-to-face market interaction would be on the wane, doomed perhaps.

Yet, it is evident that in the era of globalized business, place continues to matter, for instance, in the conditions of production (Salzinger 2003; Klein 1999), in the power and spatial significance of 'global cities' (Sassen 2001) and, as well, in social interactions among traders (Knorr-Cetina and Bruegger 2002; Zaloom 2006). Closer in form to the studies in this volume, Elizabeth Chin's (2001) ethnography of poor, African-American children in New Haven Connecticut in the 1990s demonstrates how the exigencies of place inform the meaning of goods and of social relations differently in relation to their experiences shopping at neighborhood stores and at shopping malls.

With the terrestrial market as a starting point, the chapters of *Lived Experiences* in their own ways reaffirm the significance of place in economic life. Each project focuses in some manner on the emplaced practices[1] which constitute the content, boundaries and meanings of various commercial activities under scrutiny. In so doing, none leads us down the fruitless avenue of inquiry of attempting to demarcate where the 'market' ends and 'society' or 'culture' begin. We are instead taken through the places and encounters of buyers and sellers and end up with insights that would otherwise remain obscured by the cloudy overcast of categorical assumptions about actors' motivations and dispositions.

By staying 'in place' – conceptually as well as physically – and attending to the contexts of the transactions, the contributors are also careful to avoid ignoring or marginalizing the 'economic,' calculative dimensions of the exchange situations. It would do no good to replace a one-sided economism with an equally myopic culturalism. Indeed, it is the tensions pertaining to the commingling of economic exchange value with other values like sentiment, love, care and belonging that animate the descriptive and analytical approaches the authors bring to bear on the treatment of their subjects. Throughout the various contributions that comprise *Lived Experiences*, the point is made with intimate detail that, in market/commercial contexts, economic value never stands alone on its own without being accompanied by and enfolded into exquisite human specificity.

The contents

A number of recurrent themes are imperfectly threaded throughout different chapters and different aspects of chapters – a discontinuity that speaks as much to the variety of ethno-geographical contexts of the studies as it does to the emergent novelty of many of the authors' formulations. Frederick Wherry's research in a Thai handicrafts market calls into question and confounds simple formulations of 'market action.' In relating how he 'got played' in the drama of market performances, Wherry forefronts the staging of back stages and the way consumers, sellers and the researcher sought, for their own reasons, to establish the authenticity of the crafts.

We encounter other forms of play in and about marketplaces. Joel Stillerman sees the humor among vendors and shoppers in Santiago, Chile's street markets as way of conducting 'relational work' which both furthers the strategic goals of each side pertaining to sales and deepens longstanding affective ties. In contrast, flea markets exemplify what he calls a different genre of shopping experience where the focus tends to be on the thrill of the hunt and the search for bargains and the relational work pertaining more among shoppers than between them and vendors.

The varied pleasures of shopping that Stillerman highlights take on a different hue in Jenny Huberman's study of tourists in Banaras, India. She questions what constitutes the 'object of consumption' for Western tourists who become interested in meeting, knowing and being with the young, unlicensed tour guides and peddlers on the city's waterfront. Huberman's response points to an interesting correspondence between some of Jean Baudrillard's early work and the views of the tourists themselves who are trying to stave off what they see as the alienating, dehumanizing aspects of global capitalism, even as they actively seek to partake in some of what it offers.

YuLing Chen provides us with nuanced portraits of Taiwanese mothers' personal agency as they juggle and struggle with the competing demands between employment and child/husband care. Chen poignantly illustrates that much of the 'pleasure' of shopping for these women rarely corresponds to the typical image of indulgence, except perhaps when weekend shopping at a department stores seems like a visit to a 'magical' place. It is rather a matter of ingenious necessity for them to forge something for themselves – some time or space – in the interstices of their daily rounds.

Shopping in American grocery stores, as Jan Phillips demonstrates, can be understood as a way that mothers and children together produce and reproduce family. Reminiscent of Daniel Miller's (1998) ruminations about shopping, Phillips takes the point further to argue and show that it is the notion of 'family' itself which is 'accomplished' in the relational work underlying the seemingly trivial decision of, for example, whether or not to buy certain cookies. Consumption here clearly stands for something other than purchases or pleasures as the boundaries between home, mothering and the marketplace become blurred in practice.

The play, pleasure, agency and relational work of consumers in these varied contexts stands in notable contrast to the lived experiences of Afro-Jamaican higglers studied by Winnifred Brown-Glaude. Brown-Glaude's treatment of the transient existence of these female micro-entrepreneurs exposes the social–moral organization of public space in the city of Kingston as a battle not only for physical space in which sell their wares, but a fight for discursive definitions of legitimacy. The informal, 'non-legitimate' status of their selling practices, we learn, functions as a surface condition whereby their darker, larger female bodies serve as signs both of their 'social pollution' and as instruments of their resistance to the legitimate, 'uptown' business owners and to their portrayals in the press.

Higglers' bodies and presence transgress and thereby outline the distinctions between 'legitimate' and 'illegitimate' markets in the streets of Kingston. Giovanni Semi takes us into a different kind of transgression and 'illegitimacy' occurring within and beside the officially sanctioned market of Porta Palazzo in Turin, Italy. Through the eyes and experiences of unlicensed Moroccan vendors, Semi tunes us into the varied cadences of social market life as day turns into night and how the boundaries between legitimate/legal and illegitimate/illegal are negotiated among vendors, and between vendors, patrons and the police. Through instances of aggressive, verbal sexual play with female shoppers by vendors, their joking relationship with the researcher and among themselves, we come to understand the blending of particular kinds of cultural practice in, with and sometimes in spite of the market-exchange relationships and contexts.

In privileging lived experiences, *Lived Experiences* provides vivid detail and example of how – to rephrase Geertz (1973) on culture – there are only market places, not the Marketplace. It is a point that holds beyond single-sited studies or single city marketplaces and extends into the register of global relations. Kim Humphrey examines the 'public discourse of unease' in Australia with regard to the ever-expanding presence of what he calls the 'global shop' – retail establishments that have a significant presence in many countries. He takes us through the anxieties expressed by business owners and others about the 'colonizing' and 'Americanizing' of Australian public culture by Borders and Starbucks specifically, both of which have struggled to thrive in Australia. Humphrey suggests that examining this unease as a politics of both engagement and distancing – of using and rejecting these places – will open the way to conceptualizing 'globalization' as a complex process bound up an 'embodied sense of how place should be constituted and experienced.'

Keith Brown's study of fair trade practices in and about Philadelphia handicraft stores and coffee shops provides yet another way to grapple with global issues while remaining tethered in some way to the terrestrial market context. He offers insightful description and analysis of how fair trade entrepreneurs frame the products, stores and their endeavors generally to customers largely unaware of the efforts and politics behind fair trade. Arising out of observations, interviews and his own experience working in some of these establishments, Brown outlines and gives depth to a number of tensions fair traders encounter as they seek to remain solvent in the environment of competitive capitalism.

Global tensions and interactions arise in the juxtaposition of 'the mall,' 'Bazaar' and 'the street' from Jonathan Shapiro Anjaria's fieldwork in Mumbai, India. Anjaria shows that, contrary to what many assume, the space of the mall does not overtake the less rationalized and less organized street market or Bazaar. He finds that shoppers seek different things from each place – spectacle, open space and air-conditioned comfort in the mall, personal and sometimes longstanding ties in the street, and bargains at the Bazaar. For Anjaria, we would do better to make close, embedded examinations of market places in order to ascertain how customers understand and make use of the different, non-market features each offers instead if assuming uniform effects of an overarching structure.

Anette Baldauf offers the case of Muslim women shopping in Dubai as a way to investigate multiple articulations of commercial space. She sought to understand how the She Zone, a women's-only shopping establishment, failed while a large, gender-integrated mall flourished. Juxtaposing popular media accounts which often present Orientalist interpretations of Muslim women's identities with the activities and words of the women themselves, Baldauf finds that the mall 'allows visitors to go on temporary excursions to imaginary elsewheres, where urban qualities like diversity and integration are simulated and concepts like femininity and masculinity, local and global, are negotiated.' It is this quality of consumer space, she argues which builds a particular kind of gender topography in the context of that global city.

A note on the dramaturgy of value

Varied in their intensity, intimacy, tone and tenor, the contributions which together make up *Lived Experiences of Public Consumption* each trace their own trajectory through transactions and social relations to arrive at a similar point – namely, the significance of place in the encounter with value. It is, on one level, unsurprising that place and value would be found to be closely connected given that the investigations started with this notion in mind. What we learn here, also, is how value and place inform each other with and through the embodied practices of those who inhabit and animate market spaces.

Emplaced value is embodied value. The abstract economic Value posed by the economist or theorized by Marx when discussing commodities cannot be established in, by, for or of itself. It must be located by way of identifying persons who occupy specific positions and sport specific identities *vis-à-vis* others. In market places, to encounter value is to encounter and interact with things and with others – to smell and feel the goods, to observe those others milling about buying, looking, selling, dickering, joking – that is, be in public. Seen in this way, the division between culture and economy has no force of distinction at the level of practice because value – that inescapable element of anything commercial – is *performed* in its realization. When people engage in face-to-face behavior, as Goffman (1959, 1967, 1979) demonstrated long ago, they engage in ritual performance. That is, they adopt postures and representations of typified identities. In market places and market-like situations, these postures and representations refer always in some way to exchangeable values and exchange relations.

How exchanges are conducted in markets are as relevant to the 'value' of something as what is being bought and sold. The back stages of handicraft markets, mother–child negotiations in grocery aisles, the dance between police, drug dealers and mint traders in Turin and the soft, delicate sell of the fair trade entrepreneur – these enact various dramaturgies of value. The tie between market and theatre has a strong current in Western thought (Agnew 1986). It is made material in this volume by the ways in which many of the authors integrate, and sometimes favor, the experiences and practices of the sellers in addition to the 'consumers.' 'Shopping' is not simply an activity made by shoppers on their own (cf. Miller 1998; Miller *et al.* 1998; Zukin 2003), but a co-production involving sellers, buyers as well as the setting. The stage is inseparable from the meaning and interpretation of the performance

Directed at different audiences for different purposes, these performances nevertheless demonstrate or propose how the goods and thus the social relationships are to be regarded. Stillerman and Anjaria each describe what can be thought of as a performative differentiation of market behavior given the genre of shopping – flea market, street market, Bazaar or mall – wherein different emphases on different kinds of value are signaled by allowable and expected behavior in each place. Chen's mothers also perform the value of goods and place in highly public and nuanced ways, i.e. alternatively for their children, husbands and for themselves depending on the time of day, day of week and type of establishment. Controlled and contrived spaces like global shops in Australia and malls in Dubai offer different dimensions of performativity as they brand and constrain certain kinds of practices while encouraging others.

Taken individually and together, the chapters in *Lived Experiences* show, in multiple ways, that the thrust of human effort is not myopically centered on rejecting or evading monetary calculation in favor of only particularistic, personal, or social worth, as if these are exclusive of one another. Rather, the close look that these projects give us of the practices in and of public, terrestrial, commercial market places highlight how emphasizing one kind of value over another can accomplish many social ends. They can serve as a maneuver in an overall game, an attempt to make sense out of a situation or a way to make connections between and distinctions from others. We see, for instance, how tourists in Banaras seek to counter the impersonality of the commodity relation by trading with and for the personalities of their performative guides, while Kingston's higglers would welcome being seen and treated in more general, less particularistic ways rather than simply as poor, dark, female sellers.

Lived Experiences drives home the point that there is no one market and no one kind of market behavior or motivation. Market behavior – i.e. behavior in public market places – does not seek simply to fend off the pull of commodification with highly singularized meanings, as Kopytoff (1986) has insightfully theorized. It is rather about *engaging with* the tensions and challenges posed by the inescapable presence of pecuniary valuation in market contexts. There is always a calculative dimension when exchange is at issue; but there is never only calculation. The deeply interesting and finely detailed performances of value presented in this volume illustrate not simply an impetus toward realizing vernacular value, but toward vernacular valuation. In market places, it is the active, mutual valuation of goods wherein people perform, propose and test relationships – relationships which may be fleeting, recurring or the most permanent imaginable.

Note

1. On the notion of emplacement of goods and consumption, see Sherry (1998).

References

Agnew, J. (1986) *Worlds Apart: The Market and Theatre in Anglo-American Thought.* Cambridge: Cambridge University Press.

Bahktin, M. (1984) *Rabelais and His World.* Bloomington: Indiana University Press.

Bevir, M. and Trentmann, F. (2004) 'Markets in Historical contexts: Ideas, Practices and Governance,' pp. 1–24 in *Markets in Historical Contexts.* Mark Bevir and Frank Trentmann (eds). Cambridge: Cambridge University Press.

Carrier, M. (1997) *Meanings of the Market.* Oxford: Berg.

Chin, E. (2001) *Purchasing Power.* Minneapolis: University of Minnesota Press.

Comaroff, J. and Comaroff, J. L. (2000) 'Millennial Capitalism: First Thoughts on a Second Coming,' *Public Culture* 12:2 (Spring): 291–342.

England, P. (1993) '"The Separative Self": Andocentric Bias in Neoclassical Assumptions", in M. A. Ferber and J. A. Nelson (eds), *Beyond Economic Man: Feminist Theory and Economics.* Cambridge, MA: Harvard University Press.

—— (2003) 'Separative and Soluable Selves; Dichotomous Thinking in Economics,' pp. 33–59 in *Feminist Economics Today.* Marianne A. Ferber and Julie A. Nelson (eds). Chicago: University of Chicago Press.

Frank, T. (2000) *One Market Under God: Extreme Capitalism, Market Populism, and the Economic Democracy.* New York: Doubleday.

Geertz, C. (1973) *The Interpretation of Cultures.* New York: Basic Books.

Goffman, E. (1959) *The Presentation of Self in Everyday Life.* Doubleday: New York.

—— (1967) *Interaction Ritual.* New York: Pantheon.

—— (1979) *Gender Advertisements.* New York: Harper.

Harris, J. (2004) 'Toennies on "Community" and "Civil Society": Clarifying Some Cross-currents in post-Marxian political Thought', pp. 129–44 in *Markets in Historical Contexts.* Mark Bevir and Frank Trentmann (eds). Cambridge: Cambridge University Press.

Hochschild, A. (2003) *The Commercialization of Intimate Life.* Berkeley: University of California Press.

Klein, N. (1999) *No Logo.* New York: Picador.

Knorr-Cetina, K. and Bruegger, U. (2002) 'Traders' Engagement with Markets A Postsocial Relationship,' *Theory, Culture & Society,* Vol. 19, No. 5–6, 161–85.

Kopytoff, I. (1986) 'The Cultural Biography of Things: Commoditization as Process,' pp. 63–91 in *The Social Life of Things,* Arjun Appadurai (ed.). Cambridge: Cambridge University Press.

Miller, D. (1998) *A Theory of Shopping.* Ithaca, NY: Cornell University Press.

Miller, D., Jackson, P., Thrift, N., Holbrook, B. and Rowlands, M. (1998) *Shopping, Place and Identity.* London: Routledge.

Miller, L. (2006) *Reluctant Capitalists.* Chicago: University of Chicago Press.

Polanyi, K. (1957) *The Great Transformation.* Boston: Beacon.

Salzinger, L. (2003) *Genders in Production: Making Workers in Mexico's Global Factories.* Berkeley: University of California Press.

Sassen, S. (2001). *The Global City.* Princeton: Princeton University Press.

Sherry, J. (1998) 'The Soul of the Company Store: Nike Town Chicago and the Emplaced Brandscape,' in *Servicescapes,* John Sherry (ed.). Chicago: American Marketing Association.

Slater, D. (2002) 'Capturing Markets from the Economists,' in *Cultural Economy*, Paul du Gay and Michael Pryke (eds). London: Sage.

Slater, D. and Tonkiss, F. (2001) *Market Society*. London: Polity Press.

Toennies, F. (1887 [2001]). *Community and Civil Society*, J. Harris (ed.). Cambridge: Cambridge University Press.

Zaloom, C. (2006) *Out of the Pits: Traders and Technology from Chicago to London*. Chicago: University of Chicago Press.

Zelizer, V. (2005) *The Purchase of Intimacy*. Princeton: Princeton University Press.

Zukin, S. (1991) *Landscapes of Power*. Berkeley: University of California Press.

Zukin, S. (2003) *Point of Purchase*. NY: Routledge.

Part I
Playing In and With Market Places

1

The Play of Authenticity in Thai Handicraft Markets

Frederick F. Wherry
University of Michigan

In village handicraft markets, the play is the thing wherein you'll catch the conscience of consumption. The play itself teases the (potential) buyer in the multiple meanings that play suggests – a gay distraction, a past-time without consequences, a representation of the absent, a plot in the service of greed or envy. Through amusement, ritual, or trickery, handicraft markets are spaces of performance – enacted dramas staged, blocked, and riddled with props. Is the play of authenticity the mere amusement one feels by walking into a colorful place where one can see the carver carve, the painter paint, and 'authentic' cultural traditions be born-again? Is the shopper carefree, behaving playfully from one moment to the next in the midst of a shopping experience that has more to do with what one experiences than what one can 'rationally' assess about the qualities of the objects for sale? Regardless of the seller's intentions or the irony of the outcomes, the buyer may participate in the market performance in order to be entertained, taught, or in some other way entangled. The nature of these entanglements is the subject of my investigation. Rather than exhaust the possibilities of play in a handicraft market, I will examine how I got played, and saw others in play in northern Thailand.

Disconnected lives

To get played is to get marked as a gullible individual or as an individual so full of self-confidence or of racial guilt (for exploiting brown people abroad and at home) that one believes what 'ethnic' people say about the economic and social values of their handicrafts (e.g., Causey 2003). Dean MacCannell argues that the capacity of the individual to get played grows with modernity's rise because the fragmentation and alienation so

prevalent in Western societies compels its inhabitants to seek the imme-
diacy and presence of an authentic (shorthand for unspoiled, original,
and tradition-bound) other. Played out in his or her own society, the individual revels in whatever staged deceptions might bring him or her back
in touch with a less fragmented, more pristine existence, but these deceptions do so through contrast: the old contrasts with the new; the dirty
with the sanitized clean; the dark with the white. Ironically, authenticity
takes on the quality of an unmediated experience, yet by virtue of being
marked by official guidebooks and of being put on sale in the marketplace, the experience is greatly mediated while simultaneously cloaked
in mystery.

The mysteries of the experience generate the economic value of the
product. There is much that the seller knows that the buyer does not,
and vice versa. Therefore, as the buyer bewares deception and tries to
distance her or himself enough from the experience in order to evaluate its worth, the buyer's market experience becomes disconnected
from whatever is 'real' so that the buyer can evaluate, on the one hand,
what the objects are worth in monetary terms and, on the other hand,
whether there is any artistic. Disconnected from the historical baggage
that might influence one's behavior, the buyer pretends that the price is
too high or the quality too low; the seller, that mistakes are intentional,
that there is something special about the handicraft that defies simple
cost-calculations, or that the price is as low as the seller can go. The difference in information held by the buyer versus the seller (information
asymmetry) creates opportunities for deceit – opportunities that would
have been pursued no matter the historical record. The seller does not
know how much the buyer is willing to pay for the object, and the
buyer does not know how much it cost the artisan to produce the object.
Authenticity being what it may, buyers and sellers are trying to gain as
much as they possible can in the market.

More importantly, in a market where authenticity matters a great deal
to the buyer, the price represents the object's authenticity. The fact
that the seller and producer of the crafts undertake a number of unob-
servable actions without the buyer's knowledge means that the seller
can fool the buyer with ease. Children dressed in ethnic hill-tribe garb
might be non-ethnics in drag. Reportedly hand-crafted objects might
be non-traditionally (or worse, mass-) produced. The buyer interested in
purchasing objects that represent some authentic, singular culture might
well be duped. Disoriented by the moral hazard arising from information asymmetry, the buyer cannot rely on the price as a signal of object's
inherent value. To complicate matters further, the buyer cannot question

outright the motives of the seller without the buyer her/himself appearing as insensitive or, worse, racist. This psychic cost to the buyer of disengaging the seller sends the buyer into the negotiation with her/his eyes wide shut – looking, not looking, her or his life seemingly disconnected from the social complications that entrain the buyer into the negotiation ritual and that restrict how the buyer behaves in the course of the ritual. This psychic costs spill over from other relationships, histories and shared understandings seemingly disconnected from the negotiation at hand. For the most part, standard economic assessments of these markets do not take these other relationships, histories, and understandings fully into account when accounting for the public consumption of cultural commodities.

In the market for cultural commodities, economic theory imputes, the buyer cannot assess the quality of the commodities without great difficulty. In the absence of information asymmetry, one would infer that two handicraft objects of the same size but priced differently necessarily belong to different quality classes. Out-of-the-ordinary prices put the buyer on alert. What would motivate a seller to sell an object for much less than similar objects on the market? The potential buyer might imagine several motivations for the seller: (1) the object is of lower quality; (2) the seller is ignorant of the object's value; (3) the seller wants to undercut her/his competitors; or (4) the seller does not depend on the profits from selling these objects and does so for non-economic reasons (as a personal hobby or a charity for the poor). Likewise, the potential buyer might imagine a number of reasons why an object would be sold for a price much higher than average: (1) the object is of higher quality; or (2) the seller knows that the buyer is ignorant of the object's value and wagers that the buyer will equate high price with high quality (Akerlof 1970; Dawar and Parker 1994; Kennedy 1994; Milewicz and Herbig 1996; Riley 2001; Stiglitz 1987).

Firmly believing that high price equals high quality can make it so (Akerlof 1970; Stiglitz 1987). If the buyer is willing to pay more for an object, the buyer signals to the producer that more care needs to be taken in producing the object relative to the other objects being produced. In time, the lack of attention the producer–seller gives to producing lower-priced goods and the more attention given to higher-priced goods bring the actual quality levels in line with the beliefs expressed through the price (Akerlof 1970). Buyers and sellers respond rationally to their interpretation of the price. The congruency between price and quality initially disintegrates in this example based on the buyer or seller's misunderstanding. Over time, however, the individual's behavior responds to the pricing signal and brings price back in line with quality. There is an essential value in the object that the price expresses. Misunderstandings lead to short-term price–quality deviations that longer term engagements between buyers and sellers will remedy. In this view, the play of authenticity in handicraft markets is merely manipulation through artifice, wiles, and dramaturgical skill meant to dupe foreign tourists into paying exorbitant prices for un-extraordinary things (or to inflate the economic value of extraordinary qualities).

Connected lives

How actors manipulate their authenticity for commercial gain depends on a host of other actors outside of the immediate play. David Grazian (2004) pinpoints the various actors who help to identify, attract, and mollify the (sometimes) ignorant attendees at blues clubs in Chicago. The structure of the blues industry robs the blues musicians of their autonomy because the club owners decide what the musicians perform and who among the musicians may perform it. A blues band whose repertoire has too many less-well-known songs and whose membership has too many white people will not find a sympathetic ear among club owners. Moreover, the musicians become alienated from their craft as they play 'the set list from hell.' Grazian's analysis builds on Erving Gofman's insights into the dramaturgical staging of social identities and MacCannell's (1976) notion of staged authenticity by articulating the roles that various actors play in the careful enactment of their social identities, but Grazian (2003) also recognizes that non-commercial orientations remain relevant for goals recognized and the strategies deployed in the service of these goals. In other words, the lives of these 'commercial' musicians are intimately connected to a sense of community and to a differentiated set of personal relationships (Zelizer 2005b).

I will emphasize how the objectives of staging authenticity are not connected solely to a profit motive disconnected from persons, their relationships, and their emotions. Instead, I recognize authenticity as an emergent characteristic of persons, places, and things that one feels in the act of shopping:

> [I challenge] the traditional concept of a singular authenticity, characterized by purity, bound by tradition, marking a particular time and place (Postrel 2003: 110–23). In the age of global markets, the authentic object has become differentiated by the circumstances of production and exchange as well as by the initial understandings

that guide the interactions and by those understandings that emerge between the producer and the object, the producer and the primary sellers, and the object and the final consumer. (Wherry 2006: 6)

In contrast to the discussion of staged authenticity found in MacCannell (1976), I will argue that the staging of authenticity is not a denial of the real thing. Moreover, not all artisans are actively engaged in deception, and some artisans privilege the integrity of their craft over the profitability of their creations. The way that the buyers and the sellers' lives remain connected to persons, institutions, and sentiments (seemingly) foreign to the market place informs the course of maneuver within the market. The hybridity and the ambiguities brought about by internationally mobile actors, institutions, and ideas may either firm up the 'set list from hell' or create opportunities for resisting modifying it.

To understand the ambiguities of play in the context of Thai handicrafts, I focus on how market actors involve themselves in what Michel Callon *et al.* call 'hybrid forums' (2002). Handicraft markets are forums because the buying and selling occurs in a space meant for public meetings as well as for other economic, social, and political exchanges. The markets are hybrid in that the actors and institutions involved originate from different species and sources: Tour buses from different parts of the country unload tourists from different parts of Thailand and different parts of the world into a market square where the Thai Tourism Authority and the police as well as vendors, packing and shipping businesses, peoples' homes, their children, their pets, stray pets, exotic fruit, the smell of spice, the flash of shiny cloth, the knock-knock of carved wood, the not-so-subtle interviews conducted by people from the International Labor Organization (ILO) and other supra-national organizations as well as sociologists, anthropologists, economists, demographers, and journalists. The hybridity in the types of people and institutions gathered is matched by the diversity of the issues that emerge from participating in the market (Callon *et al.* 2002: 195): Is the object somehow authentic, or is the object kitsch; the experience, a lie? Is the buyer promoting local economic development and cultural preservation or economic exploitation and cultural emasculation? Is consumption a positive social force in the lives of these artisans and their community or does the history of exploitation repeat itself in miniature?

These questions bear upon the activities in the marketplace, where 'all the world's a stage' different social scripts are featured. Charles Smith's study of auctions highlight the various scripts for strategic play in marketplaces, emphasizing the hodgepodge of instrumentally ratio-nal, affective, and conventional logics that shape the course of bids made and taken. No single logic dominates the public negotiations. Instead, '[H]uman behavior...[in the auction setting is] contextual ... [It] reflect[s] and constrain[s] ... social expectations, [and is] governed more by expressive aims than instrumental tasks ... [It is] more emotional than rational, and more interactive than self-directed' (Smith 1989: 108). The actors conceive of themselves as thespians, engaged in a drama (Goff-man 1959). Unlike a fully scripted play, however, the thespians carry partial scripts onto the stage and improvise the rest.

These scripts cross different spaces to generate what Viviana Zelizer calls 'connected lives.' What happens in one set of social relationships may spill over into what is happening in another set of seemingly non-social (business) transactions. Zelizer reminds us that the hybridity and differentiation, emphasized by Michel Callon, are part and parcel of the market experience and proposes that social analysts chart a course between the structures of play, the meaningful relationships among the players, and the meanings of play for the individuals caught up in differ-ent types of exchange. In their acts of buying and selling (among other things), Zelizer writes:

> ... people create connected lives by differentiating their multiple social ties from each other, marking boundaries between those dif-ferent ties by means of everyday practices, and sustaining those ties through joint activities ... but constantly negotiating the exact content of important social ties. (Zelizer 2005b: 32)

A handicraft seller may differentiate her/his customers by those given a back-stage tour (or not) as well as by other acts of feigned or sincere intimacy. In the hours when the sellers are selling and the buyers are not looking to buy, both buyers and sellers are constantly swapping sto-ries among themselves and between one another. In these stories, they make sense of how important or trivial different products and relation-ships are. Buyers and sellers engage in other practices as well that mark the boundaries of their social ties as well as the ease with which authen-ticity requires their trespass. For example, in their display of handicraft objects for sale, vendors may arrange the objects in the shop that rep-resent the vendor's relationships with socially significant others: some of the objects come from family members, neighbors, good friends, or friends-of-friends; others, from the vendor her/himself. If the buyer asks about the characteristics or the cost of an object, the vendor may allude to or emphasize the social relationships that resulted in the object's production and its distribution to this site of sale. At times, the person(s) evoked can be seen, spoken to, touched, or in some other way made real. The buyer then purchases a story, a direct experience, and an object that has use value, exchange value, and most importantly symbolic value.

The setting

This chapter investigates the construction of symbolic value (authenticity) through public consumption in handicraft markets in northern Thailand. The Kingdom of Thailand occupies the middle of mainland southeast Asia. Along its western border is Myanmar (Burma), to its north and northeast is the People's Republic of Laos, to its eastern border Cambodia, and to the south Malaysia. The population totals 60.7 million in 1997 and has a life expectancy of 69 years. 'Thailand' means 'land of the free,' and its people like to distinguish themselves from their neighbors saying that they have never been colonized. The 'freedom' signified by the name refers to a non-event (colonization). The official language is Thai, and the official religion is Buddhism. In the agricultural sector Thailand exports rice, cassava, and tin. In the manufacturing sector, it exports clothing, canned goods, and electrical circuits. Thailand's GDP was US$121.9 billion in 1999.

Nestled in the north of Thailand, Chiang Mai province covers 20,107.057 square kilometers and has a population of 1.6 million inhabitants (in 2000). Agricultural areas cover nearly 13 per cent of the land and residential areas 4.4 per cent. The remaining land is mountainous, with peaks reaching 500 feet above sea level. Chiang Mai city, the provincial capital, is known as the city of craftsmanship and is famous for its Night Bazaar where local handicrafts are sold. The city covers 166 square kilometers, has 260,000 residents (in 2000), and is surrounded by villages specializing in handicrafts. There have been nearly 1.3 million foreign visitors to Chiang Mai in 1999. Most foreign visitors are tourists interested in the low-priced handicrafts and the custom furnishings to be found there. International tourism has served as the starting point for many Thai handicraft enterprises.

The people of Chiang Mai boast a distinguished cultural tradition dating as far back as the Lanna Kingdom. The Lanna Kingdom, where 'Lanna' means 'land of a million rice fields,' was founded in the late 13th century by King Mengri, and was once the center of power in northern Thailand as well as part of present day Myanmar and Laos. Chiang Mai was the center of the Lanna Kingdom and came under the control of central Thailand in the late 18th century. Known for its woodcarvings and its teak forests, Chiang Mai is the handicraft center of Thailand.

Among the artisans and buyers I encountered in Chiang Mai, there was much talk of authenticity. In 2002 I spent five months in Chiang Mai interviewing artisans in their workshops and observing them producing their goods and selling them in the marketplace. Artisans would describe themselves proudly as 'real' crafts persons possessing local knowledge, and buyers would go in search of real ones (indigenous artisans) making real things. In the vignettes that follow, the question of realness remains as the subtext of the interaction. There is a mood of authenticity, an elusive sense of concrete realness. As buyers get taken on backstage rounds to see works-in-progress, the buyer might feel brought closer towards the core of a community ritual. This approach towards the core elicits an intense feeling that there is something authentic either about the artisan or the goods for sale.

Putting on the play

Staging a work-in-progress

Artisans who present themselves, their crafts, and their producers *in the raw* give the buyer a sense that he or she is observing a work-in-progress. The improvised presentation comes with its interruptions; misplaced props slow down the pace of maneuver; but the seller does invite the seller for a tour 'behind the scenes,' because however improvised the show is, it nonetheless must go on. The work-in-progress becomes a totalizing market experience, each moment stitched into a motley quilt of memories and rationalizations. About this quilt-like manner whereby individuals account for their actions, Robert Wuthnow writes:

> Rags have been used before, although quite often for a different purpose than the one to which they are about to be put. They are still usable as cloth, and this property renders them more useful for some purposes than for others. To make something elaborate such as a quilt, we . . . have to piece together our projects by using a variety of rags. (Wuthnow 1996: 95–6)

Not from making the rags uniform to ease comparison but from making a grab bag of misfit bits and pieces does the buyer stitch together an account of what is being sold, how sincere the seller is, how sincere the artisans are, and how much the buyer should be willing to pay for the object and for the experience of (now) buying and (later) displaying it.

The Thawai village handicraft market offers an excellent space for buyers to walk into a performance *in medias res*. I recall walking down the main street of the village market along the canal, with two wooden platforms astride the canal on which groups of three women sit cross-legged putting finishing touches on bowls and wooden figurines using small tools (a skinny paint brush, a small brush, a small etching nail). On both sides of the canal, I notice the variety of activities going on as they would have with or without me present. Artisans are talking about food, television programs, the foreigner passing by: 'Look, he's so black!' They assume that I can't understand what they are saying, and for now, it is better so.

I slow my step before an open-front shop. A man in his 30s peers at the details of a small wood panel, flicks etchings onto a fold of the wood, blows from parted lips to remove the debris and to get a better look. He seems to be 'caught up' in performing his own work, and I am carried along with him as I hesitantly step toward him for a closer look. 'Hello,' he begins, in English spoken as if it too were a tonal language, the 'O' arched upward in pitch before careening down. He introduced himself as Mr Nui, mispronounced my name as Fresh, until reminded of Fred Flintstone, and he offered the usual inquiries: where-are-you-from, are-you-on-holiday, can-you-eat-spicy-food, you-like-the-Thai-people, do-you-have-a-girlfriend? Mr Nui did not talk immediately about his carving and about the crafts in his shop. Remarkable to me as a potential buyer, Mr Nui did not try to rope me into buying his crafts because of their cultural significance but tried instead to impress the personal investment he had in each piece.

His shop is a place of personal memories. Not only does he contrast how long it takes (over a month for that one over there) to carve some of these objects but he also talks of his physical travails: He squints as he etches marks with a scalpel into the wood. He was hurt in a car accident, he tells me, so has to avoid heavy lifting and sticks to carving small objects. He offers me a glass of water and insists that I find comfort in the shade of his shop, for he has more stories to tell. His brother painted the water color on the wall, he tells me. His cousin, who lives in the Isarn region, painted the oil beside the water color. Because his cousin studied design at the university, Mr Nui states, the quality of the design is superior that that one might find among the village artisans who paint similar pictures. Most of what he has to sell are woodcarvings, made by his uncles (Fieldnotes, 31 July 2002).

Mr Nui then entangles me further in his personal narrative by demonstrating his love for traditional Thai folk songs. He unhooks one of the three small, wooden guitars from his wall display, informs me that the guitars are hand carved, and proceeds to demonstrate the usefulness of the also-beautiful. As he plucks the strings, he beckons me to stroke the wood, to feel the taunt line, to flick it with my fingernail. 'You could learn how to play. I could help you.' I express interest in learning to play and in buying the guitar. I also begin to transform myself into a researcher: 'I'm here to shop but I'm also here to start my research project.' Those are not my exact words, but that was my general sentiment, expressed in Thai, which delighted Mr Nui. 'Good. You speak Thai. Good. But do you speak the northern dialect?' Before I could express my interest in learning it, he offered, 'I can teach you. This will be fun.' Without missing a beat, he returned to the subject of selling. 'You don't have to buy the guitar today. I'll see you around. And if you come back tomorrow, I can show you something. This woman is coming to buy some of these instruments. You will want to be here for that, and I can introduce her to my new American friend.' Before I could leave him that day, he insisted on giving me a gift – a wooden coaster with a silver inlay of an elephant in the forest. 'I carved it myself.' Mr Nui reminded me that Thais love their fun (*sanuk sanaan*) and implied that so long as I was willing to go on an occasional drinking spree (*bpai thiaw*), I could ask whatever I liked (Field notes, 31 July 2002).

Backstage rounds

I returned at 9:30 the next morning to begin the backstage rounds. In contrast to seeing the work-in-progress, I left my role as a member of the audience and became an informal inspector of the stage props, producers, stage hands, and of the stage itself. I was being invited to meet his uncle, cousins, and friends who were situated nearby but out of sight. Mr Nui and I spent nearly two hours on the rounds. First he took me to the neighboring shop that his older sister manages. In the back of the shop, she was painting and applying black resin to a pot. To her left nearly out of sight was an old man carving a mystical animal into a piece of wood about three and a half feet long. He was in no hurry, because the work required great care to detail, but he could not lose too much time because the patience of the customer is not, he realizes, unlimited. Mr Nui and I walked away from his uncle into a slightly wooded area, where we found a small workstation: a rectangular board nailed to trees to create a roof, no walls, wooden planks assembled into benches, and enough space on the dirt floor for four men to sit comfortably. A calendar with a topless Thai woman and an old television and cassette player were set against a pole where an electrical outlet offered the only source of electricity. In the center of the workstation, there was a guy carving. Along the benches, three men watched, another was in a hammock resting, and another was lying flat on his back along a bench, sleeping. The guy carving was working on the face of a Buddha. Beside his foot was a glossy picture from a magazine of the Buddha face designed in the Sukhothai style, with the Buddha's hair represented by symmetric rows of small knots. There were several rough hewn pieces of wood with the outlines of a head, lying about the floor, waiting to be transformed into the faces of Buddha.

Our inspection done and introductory remarks made, Mr Nui and I jumped a small ravine and approached a house. At home in his kitchen, a man sat on the floor working on a flat piece of wood. It was probably five feet long and two and a half feet wide. He was carving a face into it – another Buddha! He used one tool to carve the motif along marks already made by a black magic marker with more subtle marks made in pencil for the artistic etch. We left him after a few minutes for another outdoor shop nearby where a man was carving scenes from Thai folklore onto a large panel of wood. Overwhelmed by how similar and different all the scenes were, I breathed a sigh of relief when Mr Nui asked me if I was hungry.

Over lunch and over the course of the next five months, I learned that backstage rounds were not uncommon, especially for buyers expected to purchase in bulk. The village adventure was expected by those who had seen it all. The rounds reconfirmed their interest in the lives of the artisans and the ongoing integrity of the performance: the diligence of artisans supervised only by no one; the use of electricity for entertainment rather than production; the integration of craft work into the rhythms of the household; all these elements became part of the object's identity.

After lunch, on our way back to the shop, we found three Thai women waiting at Mr Nui's shop, wanting to buy the types of instrument that I had almost purchased the previous day. Their requirements were more specific than mine, and Mr Nui didn't have exactly what they needed, so he asked for their patience as he initiated several phone calls. Within ten minutes, he reached for my mobile phone, asking only, 'No problem, right?' Within two phone calls, he had located the instrument (or rather, he had confirmed a meeting). We all piled into Ms Oi's car and traveled less than ten minutes to a nearby village. We walked down a narrow lane of tall shrubs that opened onto a small yard and a tall house. On the side of the house was a cottage containing the artisan's workshop. Inside, there were several large power tools and four men in the shop. In the anteroom, an older gentleman and a teenage boy sat as the older man tuned a traditional Thai instrument similar to a guitar. The women selected her instrument from those assembled by the feet of the man. Looking down on the scene from the wall was a photograph of the Thai princess (I do not recall which one) with the older gentleman. Outside of the photograph, that same older gentleman sat in still life, not bothered by what the women wanted or needed. The tableaux shifted: He blew into what looked to be a recorder as the teenage boy plucked a traditional folk song on the copper-colored strings of the instrument the woman soon selected.

I was witnessing a play-within-a-play: We the buyers were treated as if we were invisible non-persons – there, but not there as was the status of Clifford Geertz and his wife upon entering a Balinese village (Geertz 1973). Life at this site of production moved on, unencumbered by the preoccupation of attending to bewildered guests. From the social organization of work, I could interpret the meanings of age, sex, experience, and talent in this artisan's community. The old man and the young boy embodied the inter-generational transfer of cultural practices. The men remain close to their wood and their tools; the women find themselves in the showroom to sell, but few women are seen in these traditional sites of production. The women do not carve large pieces of wood; instead, they paint and they perform intricate etchings to finish products. This gendered and generational division of labor harkens a time thought to be obsolete in a 'gender-blind' economy. The men I encountered at this site seemed disinterested in the commercial transactions underway, and the photograph of the Thai princess (a verification of the artisan's authenticity and status) certified the disinterested stance of the artisan as real. The multiple issues evoked by the play-within-the-play deserve mention: How does Mr Nui know them? Did the actors alter what they were doing in any way after receiving Mr Nui's phone call to alert them to our approach? What story would Ms Oi and her friends tell about their experience of searching for and selecting the instrument? Would she focus on the 'realness' of her experience backstage, or would she talk about her concerns for the quality of the craftsmanship? Because she is purchasing a traditional musical instrument, I assume that she wants to make sure that the production process for the instrument is traditional enough (a component of authenticity) that it will serve its intended purpose. I did not ask Ms Oi these questions, in part, because I did not want to intrude on the purchase or sway how she might frame the interaction. What I observed was the creation of a mood of reverence that differed from the mood that I felt while in the marketplace. Perhaps I was the only person on site feeling the mood. This is a question that I cannot answer, but I seriously doubt that I had been that thoroughly duped. I had been on enough backstage rounds and felt enough variations of reverence for the work and the space of work that this particular episode emerged from my notes as a significant demonstration of how the mood of authenticity gets played.

Playing up authenticity by not playing it up

There are more subtle ways to play authenticity; rather than play up one's authenticity, the artisan may choose not to play it up, and in doing so, the artisan highlights her/his own authenticity. Nopphadohl, the woodcarver in the Thawai village, was satisfied that he could make a living by carving Thai pastoral scenes. When he was not carving pastoral scenes to be hung on the wall, he was meeting the requests of local Thai temples for wooden doors composed of carved lotus flowers in relief, the entangled stems nearly indistinguishable from one another, their mesh constituting the door's surface. These were the local traditions that generated work and pride for the talented. The thought of turning his artwork into work appropriated by Europeans, Americans, or any other outsiders, triggered an automatic response: No, thank you.

The German fellow who had come to give Nopphadol the chance to 'go global' was not accustomed to such refusals. The German had traveled throughout Asia to identify and purchase high-quality, authentic handicrafts. En route to Bali, he stopped in Chiang Mai, a region well known for the craft villages scattered across its territory. Like many others before him, the German searched for only those villages with a reputation for having authentic artisans. The village found, the most talented artisans could then be identified. The more Nopphadol refused to prospects of making great profits, the more confident the German became that Nopphadol was 'a real one' (Wherry 2006).

Not Nopphadol's position (in the right place at the right time) but his disposition toward the commercial market presents the greatest puzzle. Ironically, Nopphadol's refusal to go global and his sincere reticence seems to have been exactly what the German sought. Not money, not fame, but caution and sincerity blocked the deal. The artisan wanted to protect a socially valued tradition and seemed savvy enough to understand how messy and duplicitous commercial relationships could be in the modern world too caught up in its getting and spending (Wuthnow 1996; Zelizer 2005a). Here was an artisan who would not lay waste his local traditions nor cheapen them for sale. In the local environment, the artisan found all he needed (materials, hand-made equipment and tools, consumers, civic pride and regional fame). The German did not doubt that Nopphadol was an authentic local artisan worthy of pursuit, but

Nopphadol's refusal clinched the deal. He now hosts his own website selling his carvings and conducts workshops on woodcarving attended by international tourists and woodcarving enthusiasts. Well respected at home and abroad, this humble man has reaped the profits of global markets by being seen as not wanting to play up his authenticity for commercial gain.[1]

Awkward play

My interaction with one entrepreneur highlights how awkward playing up authenticity can be. While attending the Small and Medium Enterprise Day Fair at Chiang Mai University, I encountered Mark Narongsak of King's Collection. Mark speaks English fluently and is well read. As we discussed the items on display at his booth, one of his managers handed me a business card. I noticed right away that 'Collection' of 'King's Collection' is missing the 'c' just in front of the 't.'

> 'What's missing?' Mark asked, pointing to his associate's card.
> With unease, I responded, 'C.'

His lips broaden into a smile. Strange, I thought, he seems pleased that there is a misspelling on the business card and that I noticed it right away. Before I could conjure a cultural explanation about how the smile might be his way of concealing embarrassment, he flipped the card over to reveal a bold message: 'The C that is lost is *Culture.*' I became immediately aware of and uncomfortable with the assumptions I had made in an instant. Had I, a politically liberal and multi-cultural omnivore, taken a patronizing attitude toward Mark? Had I seen him as an 'equal,' I would have lost no time in telling him that there was a minor mistake on his business card. As soon as he flipped over the card, my mood changed. I felt immediately relieved that I had been played a fool in the service of a good cause. (With too much reflection, I feared the return of my patronizing attitude and ignored it. After all, I the joke was on me.) Mark continued his explanation which I remembered especially well because it coincided with a moment of personal discomfort. He reminded me that the lost C of authentic culture alluded to the forgotten history of the Lanna Kingdom which Mark hoped to revive by playing up local traditions under the Lanna brand name (Thailand, interview with author, 12 October 2002). By disarming the potential buyer through staging an awkward situation, Mark had created a hybrid forum for the exploration of several non-commercial concerns. He had, in short, connected other concerns in my life with my current market interaction.

The awkward and smooth social interactions are responsible for the creation of markets. It is well known among economic sociologists that markets do not create sociability; instead, sociability creates markets (Abolafia 1996; Callon 1998; Smith 1989). In order for financial transactions to obtain, the buyer and seller feign some kind of intimacy in order to begin the transaction. This intimacy, however affected, depends on the practices and understandings well known in other areas of social life (e.g. Bandelj 2002). Georg Simmel likens economic transactions to romantic exchanges:

> Competition compels the wooer who has a co-wooer, and often in this way alone comes to be a wooer properly speaking, to go out to the wooed, come close to him, establish ties with him, find his strengths and weaknesses and adjust to them, find all bridges, or cast new ones, which might connect the competitor's own being and doing with his. (Simmel 1955: 61)

Buyers and sellers do not necessarily learn to intuit the predilections of their customers as a result of market participation but rather as a spillover from their participation in intimate (non-economic) relationships (Zelizer 2005b). Sellers must learn how to sell their products within different expectation sets for behavior. Participation in a whole range of social institutions provides individuals with the tacit knowledge they need for understanding these expectation sets. Often, these expectations are breached, highlighting the tacit knowledge required to engage successfully in market transactions.

One entrepreneur laments how his salespeople do not anticipate the scripts that western customers expect performed. For example, a potential buyer entered the informant's shop and asked the salesperson how much a small lacquer-ware box, with four by six inch dimensions, would cost. The salesperson quoted the price which exceeded the customer's expectations. The customer expected that the box would be a third of the quoted price, and indeed, there were other boxes with the same diameters available in the shop for the expected price, unbeknownst to the customer. The salesperson failed to explain that the expensive box was real lacquer-ware made in the Japanese style whereas the cheap boxes that one usually finds is made with a simple finish and is of lower quality. The salesperson also failed to inform a buyer why one bed (made of teak) was twice the price of another bed (made of plywood). The expectations for who would ask what questions were being breached on both sides of the interaction (Thailand, interview with author, 21 September 2002).

The informant had to intervene in both situations and set the inter-action back on course. This informant has studied and worked in the United States. His experience working in a mall helped him to learn how one plays the game of engaging one's customers. He also learned the importance of timing: when customers would expect what and in what manner they would find acceptable for its delivery. There are rules of hos-pitality, even in a shop or a showroom. Customers wait for cues before asking more detailed questions about how something was made and how much an object costs. If the seller forgets to deliver a cue, or if a cue prop-erly delivered is missed by the buyer, the transaction risks being aborted. With all this in mind, the informant has considered hiring a westerner who has a 'feel' for the game to work in his salesroom. In the meantime, he continues to explain to his salespeople that western customers have expectations about what they will be asked and told and what the timing of these questions and answers should be. The sales people need to have a 'feel' for the customer's expectations. 'The feel' is the hardest thing to teach and is reinforced by institutions and practices outside of the train-ing room. When asked if 'the feel' for the transaction might simply be the lack of English proficiency, the informant objected. His main sales people do speak English and speak it quite well. Lacking international experi-ence abroad, they also lack 'the feel.' They miss the meaning between the lines that may not be consciously recognized by either partici-pants in the transaction but that may nonetheless guide their behaviors. Following her own mental map, the sales person finds herself at a differ-ent topical destination than her potential buyer. The sales person cannot play (deceive) the buyer having already played (confused) herself; the plan for deception seems to have failed to cross her mind. The sales per-son under consideration lacks the tacit knowledge of how such games are played, and in the context of the formal show room, this play of sim-plicity does not play up the economic value of authenticity. Instead, the sales person's simplicity (though 'real') plays down the legitimacy of the show room as a place for high-end display and higher-end purchases.

Conclusion

Authenticity comes into play in diverse contexts in this chapter. One sees authentic cultural practices in the raw during visits to the sites of active production. It feels as if one has been given a backstage tour in the middle of an onstage performance. The realness of the tour mani-fests itself in the stories bandied among the artisans, their families, and their friends as well as the feel that one gets, ever so briefly and ever more intensely, for the game. The games are played 'deep' and 'shallow' (Geertz 1973), with the former associated with tradition and status but the latter associated with making an economic profit, by histrionic hook or stealth crook. Likewise, the fact that one inhabits a 'live' market where no single thing happens without reference to, ignorance of, or regard for something else means that the marketplace accommodates hybrid forums and simultaneous 'deep plays' along with 'shallow plays' in close proximity.

It would be a mistake to treat the public consumption of handicrafts as a purely economic act perpetrated by people whose social lives are disconnected from their market practices. The multiple relationships held by producers, sellers, and buyers come to the fore. The back stories reveal themselves in snippets of conversation and in the way that the actors themselves mediate otherwise straightforward business transactions. The connected lives that the actors weave explain the variations in why some things are crafted and by whom as well as what gets sold (and for how much) versus what remains not-for-sale. Flat accounts of cost-benefit calculations obfuscate the meaningful social actions that take place in the market, the differentiation of transactions according to these worked out meanings, and the ongoing negotiations for each individual's place within such dense webs of social affiliations as those found in the market for authentic handicrafts. The play among these relationships, the negotiation among threads already spun and the spinning of new ties, help us better understand the life of the market and the importance of public consumption within it.

Note

1. The author is indebted to Amornrat Wattanatorn, a PhD candidate in the faculty of education at Chulalonghorn University (Bangkok, Thailand), for providing the transcript of her interview with Nopphadol. The interview was conducted on 19 November 2002. Any errors of interpretation are entirely my own.

References

Abolafia, Mitchell Y. 1996. *Making Markets: Opportunism and Restraint on Wall Street.* Cambridge, MA: Harvard University Press.

Akerlof, George A. 1970. 'The market for "lemons": Quality uncertainty and market mechanism.' *Quarterly Journal of Economics* 84: 488–500.

Bandelj, N. 2002. 'Embedded economies: Social relations as determinants of foreign direct investment in Central and Eastern Europe.' *Social Forces* 81: 411–4.

Callon, Michel. 1998. 'The embeddedness of economic markets in economics.' pp. 1–57 in *The Laws of the Market*, edited by M. Callon. Malden, MA: Blackwell.

Callon, Michel, Cécile Méadel, and Vololona Rabeharisoa 2002. 'The economy of qualities.' *Economy and Society* 31: 194–217.

Causey, Andrew 2003. *Hard Bargaining in Sumatra: Western Travelers and Toba Bataks in the Marketplace of Souvenirs*. Honolulu: University of Hawaii Press.

Dawar, Niraj and Philip Parker. 1994. 'Marketing universals: Consumers' use of brand name, price, physical appearance, and retailer reputation as signals of product quality.' *Journal of Marketing* 58: 81–95.

Geertz, Clifford 1973. *The Interpretation of Cultures*. New York: Basic.

Goffman, Erving 1959. *The Presentation of Self in Everyday Life*. Garden City, NY: Doubleday.

Grazian, David 2003. *Blue Chicago: The Search for Authenticity in Urban Blues Clubs*. Chicago: The Chicago University Press.

—— 2004. 'The production of popular music as a confidence game: The case of the Chicago Blues.' *Qualitative Sociology* 27: 137–58.

Kennedy, Peter W. 1994. 'Word-of-mouth communication and price as a signal of quality.' *Economic Record East Ivanhoe* 70: 373.

MacCannell, Dean 1976. *The Tourist: A New Theory of the Leisure Class*. New York: Schocken.

Milewicz, John and Paul Herbig. 1996. 'Differences in market signaling behavior between manufacturers and service firms.' *Journal of Professional Services Marketing* 14: 65–79.

Riley, John G. 2001. 'Silver signals: twenty-five years of screening and signaling.' *The Journal of Economic Literature* 39: 432–78.

Simmel, Georg 1955. *Conflict: The Web of Group-affiliations*. Glencoe, IL: Free Press.

Smith, Charles W. 1989. *Auctions: The Social Construction of Value*. New York London: Free Press; Collier Macmillan.

Stiglitz, Joseph E. 1987. 'The causes and consequences of the dependence of quality on price.' *The Journal of Economic Literature* 25: 1–48.

Wherry, Frederick F. 2006. 'The social sources of authenticity in global handicraft markets: Evidence from northern Thailand.' *Journal of Consumer Culture* 6: 5–32.

Wuthnow, Robert 1996. *Poor Richard's Principle: Recovering the American Dream Through the Moral Dimension of Work, Business, and Money*. Princeton, NJ: Princeton University Press.

Zelizer, Viviana A. 2005a. 'Circuits within capitalism.' Pp. 289–322 in *The Economic Sociology of Capitalism*, edited by V. Nee and R. Swedberg. Princeton, NJ: Princeton University Press.

—— 2005b. *The Purchase of Intimacy*. Princeton, NJ: Princeton University Press.

2
Tradition, Adventure, and Pleasure in Santiago, Chile's Informal Markets

Joel Stillerman
Grand Valley State University

A young woman approached a clothing vendor's stall with her two small children.
Julio: [Shuffles index cards until finding the right one.] 'Mrs. Pérez, right?'
Mrs Pérez smiles, nods, and hands him some money.
Julio: 'Paying up for this week?'
Mrs Pérez: 'Yes.'
Julio: 'Thanks. How have you been?'
Mrs Pérez: 'Great. The kids have winter vacation this week, so the other day we went to the mall and saw "Shrek" – have you seen it?'
Julio: 'No, but I've heard of it.'
Mrs Pérez: 'We thought it was really funny. Afterwards, we stayed for lunch. It was a great time!'
She examines the sweaters hanging in the stall, feeling the fabric, and checking the size. She points to one.
Mrs Pérez: 'Oh, that one looks nice. How much?'
Julio: 'It's made of really good material, too. Ten dollars. Take a look.'
Mrs Pérez: 'It looks really nice. I've got to go talk to my husband after he gets off of work. How late will you be here?'
Julio: 'I'm here until 2 today, and then I'm back on Saturday if you miss me.'
Mrs Pérez: 'OK, I'll come back. Bye, *casero* [shopkeeper].'
Julio: 'Bye, Mrs. Perez.'
She returned a short while later and purchased the shirt (Field notes, Santiago, Chile, 27 July 2001).

Scholars argue that Chileans are increasingly individualistic, hedonistic, and status conscious consumers attracted to a growing shopping mall, department store, and big box grocery chain sector (Moulián, 1997, 1998; Tórche, 1998; Tironi, 2002; Márquez, 2003; Dammert, 2004). Yet the above exchange in a Santiago, Chile neighborhood street market underscores the complex social dynamics of consumption in alternative settings missed in scholarly accounts. The extract illustrates how consumers and vendors engage in 'relational work' (Zelizer, 2005), which simultaneously favors their strategic goals in the market encounter and draws them into deep and wide ranging affective ties. Mrs Pérez works to gain Julio's trust in order to access credit and favorable payment arrangements while Julio maintains a friendly demeanor to retain her loyalty and patronage. In this process, Mrs Pérez shares details of her family life and refers to her married status and the negotiations it implies, while both have a pleasurable exchange.

This example underscores the need to understand the diverse elements of public consumption in Santiago, Chile's street and flea markets as distinct from shopping in standardized mall and chain store environments. With this goal in mind, I draw on ethnographic observation of shopping practices and the meanings of consumption as found in street and flea markets as well as semi-structured interviews conducted in Santiago, Chile between 2001 and 2006.[1]

Chile's changing retail environment since the 1973 military coup, but particularly since civilians took over government in 1990, might suggest that traditional markets are decreasing in importance as shopping venues. The liberalization of trade and land markets under the dictatorship lowered the relative prices of imported consumer goods and created incentives for shopping mall and big-box store construction. During the 1990s, the expanded availability of credit cards to middle and lower income groups also widened the array of non-essential goods available to the poor. With rising wages and easy credit, Chileans at all income levels began to purchase more sophisticated durable goods, increase their debts and frequent western style stores (Schkolnik, 1983; Cámara de Comercio de Santiago, 1996; Moulián, 1997, 1998; Cáceres and Farías, 1999; Frigolett and Sanhueza, 1999; INE, 1999; Consumers International, 2000; Sabatini and Arenas, 2000; CEP, 2001).

Nonetheless, in 2002, small traditional stores and street markets sold almost half of all food and personal items (D'Andrea, *et al.*, 2004, pp. 4–5). Neighborhood street markets, which predate the 16th century Spanish conquest of Chile, have more than US$2 billion in officially recorded annual sales,[2] and the metropolitan region hosts over 400 street markets (Salazar, 2003).[3] These markets form part of Chile's informal economy, which makes up almost one-third of the urban economically active population (Portes and Hoffman, 2003: 56). Thus, Santiago's new retail infrastructures and practices coexist with significant traditional venues that have distinctive characteristics.

Understanding the complex dynamics of consumption in Santiago's street and flea markets will help rectify an emphasis on the surface features of new retail forms that seems to indicate that Chileans are becoming more like the common image of hedonistic, status-conscious middle class western consumers (Campbell, 1987 [2005], 2004; Schor, 1998; for critiques, see Miller, 1998; Miller *et al.* 1998, and Zukin, 2004). Yet analyses of consumers in México (García Canclini, 2001), Brazil (O'Dougherty, 2002), Trinidad (Miller, 1997) and Ecuador (Colloredo-Mansfeld, 1999) demonstrate that they are engaged in a complex negotiation between global and local identities, attempt to reinforce or reinvent their class and ethnic affiliations via consumption, and improvise creative strategies to retain locally meaningful consumption-based identities.

Following this focus on locally meaningful consumption practices, I contrast the distinct, but overlapping *genres* of shopping in Santiago's street and flea markets. Miller (1997, p. 301) argues that these genres are distinctive aspects of shopping present in different retail locales, such as tourist areas, corner stores, or shopping malls. In Santiago, street markets are intimate settings in which ritualized weekly purchases help shoppers form strong social bonds with particular vendors, shoppers there feel comfortable engaging in playful joking, consumers make purchases to satisfy family members' daily needs or to purchase gifts, and shoppers buy goods for resale. Through these activities, they reinforce gender and generational categories and relationships (Douglas and Isherwood, 1979[1996]: 38–9) and become skillful shoppers. Shoppers also engage in creative 'tactics' (De Certeau, 1984) whereby they recycle goods or purchase ingredients for preparation and resale.

Flea market shopping is primarily focused on the challenge and excitement of the 'hunt' for bargains, used goods (for collections or resale), and stolen goods to be repurchased (Belk *et al.*, 1988; Sherry, 1990b; Prus and Dawson, 1991; Gregson and Crewe, 2003: 9). Shoppers and vendors are engaged in competitive, short-term transactions in which guile and deceit are ever-present. Shoppers also enjoy a carnivalesque street scene full of performances and itinerant vendors, in which consuming the 'spectacle' appears more appealing than consuming goods (Sherry, 1990b; Falk, 1997; Lehtonen and Mäenpää, 1997).

These two environments demonstrate that shopping is a challenging, pleasurable and meaningful activity in which multiple logics operate simultaneously. Shopping cannot be reduced to the single logic of individuals' search for status (Schor, 1998), pleasure and novelty (Campbell, 1987 [2005], 2004), or the fulfillment of family obligations (Miller, 1998). Moreover, shopping is situated in specific territorial and relational contexts that fundamentally shape consumers' practices and understandings of these activities (Gregson and Crewe, 2003: chs 2–3). While these findings are specific to alternative markets, they have implications for standardized retail venues like grocery stores or malls (see Miller *et al.*, 1998). The results call for an understanding of how the relational contexts of specific retail sites shape the character and meaning of shopping.

Relational work in street markets

Street markets are settings where shoppers meet weekly with their regular vendors and with neighbors and thus sustain relationships that are simultaneously practical and intimate. These long-term ties allow vendors and shoppers to mark the passing of time through transitions and rites-of-passage within their families; familiarity also encourages playfulness and the use of humor. The family context for shopping predominates given consumers' focus on food and gift purchases as well as the ingredients for food prepared at home for resale.

Shoppers meet weekly with their regular vendors and neighbors in street markets and thus sustain simultaneously practical and intimate relationships. For women, who are the markets' principal consumers, building and maintaining relationships with friends, family, and vendors is a principal element of shopping; and shopping, in turn, intensifies these relationships (Douglas and Isherwood, 1979[1996]: 37; Dimaggio and Louch, 1998; Miller, 1998; Zelizer, 2005). Additionally, shoppers use creative 'tactics' (De Certeau, 1984) to recycle found objects for use in the market, while others purchase ingredients for home preparation and resale (compare Gregson and Crewe, 2003: ch. 5).

Predating the Spanish conquerors' arrival in the 16th century and having survived political repression in the 19th century, neighborhood farmers' markets were legalized in 1939 to control food prices by a center-left administration, though small-scale merchants replaced farmers as the majority of vendors (Salazar, 2003). Today, almost all Santiago neighborhoods in mixed- and low-income areas have street markets (*ferias*) operating on a given street on specified days of the week. Though originally fresh food markets, today, processed foods, household goods, clothing, and entertainment items are sold. Licensed vendors (*feriantes*), who pay an annual fee to their local government office, park their cars or pickup trucks and set up tables in front with a tarp or awning overhead.

Processed food and household goods salespeople have more elaborate, store-like carts, as do fish and meat salespeople. Unlicensed vendors (*coleros*) lay their products on blankets on the ground, tend to work alone, squat at the market entrance or along adjacent streets (where police may remove them), and sell clothes, recorded music and films, and small electronic items (Salazar, 2003: 87–89; Leemira Consultores, 2004: 6–7, 126–7, 132; Stillerman, 2006). Family members conduct daily shopping for produce, meat and fish, medicine, and household items. Multi-generational families, groups of young women, or young mothers with children are the primary weekday shoppers, though young and elderly men (the former sometimes riding bicycles) are also present. Weekend shoppers include entire families or groups of friends, and crowds are much larger.

In my observations of social processes in ferias and flea markets, I relied on the good will of shoppers who allowed me to accompany them through the markets and/or vendors with whom I conversed in their stalls while they were working. I had developed entrée with these individuals via referrals from other researchers or through preexisting personal relationships. In the ferias, shoppers confront a lively and pleasant ambience, which includes the smells of fresh produce, fish, and barbecued food, the din of music or soccer games played on the radio, and the characteristic calls of produce vendors who utilize humor to amuse shoppers and thereby attract their attention, or inform customers about sales. For example, a fruit vendor in the southern Santiago Los Carolinos street market frequently calls out '*Kiwis hay*' (I have kiwi fruit). Because Chileans often do not pronounce the final consonants in words, 'Kiwis hay' comes out sounding more like '*Qué huevai?*' *Huevon* is a commonly used colloquial term. It literally means 'testicle,' but colloquially, it can mean 'dude,' 'buddy' or 'fool,' depending on the context of use. The verb, *huevear*, can mean fooling around, wasting time, or engaging in an amorous relationship. Hence, 'Qué huevai?' means something like, 'Why are you messing with me?' – a question shoppers usually greet with amusement (Field notes, 5 July 2003).

In this context of humor and flirtation, shoppers may initiate sexualized humor, as in the following example. An elderly woman approached a clothing vendor's stall holding two bags, one with a shirt to be exchanged, and another containing the remaining crumbs from a *churro*: a fried pastry covered with powdered sugar. She mistakenly gave the vendor's husband the wrong bag with churro crumbs, and said, laughing, '*Le dí el churro*,' to which the husband replied, '*me dió el churrazo*,' both of which literally mean, 'I gave you/you gave me the churro.' Nonetheless, colloquially, churro means 'good looking' or 'attractive' man. Also, the pastry's cylindrical shape has phallic connotations. Thus, the woman was embarrassed, and amused, that the vendor's husband might have interpreted the joke as a 'come on.'

Shortly afterward, a younger woman looked at a low cut shirt hanging from the stall and placed it in front of her to check its fit. Laura, the vendor, said, 'Hi, my dear, what can I do for you?' She responded, standing directly in front of Laura's husband, 'I have to pull this down really low so it fits right' (laughs). Pablo responded, turning away and smirking, 'I didn't say anything.' The shopper suggested that since the shirt was so low-cut, if she pulled it down to her genital area, it would provide easy access for a sexual encounter: an embarrassing but outrageously funny joke to make to a married man in his wife's presence (Field notes, 22 December 2005). Our first glance at ferias shows us that play and humor (often with romantic themes) are central to the experience and practice of shopping, which is part of its appeal.

Ferias nonetheless play a central role in household food and clothing provisioning and thus fit into a set of weekly routines and relationships. Customers shop for food and clothing items once or twice a week. In Chile and elsewhere in Latin America, low- and moderate-income shoppers split their food purchases between small, local markets and supermarkets. Shoppers buy fresh produce, bread and meat locally, and bulk goods on a weekly or monthly basis at supermarkets. Consumers divide purchases in this manner in order to reduce transit costs, purchase foods in smaller, fractionated quantities, and enjoy better quality, fresher, and less expensive produce and bread (Bromley, 1998; Salazar, 2003, pp. 87–93; D'Andrea *et al.*, 2004; Leemira Consultores, 2004, pp. 6–7, 126–7; Stillerman, 2004; ASOF, 2005; Stillerman, 2006).

Women try to ensure they are purchasing high quality and reasonably priced produce and that vendors do not cheat them, developing alliances with specific vendors, who they call *caseros* (Stillerman, 2006; compare Polakoff, 1985 for Cochabamba, Bolivia). Vendors also address their regular customers as *casero* or *casera*. The term originated with door-to-door salesmen selling fresh foods or household items and often extending credit to customers.

Customers develop close, trusting, and long-term relationships with caseros, often jointly observing their children grow up, as customers bring their children to the feria and vendors often rely on family labor. This is particularly true for vendors who sell more expensive items. Here, caseros offer them credit at 40 per cent or 50 per cent interest but allow them to pay off debts in small weekly, biweekly, or monthly installments.

As Pablo, a shoe vendor comments, 'I offer credit and give the shoes to a customer before they have paid in full if I have known them for a long time. I have known some of my customers since they were little kids' (Field notes, 13 July 2003). Many young mothers are unemployed and hence have neither an independent income nor the qualifications to access department store credit cards. As a consequence, they, along with sporadically employed youth, take advantage of this source of credit. Paying regular installments creates another ritual similar to the visit to the produce stand. Shoppers visit their merchant-creditors at the market, or the former visit them at home to collect payments.

The long-term ties between merchant creditors and shoppers noted above help notch off short-term and long-term passages of time: shopping is a semi-weekly ritual, and long-term relations with vendors allow shoppers and vendors to share and remark on life transitions (Douglas and Isherwood, 1979 [1996]: 43–4). These credit arrangements also project the relationship into the future and spill over into affective connections, thereby diverging from the image from neoclassical economics that market transactions are one-time, arms-length encounters (Granovetter, 1985; Zelizer, 2005).

Gift purchases in the feria have a different characteristic than routine and ritualized food and clothing purchases. Nonetheless, much like these other purchases, they are often oriented toward the satisfaction of family members' needs or desires. Gifts are often 'treats' (Miller, 1998) given to children, and gift-giving also serves as a medium for asserting family roles and responsibilities (Douglas and Isherwood, 1979 [1996]: 37): I have observed mothers purchase items for their children and then kiss them, thereby reframing an economic transaction as representing an intimate relationship (Field notes, 22 July 2003).

Shoppers also assert their family roles through everyday purchases: *Paula and Georgia, her mother-in-law, were shopping for fruit.* Paula asked, 'I bought *pepinos* [a locally available small melon] over here, are you going to buy them here, too?' Georgia responded, 'I don't like them here, they're too small. I go to the stall further down.' *Paula turned to me and shrugged her shoulders* (Field notes, 5 July 2003). Paula expresses uncertainty about her decision, seeking her mother-in-law's approval, and thereby defers to her authority. When Georgia asserts her superior wisdom, Paula withdraws rather than defending her decision, thereby acknowledging Georgia's authority and judgment.

In another form of relational work, shoppers converse with and offer gifts to friends from their neighborhood. In a visit to a Southern Santiago feria, Raquel, a low-income resident, cheerfully greeted many of the vendors. She had purchased a bag of oranges and offered some of them to several older female shoppers, who gratefully accepted the oranges, peeled and ate them (Field notes, 5 August, 2001). It is also common for shoppers to stop and chat with neighbors they encounter in the feria (Field notes, 3 July 2001). Many vendors and shoppers also describe a visit to the feria as an 'outing.'

In addition to engaging in relational work, some customers devise creative uses for commodities, or 'tactics' (De Certeau, 1984). For example, consumers use recycled goods for carrying groceries or family members. On a number of occasions, I observed shoppers carrying groceries in wheelbarrows or laundry hampers, or pushing a spouse or mother in a wheelbarrow or wheelchair. The appropriation of these makeshift items (De Certeau, 1984) would seem out of place in a supermarket or mall, yet they occur without comment in the feria (Field notes, 5 July 2003, 23 December 2005, 22 December 2005).

Many also purchase ingredients in ferias for household preparation and resale. To be successful in such creative entrepreneurship requires prior comparison shopping and the identification of profitable sales venues (compare Sherry, 1990b; Morales, 1993). A college student comments, 'I sold *empanadas* [meat pies] at the University and a few housewives prepared them with me. We bought some ingredients at the feria and others at the supermarket depending on where they were least expensive' (Field notes, 14 July 2001). Raquel, interviewed above, states: 'At times I've sold food from my home and bought the ingredients in the feria because it's cheap.' (Interview, 13 July 2001). She demonstrated her ability at creative self-provisioning when, on a visit to the feria, Raquel purchased cloth to make bed sheets (Field notes, 5 August, 2001).

Street market consumers, as we have seen, are embedded in long-term reciprocal ties *through* and not in spite of the market. They imbue economic transactions with emotional and relational meaning, all the while appropriating and recycling found objects, and strategically purchasing raw materials for preparation and resale. Shoppers in the ferias, when examined on their own terms and *in situ*, are not recognizable as the hypothesized hedonistic or status-conscious individual consumer familiar in much consumption theory.

The thrills of the hunt and other pleasures in flea markets

In contrast to street market customers, flea market shoppers primarily focus on the search for bargains, unique second-hand goods, or goods for resale. They also partake in a carnivalesque street spectacle. Shoppers and vendors engage in a strategic game to gain value through one-time transactions. Vendors may attempt to gouge naïve shoppers, while the latter may haggle vociferously or frustrate vendors by engaging in comparison shopping or 'just looking' (Sherry, 1990b; Wherry, this volume). Unlike street markets, where vendors' or shoppers' humor greases the wheels of a sale, attracts customers, or adds a pleasurable element to the shopping experience, much of flea market vendors' humor is 'backstage' commentary (Goffman, 1959) that celebrates having tricked a customer, or quietly insults shoppers who refuse to make a purchase. When vendors try to lure shoppers with jokes, they often fall flat.

Second hand goods sales within the flea markets include considerable 'role fluidity' (Sherry, 1990a, p. 21) in that shoppers may attempt to gain 'deals' from naïve vendors on goods intended for resale. These consumers develop a sophisticated understanding of goods' potential market value, rely on personal networks for sourcing goods, and have extensive knowledge of customers' tastes and potential resale venues (Sherry 1990b; Gregson and Crewe, 2003, ch. 5).

Used goods sales, by definition, require initial owners to divest themselves of their products (Belk *et al.*, 1988; Gregson and Crewe, 2003, ch. 5). In the flea markets, resale vendors capitalize on the inexperience or personal misfortune of vendors who seek to quickly liquidate their assets. Other vendors sell stolen goods, and theft victims repurchase these goods after learning of their location at the market. Additionally, collectors seek unique or authentic goods to fashion a distinctive identity by displaying these products in their homes (Gregson and Crewe, 2003, ch. 7).

On weekends, there is a festive street environment outside the markets as onlookers crowd the streets to hear free concerts, observe impromptu performances, purchase inexpensive foods and goods on the streets, or as part of a trip to the indoor markets. This outdoor scene is a particularly pronounced example of the festive and carnivalesque element present to a greater or lesser degree in most markets (Sherry, 1990a, pp.16–18), in which one's sensory experience may be more important than purchasing or using a product (Falk, 1997; Lehtonen and Mäenpää, 1997; Zukin, 2004). In contrast to street markets, where shopping practices reinforce shoppers' gender and family identities, this street scene permits the temporary or simulated inversion of social hierarchies—a place where shoppers can experience a momentary sense of freedom from societal controls (Sherry, 1990a; Belk *et al.*, 1998).

Flea markets originated as antique stores near the center of Santiago, but the markets today offer a more diverse array of products. Santiago has several indoor markets; the Bío Bío market observed for this study is the best known and is located in an older neighborhood near downtown Santiago. Vendors work in small stalls in defunct factory buildings that cover about one square mile. Though the Bío Bío began as a street market, the mayor forced vendors indoors during the 1970s and again in 1995 (Salcedo, 2004, p. 95), though a few street vendors today still work on the sidewalks, especially on weekends.

Merchants sell clothing, furniture, computer goods, antiques, tools, and bric-a-brac. Individual vendors or families rent stalls and different types of products are grouped in specific sections of a building or in different buildings. For example, used goods and hardware share space with antiques in some buildings; separate buildings house computers, furniture, and bicycles.

The market sits alongside the city's former stockyards, which were moved to a peripheral zone in the city in the 1960s, but restaurants, butchers, and fresh fish stores remained in the area. A great deal of the clothes, CDs, and DVDs sold there are evidently pirated merchandise, and citizens widely believe that many of the used goods available at the market are stolen. In addition to its reputation as a thieves' market, the neighborhood is known for high assault rates, though the markets remain popular shopping destinations.

The markets attract a variety of shoppers whose social backgrounds and lifestyle orientations vary considerably. We conducted most of our observations in a furniture business in the *Las Gangas* building. This area attracts families (often young couples expecting a child) with varying class backgrounds; a smaller group of wholesale buyers for restaurants or offices are also regular patrons. These shoppers are price conscious, seeking written estimates from different stalls.

Since most shoppers have no long-term attachments to a given vendor or stall, though they may receive a referral, vendors must use their wiles to 'reel them in.' They do so with calls emphasizing the quality and low costs of their merchandise, or through flattery or humor, mimicking feriantes to some degree. Transactions are a strategic game between vendors and shoppers as vendors have a reputation for trickery and shoppers have little or no loyalty to individual merchants (Stillerman and Sundt, forthcoming). Vendors may persuade shoppers to purchase an item based on their claims regarding its reputed quality, low delivery fees, warranty, or their willingness to haggle. It is with good reason that shoppers treat vendors with caution, as the latter may hide aesthetic defects in goods or overcharge customers who appear affluent (Field notes, 11 July 2003).

As is true in the ferias, family members shop in groups of two or more; and once they politely gain a vendor's attention, they ask several questions about price, styles, options, and durability. They often sit on chairs or at tables to test their comfort and durability. After learning of the different available designs, prices, and options, the family members then confer. They may request a price estimate and offer to return. In contrast, if they are convinced they have found the right dining room set or chairs, they will close the deal, which entails sitting down with the salesperson at a table in the back of the stall in order to pay, receive their receipt, and arrange for pickup or delivery. As sales staff wrap up the chairs and table in plastic to protect it and contact one of the building's delivery men to arrange for shipment, very often the family members sit or bounce on display chairs and smile or laugh with satisfaction at their new acquisition (Field notes, 24 December 2005).

Based on my many visits to Chileans' homes during sixteen years' of travel to the country, I argue that we here see Bourdieu's (1977, 1984) *habitus* at work: these consumers operate within an aesthetic universe that they seek to reproduce due to its familiarity. I would describe the furniture at this stall (and most of the others in *Las Gangas*) as typical in style for working- and lower middle-class households. Glass or wooden tables are accompanied by straight-backed chairs with aluminum or metal frames and cushions covered with simple, bright designs in cloth, velour or imitation suede. I hypothesize that the satisfaction customers show upon purchasing dining room sets or chairs reflects two phenomena. First, these consumers have identified a style with which they are familiar – it is seen as acceptable and attractive within their milieu. Because it is familiar, and for young families is likely a first-time experience, it may signify either upward mobility to a desired, but familiar social status, or acquisition of a level of comfort achieved by parents or other family members. Hence, the goods function communicatively within these consumers' family and class contexts (Douglas and Isherwood, 1979[1996]: 38–9, 43).

There are some minor variations on the scenario described above. Self-appointed brokers (or *piratas* [pirates] in the vendors' lexicon) approach shoppers at the door and offer to show them furniture at various stalls. If a shopper decides to make a purchase, the sales price includes a 'finder's fee' that the brokers retain and then give the actual sales price to the vendor. Additionally, shoppers may want one item available at a stall, but wish to combine it with another that is either out of stock or not carried by that vendor. Merchants use their personal networks to acquire the desired item at another stall to complete the 'combination' for the customers (Field notes, 18 and 26 July 2003).

The dynamic of customer-vendor interactions in the markets is sharply different from the patterns observed in street markets. Shoppers collect cards with estimates from several different shops, seeking the lowest price. Especially when business is slow (as in our 2003 observations when Chile was ending a long recession), vendors become frustrated with buyers' ability *not* to make purchases: *A couple walked by and commented,* 'What a nice looking living room set.' As they walked away, a vendor saw a business card in the man's hand and asked, 'What does that card have that we don't?' (Field notes, 12 July 2003). Manuel, a security guard, echoed vendors' complaints that shoppers only compare prices but do not purchase goods (Interview, 26 July 2003). María, the business co-owner, complained about customers' haggling: 'We don't get too many middle and upper class patrons. It's probably for the best because we've had problems with them. They'll fight you for a US$2.00 discount even though they have tons of money. Another wealthy customer gave us a bad check' (Field notes, 1 July 2001). Consumers' price conscious orientations, effective haggling, and unwillingness to socialize with vendors would be atypical in the feria setting, where vendors expect shoppers to socialize with them and shoppers assume they are receiving the best price and quality from their casero.

The absence of close, affective vendor-customer ties is also evident in vendors' use of humor or flirtation, as in the following example: *Three young women approach Israel, the business co-owner, looking for Carlos, a younger employee. Israel opens his arms, as if to hug one of them, smiles, and says, 'I'm the one you're looking for!' The women did not play along with the joke, and asked again when Carlos would return, so Israel responded to their question and they walked away* (Field notes, 11 July 2003). While these efforts often fell flat, ironic jokes among vendors went over well: *Carlos tried to sell a corner table to an older woman*: 'You can use it to hold a flower vase.' *After she walked away, María turned to me and said*, 'She can use it to hold her dentures' [we laughed] (Field notes, 26, July 2003). Thus, unlike the humor and romantic play common between shoppers and feria vendors, flea market vendors lack the level of trust and rapport with shoppers for such efforts to be effective. Facing their fragile influence over shoppers, vendors attempt to compensate for their frustration through ironic backstage jokes that express contempt toward shoppers.

The 'treasure hunt' is essential to the modus operandi of many shoppers at the Bío Bío markets as well as other less well-known flea markets. As Belk *et al.* (1988), Sherry (1990a, b) and Gregson and Crewe (2003) found, one of the chief pleasures and challenges of shopping for used goods is having the ability to differentiate 'treasure' from 'trash,' and seasoned vendors or customers often take advantage of novice merchants, buying their goods at a large discount. Additionally, purchases of goods for resale and fencing stolen goods are examples of Certeauian tactics whereby consumers appropriate goods creatively (though in these examples, these actions affect subordinate rather than dominant groups). Arturo, an industrial worker who sells used goods to supplement his income, comments: 'I once bought an electric generator at the Bío Bío market for US$400 that was worth US$3,000. The guy didn't know what he was selling. You need to look for opportunities. I know what things are worth because I went to trade school – I recognize the manufacturer's trademark' (Interview, 24 July 2003).

In addition to knowledge of the market value of used goods, second hand entrepreneurs rely on personal networks to source goods. Thus, Arturo maintains contacts with unlicensed vendors in street markets who identify goods he might wish to purchase for resale. Because his peers share his expertise, they can take advantage of other unlicensed vendors who liquidate their possessions under severe financial pressure. Arturo comments, 'A lot of the coleros are unemployed young people who need to obtain cash quickly. They don't know what they're selling and they practically give the stuff away' (Interview, 24 July, 2003). Similarly, Raquel, interviewed above, observes, 'They sell everything in the feria! Sometimes they sell enormous TV sets at such low prices. When people are in bad financial shape, they get desperate and sell their things at ridiculous prices. ... That's really sad. ... Happily, when I was in bad shape, I solved my problems without having to sell my important things' (Interview, 13 July 2003). Thus, shoppers' opportunities for purchase and profitable resale are often predicated on others' misfortunes and sale of prized possessions. This fact underscores the importance of understanding the cultural biographies of goods (Gregson and Crewe, 2003).

Used goods vendors also build their inventory through theft or by acting as fences for thieves. Arturo, quoted above, comments, 'There are lots of stories about the area. A guy had a car part stolen. He went to Bío Bío to buy a replacement, and he found the part there. One time, a guy had his Rottweiler dog stolen and a friend led him to the person who had stolen it so that he could buy it back.' (Interview, 24 July 2003). Similarly, Marcos Medina, a retired industrial worker, recounts: 'A friend of mine is a carpenter and he had a very expensive tool stolen from his home. He asked around in the neighborhood, and someone brought him to Bío Bío to the thief. He had to go through the humiliation of buying it back because he didn't have any other choice; he needed the tool to work' (Interview, 29 July 2003).

Other shoppers seek out novel or peculiar used goods at the Bío Bío and other flea markets. One couple, who are themselves feriantes, comment,

'We found about 75 per cent of the decorations in our house at the Lo Hermida flea market [an eastern Santiago outdoor flea market]. You need to have a lot of patience, though, to find really nice stuff. They have all kinds of odd and really interesting things here' (Field notes 28 July 2001). Used goods allow the purchaser to fashion a unique identity built on the aestheticization of nostalgia (Gregson and Crewe, 2003; Sherry, 1990b).

In addition to shoppers, the markets attract massive crowds of onlookers on weekends. On numerous occasions when I was leaving the markets in the mid-afternoon on Saturday and Sunday, I was greeted by a 'wall' of teenagers and young adults, dressed in rock t-shirts and worn jeans, often eating inexpensive snacks sold on outdoor vending carts. They find in the street an array of activities – outdoor concerts, young men selling puppies, record vendors singing along to the music, street vendors, and a male-to-female transvestite dancer accompanied by a drummer.

The dancer regularly attracted large groups who formed semicircles around her, looking on in puzzled amusement. Her dance included a gag in which she would move around large, fake breasts located under her silver dress (they appeared to be large inflatable balls) in sync with the rhythms. Homosexuality has only recently become a topic of public debate in Chile, and most often highly educated segments of society dominate this discussion. The fact that a largely poor and lower middle class audience would laugh and applaud for a transvestite underscores the suspension of rules and norms that occurs on the streets outside the markets. This carnival atmosphere, intensified by the large crowds, as well as circus-like attractions such as pantomime artists and the sale and display of live animals, creates a feeling of momentary liberation from everyday routines. In this regard, the Bío Bío markets are distinct from the ferias, where shoppers share humor and enjoyment in one-on-one interactions through which they enact and refer to traditional roles and relationships. The flea market, by contrast, inverts those rules through the unusual attractions it hosts that seem to soften onlookers' attitudes toward unusual and different experiences (Field notes, 12 July 2003).

Conclusion

In this analysis of Santiago's street and flea markets, we found consumers who have little in common with the isolated, hedonistic and status conscious individuals often identified by some scholarly observers.

In contrast to this flat analysis of consumption processes, this research dramatizes the distinctive aspects of public consumption in street and flea markets. Street markets are quintessentially family settings, where the enactment of traditions, friendship, and humor abound. Thus, in important respects, these settings reflect the traditionalist model of consumption outlined by Douglas and Isherwood (1979 [1996]), conform to the view that shopping is primarily family oriented (Miller 1998), and fit within a broadly relational account of consumption (Zelizer, 2005). Nonetheless, these markets also evidence elements of Certeauian resistance that demonstrate that shoppers are not only carrying out traditional behaviors, roles, and obligations, but behaving instrumentally as well. The family context shapes these creative activities to give them a different hue than they might have in other contexts.

Shopping at flea markets is a high risk, high return strategic game where experience, cunning, and luck all figure in the outcome for shoppers and vendors. In addition to hardnosed and emotionally distant merchant-vendor encounters, the used goods business facilitates role fluidity through which consumers become vendors and vice versa (Sherry, 1990b). Astute entrepreneurs prey on the naiveté or misfortune of vendors seeking to liquidate assets, while thieves or fences sell stolen goods. Thus, undergirding the 'thrill of the hunt' are biographies of goods acquired as the result of human misfortune. Collectors also hunt for unique goods, seeking to fashion a distinctive identity (Gregson and Crewe, 2003). While the flea market is a playful and festive environment, much of consumers' ludic experiences occur outside the markets as part of the circus-like events on the street where commonplace norms are temporarily suspended.

Critics might argue that these findings refer to an archaic sector whose share of sales is declining while malls, department stores and big box supermarkets expand. While these new retail forms are indeed more profitable, the more interesting question to ask is whether the dynamics of consumption found in these alternative markets might also be found in modern retail areas. Evidence from other contexts suggests that these dynamics are indeed present. Prus and Dawson (1991) found that Canadian suburban mall shoppers find 'the thrill of the hunt' enjoyable, which closely mirrors our examination of Santiago's used goods market. Additionally, Dimaggio and Louch (1998) argue that used goods shoppers express greater satisfaction when they purchase products through friends, a finding that sounds remarkably similar to the casero relationship found in the ferias. In my own observations of Santiago, Chile's shopping malls, I found resale economies and theft/fencing activities operating within these 'cathedrals of consumption' (Stillerman, 2006), while Ortiz (1994) sees malls as spaces of sociability.

This chapter's findings and their broader applications suggest that we need to ground overarching definitions and theories of consumption in the situated practices of consumers in specific sites, which will lead us to the mechanisms undergirding consumption practices. While broad economic and cultural changes do have profound effects on consumption and subjectivity, these shifts occur in the context of existing retail infrastructures, traditions, practices, and patterns of informal resistance. Shoppers undoubtedly pursue pleasure and status, but they also seek adventure and conduct relational work. Additionally, some shoppers chart 'errant trajectories' (De Certeau 1984) through the world of commodities. Tracing these trajectories will provide important insights into their contributions to the structuring of everyday life.

Acknowledgements

I gratefully acknowledge funding support for portions of this research from the Padnos International Center and Office of Research and Development, Grand Valley State University. Tomás Ariztía and Patricio Garcia offered excellent and much appreciated research assistance for this chapter. I wish to thank volume editor Dan Cook, John Sherry, Viviana Zelizer, Catherine Sundt, and Tomás Ariztía for their very helpful comments on earlier versions of this chapter.

Notes

1. During June and July 2001, July 2003, and December 2005–January 2006, I conducted 120 hours of ethnographic observation (with two research assistants) in several Santiago, Chile street and flea markets in mixed and low income communities and in meetings of the national street market vendors' association (ASOF). I also conducted 24 interviews with vendors, consumers, marketing professionals, and scholars. Finally, I collected relevant documentary evidence. All translations by author, pseudonyms appear as first name only, and individuals who wished to be identified appear with first and last name.
2. 'Santiago: Mas de US$173.000 milliones anuales venden ferias libres,' *El Mostrador*, 13 January 2005, http://www.elmostrador.cl/modulos/noticias/constructor/noticia.asp?id_noticia=151813 (accessed 5 July 2005).
3. 'Ferias libres contra Goliat,' *Punto Final*, 27 May–9 June 2005, www.puntofinal.cl (accessed 7 July 2005).

References

Asociación Chilena de Organizaciones de Ferias Libres (ASOF). 2005. *Sistema primario de información feria libre, S.I.F.L.*, power point presentation given at Universidad ARCIS, 18 April, Santiago, Chile, 62pp.

Belk, R.W. 2004. 'The Human Consequences of Consumer Culture.' pp. 67–86 in *Elusive Consumption*, edited by K.M. Ekstrom and H. Brembeck. Oxford and New York: Berg.

Belk, R.W., M. Wallendorf and J.F. Sherry, Jr. 1988. 'A Naturalistic Inquiry into Buyer and Seller Behavior at a Swap Meet,' *Journal of Consumer Research* 14: 449–70.

Bourdieu, P. 1977. *Outline of a Theory of Practice*. Cambridge, UK: Cambridge University Press.

——. 1984. *Distinction: A Social Critique of the Judgment of Taste*, translated by R. Nice. Cambridge, MA: Harvard University Press.

Bromley, R.D.F. 1998. 'Market-place Trading and the Transformation of Retail Space in the Expanding Latin American City,' *Urban Studies* 35(8), 1311–33.

Cáceres, G. and L. Farías. 1999. 'Efectos de las grandes superficies comerciales en el Santiago de la modernización ininterrumpida, 1982–1999,' *Ambiente y Desarrollo* 15(4), Santiago, 36–41.

Cámara de Comercio de Santiago (Santiago, Chile Chamber of Commerce). 1996. *Deudas de Consumo Consolidadas por Estrato Socioeconomico* (Consumer Debts Disaggregated By Socioeconomic Groups). Mimeo. Santiago, Chile: 10pp.

Campbell, C. 1987 [2005]. *The Romantic Ethic and the Spirit of Modern Consumerism*, 3rd edn. London: Alcuin Academics.

——. 2004. 'I Shop Therefore I Know that I Am: The Metaphysical Basis of Modern Consumerism.' pp. 27–44 in *Elusive Consumption*, edited by K.M. Ekstrom and H. Brembeck. Oxford and New York: Berg.

CEP (Center for Public Studies). 2001. Estudio de Opinión Pública No. 41: Cómo hemos mejorado en los últimos diez años? (http://www.cepchile.cl), accessed 28 February, 2003.

Colloredo-Mansfeld, R. 1999. *The Native Leisure Class: Consumption and Cultural Creativity in the Andes*. Chicago: University of Chicago Press.

Consumers International. 2000. *Cambios en los patrones de consumo y sustenabilidad en Chile*. Santiago, Chile: Consumers International.

Dammert, L. 2004. 'Ciudad sin ciudadanos? Fragmentación, segregación y temor en Santiago,' *Eure* 30 (91), 87–96.

D'Andrea, G., A. Stenger and A. Goebel-Krstelj. 2004. 'Six Truths about Emerging Market Consumers,' *Strategy + Business* 34, 2–12.

De Certeau, M. 1984. *The Practice of Everyday Life*. Berkeley: University of California Press.

Dimaggio, P. and H. Louch. 1998. 'Socially Embedded Consumer Transactions: For What Kinds of Purchases do People Most Often Use Networks?' *American Sociological Review* 63, 5 (October): 619–37.

Douglas, M. and B. Isherwood. 1979 [1996]. *The World of Goods: Towards an Anthropology of Consumption*, 2nd edn. London and New York: Routledge.

Falk, P. 1997. 'The Scopic Regimes of Shopping.' pp. 177–85 in *The Shopping Experience*, edited by P. Falk and C. Campbell. London: Sage.

Frigolett, H. and A. Sanhueza. 1999. *Evolución del gasto del consumo de los hogares en Chile, 1985–1995*. Santiago, Chile: Ministry of Planning.

García Canclini, N. 2001. *Consumers and Citizens: Globalization and Multicultural Conflicts*, translated by G. Yúdice. Minneapolis: University of Minnesota Press.

Goffman, E. 1959. *The Presentation of Self in Everyday Life*. New York: Doubleday.

Granovetter, M. 1985. 'Economic Structure and Social Action: The Problem of Embeddedness' *American Journal of Sociology* 91, 3: 481–510.

Gregson, N. and L. Crewe. 2003. *Second-Hand Cultures*. Oxford, UK and New York: Berg.

INE (Chilean National Statistics Institute). 1999. *V Encuesta de Presupuestos Familiares, 1996–1997*. *Versión Resumida*. Santiago, Chile.

Leemira Consultores Asociados Limitados. 2004. *Estudio y catastro de las ferias libres del Gran Santiago*. Santiago: Leemira Consultores Asociados Limitados.

Lehtonen, T.-K. and P. Mäenpää. 1997. 'Shopping in the East Centre Mall.' pp. 136–65 in *The Shopping Experience*, edited by P. Falk and C. Campbell. London: Sage.

Márquez B., F. 2003. 'Identidad y fronteras urbanas en Santiago de Chile,' Presentation at 8 Simposio, 'Transformaciones metropolitanas y planificación urbana en América Latina,' abril, 15 pp. (accessed 3 December 2005 at http://www.identidades.cl/indexb.htm).

Miller, D. 1998. *A Theory of Shopping*. Chicago: University of Chicago Press.

———. 1997. *Capitalism: An Ethnographic Approach*. New York: Berg.

Miller, D., P. Jackson, N. Thrift, B. Holbrook and M. Rowlands. 1998. *Shopping, Place and Identity*. London: Routledge.

Morales, A. 1993. 'Making Money at the Market: The Social and Economic Logic of Informal Markets.' PhD diss., Dept. of Sociology. Northwestern University Evanston, IL.

Moulián, T. 1997. *Chile Hoy: Anatomía de un Mito*. Santiago, Chile: LOM Ediciones.

———. 1998. *El Consumo me Consume*. Santiago, Chile: LOM.

O'Dougherty, M. 2002. *Consumption Intensified: The Politics of Middle-class Daily Life in Brazil*. Durham, NC: Duke University Press.

Ortiz, S.M. 1994. 'Shopping for Sociability in the Mall.' *Research in Community Sociology*, Supplement 1, 183–99.

Polakoff, E.G. 1985. *Butchers, Bribes and Bandits: Market Relations in Cochabamba, Bolivia*. PhD diss. Dept. of Sociology, Cornell University: Ithaca, NY.

Portes, A. and K. Hoffman. 2003. 'Latin American Class Structures: Their Composition and Change during the Neoliberal Era,' *Latin American Research Review* 38(1), February, 41–82.

Prus, R. and L. Dawson. 1991. 'Shop 'Til You Drop: Shopping as Recreational and Laborious Activity' *Canadian Journal of Sociology/Cahiers canadiense se sociologie* 16, 2: 145–64.

Sabatini, F. and F. Arenas. 2000. 'Entre el estado y el mercado: resonancias geográficas y sustentabilidad social en Santiago de Chile,' *EURE* 26, 79: 95–113.

Salazar, G. 2003. *Ferias libres: espacio residual de soberanía ciudadana*. Santiago: SUR.

Salcedo, R. 2004. Towards a Reconceptualization of Post-Public Spaces. PhD diss., Political Science. Chicago: University of Illinois at Chicago.

Schkolnik, M. 1983. *Transformaciones en las pautas de consumo y políticas neoliberales. Chile: 1974–1981*. Santiago, Chile: Programa de Economía del Trabajo.

Schor, J. 1998. *The Overspent American: Why We Want What We Don't Need.* New York: HarperCollins.

Sherry, J.F., Jr. 1990a. 'A Sociocultural Analysis of a Midwestern American Flea Market.' *Journal of Consumer Research* 17: 13–30.

——. 1990b. 'Dealers and Dealing in a Periodic Market: Informal Retailing in Ethnographic Perspective,' *Journal of Retailing* 66, 2 (Summer): 174–200.

Stillerman, J. 2004. 'Gender, Class, and Generational Contexts for Consumption in Contemporary Chile,' *Journal of Consumer Culture* 4 (1), March, 51–78.

——. 2006. 'Private, Parochial and Public Realms in Santiago, Chile's Retail Sector' *City & Community* 5, 3 (September): 293–317.

Stillerman, J. and C. Sundt. forthcoming. 'Embeddedness and Business Strategies among Santiago Chile's Street and Flea Market Vendors,' in *Street Entrepreneurs: People, Place, & Politics in Local and Global Perspective*, edited by J. Cross and A. Morales. London: Routledge.

Tironi, E. 2002. *El cambio está aquí*. Santiago, Chile: Editorial Sudamericana.

Tórche, F. 1998. 'Consumismo: Alcances y Limitaciones de Un Fenómeno en Expansión' *Revista Universitaria* 59: 53–7.

Wherry, F. forthcoming. 'The Play of Authenticity in Thai Handicraft Markets,' in this volume.

Zelizer, V. 2005. 'Culture and Consumption.' In *Handbook of Economic Sociology*. 2nd edn, edited by N. Smelser and R. Swedberg. Princeton, NJ: Princeton University Press, and NewYork: Russell Sage Foundation.

Zukin, S. 2004. *Point of Purchase: How Shopping Changed American Culture.* New York and London: Routledge.

3
Shopping *for* People, or Shopping for *People?*: Deciphering the Object of Consumption Among Tourists in Banaras

Jenny Huberman
University of Missouri

Introduction: something extra

Jorgen was a 31-year-old Dutch tourist who was visiting the city of Banaras, India. On the afternoon of his arrival, as he sat along the city's scenic riverfront sipping tea, he was approached by a twelve-year-old boy named Mohan who began asking him questions about where he was from, what he did for a living, and how he was enjoying his travels in India. After an hour or so of conversation, Mohan offered to guide Jorgen around the city. Jorgen agreed and the next morning they set out on their first excursion. For the next eight days of Jorgen's stay, Mohan accompanied him virtually everywhere, and he even invited Jorgen home to meet his family. In describing the relationship that was developing between them, Jorgen commented: 'I know that he's selling me something but it doesn't feel like he is. There is something extra. I am very lucky that I met him.'

Like Jorgen, other Western tourists also had powerful reactions to the children who worked as unlicensed guides and peddlers along the city's famous riverfront. While some tourists complained that the children's 'relentless sales tactics' destroyed their experience of the riverfront and made them feel like 'walking dollar signs,' many others came away from these encounters wanting to buy these youngsters gifts, take them on outings to restaurants and movies, and even send them presents and money when they returned home from their vacations. Like Jorgen, they too felt they were getting 'something extra from these children; something that went far beyond guiding services or the sale of postcards and souvenirs.'

In this chapter, I ask: what was the 'something extra' that tourists sought to consume from these youngsters? What might this tell us about the nature and object of Western tourist consumption in Banaras? And, how might these ethnographic examples speak to a larger set of scholarly concerns regarding the lived experiences of public consumption, particularly within informal markets, where the production and consumption of values is much more ambiguous and contingent than rationalized and disciplined, and where the boundaries between consumption and symbolic exchange are more difficult to disentangle?

Consumption and symbolic exchange

In pursuing these questions, I will draw upon some of Jean Baudrillard's early writings on consumption, and more specifically his distinction between consumption and symbolic exchange. While Baudrillard is perhaps better known now as a post-modern theorist whose writings on hyper reality and the simulacrum challenge the very distinction between an authentic and inauthentic sphere of human relations and experience, in his early, more modernist writings the passage from symbolic exchange to consumption clearly marked such a transformation. For Baudrillard, to study consumption was examine the ways that people attempt to locate themselves along the social hierarchy through the appropriation and manipulation of a code of signs, and in differentiating 'the object of consumption' from other objects that people exchange, possess, or relate to, he wrote:

> an object specified by its trademark, charged with differential con-
> notations of status, prestige and fashion. *This* is the 'object of
> consumption'.... The object does not assume meaning either in
> a symbolic relation with the subject (the Object) or in an opera-
> tional relation to the world (object-as-implement): it finds meanings
> with other objects, in difference, according to a hierarchical code of
> significations.... Instead of abolishing itself in the relation that it
> establishes, and thus assuming symbolic value (as in the example
> of the gift), the object becomes autonomous, intransitive, opaque,
> and so begins to signify the abolition of the relationship (Baudrillard,
> 1981, pp. 64–5).

Thus, while consumption marks a highly rationalized and reified world of social relations where exchange is made possible precisely by replacing the ambivalence of personal interactions with codified schemes for assessing the value (both economic and sign) of goods and people, symbolic exchange, Baudrillard posited, is driven by the logic of ambivalence and the item transferred, such as the gift, derives its significance from the unique relationship that it establishes. In this regard, 'the object' transferred in symbolic exchange is not really an object. As Baudrillard noted, it is 'inseparable from the concrete relation in which it is exchanged ... the objects given, are not autonomous, hence not codifiable as signs'(ibid.: 64–5). As such, Baudrillard suggested that symbolic exchange stands 'beyond' the code:

> All forms of value (object, commodity or sign) must be negated in order to inaugurate symbolic exchange. This is the radical rupture of the field of value ... the symbolic is not a value (i.e., not positive, autonomisable, measurable or codifiable). It is the ambivalence (positive and negative) of personal exchange – and as such it is radically opposed to all values (ibid.: 125–7).

For Baudrillard, therefore, consumer society marked a fundamental 'loss of (spontaneous, reciprocal, symbolic) human relations' (Baudrillard, 1998: 16) and yet, as he observed it was simultaneously rife with quests for 'personalization.' On this basis, he argued, 'we are seeing the systematic reinjection of human relations-in the form of *signs* – into the social circuit, and are seeing the *consumption* of those relations and of that human warmth *in signified form* (ibid.)'. Consequently, he proposed that consumer society implies not just a dramatic shift in the organization of exchange but, that it also entails a radical transformation in the way people relate to each other. To relate to someone as a sign object, or, as Baudrillard suggested, even to relate to one's self as such, is *not* to recognize or appreciate them for their unique or 'genuine' human qualities, but rather, it is to acknowledge them precisely because they recall an image or 'model' that is already located within a code of differences (ibid.: 95). As such, even though human beings may still desire spontaneous, personal relationships, or unique and meaningful experiences, from this perspective, the mediations of the semiotic code ensure that most attempts at distinction ultimately result in conformity, and that 'personal' encounters invariably bespeak a 'a system where social distance and the atrociousness of social relations are the objective rule' (ibid.).

Baudrillard's overall description of consumer society may be read as part of a longstanding tradition of scholarship which has posited an inherent tension between the development of a capitalist commercial society that subordinates human relations to the homogenizing calculus of exchange value, and the maintenance of a more intimate and 'authentic' social sphere where human relations and individuals are still valued and recognized for their qualitatively unique features and attributes. And, it is important to note that such representations have been countered by numerous scholars. For instance, Viviana Zelizer suggests that this kind of argument is often un-problematically assumed rather than empirically validated, and in many cases, she argues, people not only find ways of integrating personal and market life, but the two may be used to sustain each other (Zelizer, 1994; 2005). Daniel Miller warns that such narratives, which are 'identified with an exploitative, alienating, modern, capitalist culture' 'exploit' a set of core 'myths and clichés' about the nature of consumption and consumer society (Miller, 1995: 20) and tend to be premised upon 'a myth of the past' which views 'the primitive' as 'the possessor of a true unmediated sociality' and which regards pre-capitalist society as more 'authentic' than its successor (ibid.: 23). He also cautions that these critiques are often linked to 'an increasingly meaningless debate' about the morality of consumption which, 'seems to depend almost entirely on whether consumption is seen as a passive process reflecting producer interests or an active process representing consumer interests' (ibid.: 28).

Certainly, these criticisms may be reasonably applied to Baudrillard's early writings on consumption. However, despite these shortcomings, I want to suggest that in this analysis there is still something important to be gained by drawing upon, as well as interrogating the limitations of his early work. First, as will be seen in the coming sections, Baudrillard's early, more modernist critique of consumer society and his tendency to view it as a dehumanizing development, actually echoes many of the views that Western tourists themselves espouse. In that sense, his characterization, whether empirically accurate or not, may be seen as reflective of a broader set of shared cultural beliefs about the relationship between capitalist market society and the 'deterioration' of social values and relations. While it is certainly valid to caution that such portrayals of consumer society demand empirical investigation and require more careful ethnographic analysis, it is also a mistake to simply discount these representations as baseless 'myths,' or overlook the ways they operate as powerful narratives which orient and shape consumers' lived experiences, motivations, and desires. Second, although Baudrillard's attempt to differentiate between consumption and symbolic exchange reflects a modernist nostalgia for the decline of a more 'authentic' era in human social relations, as an *analytical* distinction, these categories, and the differences they reference are useful to retain, even if in the end, it can be demonstrated that the instantiation of consumption and symbolic exchange may be intimately connected rather than diametrically opposed.

Indeed, in the remainder of this chapter, I will argue that instead of being radically opposed to each other, as Baudrillard tended to present them, the instantiation of symbolic exchange and consumption may be intimately connected and even exist simultaneously. That is, I will argue that tourists' desires to enter into relations of symbolic exchange with these children may be seen as a *response to*, rather than a *transcendence of* a regime of consumption and commercialization which they viewed as fundamentally alienating and dehumanizing. Thus the personal relationships that tourists established with these children through symbolic exchange subsequently emerged as sign objects which tourists appropriated in their efforts to create and consume more compelling and 'authentic' travel experiences in India, and as such, they were integrated into a larger code of signs that tourists drew upon in their efforts to distinguish themselves as particular kinds of consumers/travelers in India. Finally, in viewing these interactions as instances of *both* symbolic exchange and consumption I want to suggest that instead of starkly opposing a more 'authentic' and personal world of symbolic exchange against an abstract reified world of consumption, it seems more productive to try and illuminate how the realm of personal, intimate exchange is never free from broader processes of rationalization, and yet also, how processes of rationalization frequently escape total reification; they too can resonate with traces of ambivalence and elements that may be more difficult to codify.

The tourists

The data used in this chapter was gathered during twenty months of fieldwork that I conducted in Banaras between January of 1999 and November of 2001. My research objective was to analyze interactions between Western tourists, and the lower class and lower caste children who work as unlicensed peddlers and guides along the city's famous riverfront, particularly near the Main Ghat of Dasashwamedh. The primary means of data collection consisted of participant observation and formal and informal interviews which were conducted with tourists, the children who worked along the riverfront, and local residents in the neighborhood where the research was based.

From expressions of utter adoration, to hostile disdain, the reactions that tourists had to these children were rarely neutral and the primary goal of the study was to examine why and how these children elicited such powerful responses from tourists, and how they came to mediate and signify a much larger set of social, cultural, economic, and interpersonal relations and tensions. Consequently, the tourists who were selected as informants were primarily those who were observed interacting with these youngsters. Most of these tourists were self-proclaimed 'low budget travelers' or 'backpackers' who were on extended tours throughout India and Asia but, who usually visited the city for no more than a week, and often times, just a few days. As other scholars have noted, such travelers typically come from middle class backgrounds, prefer to travel alone or in small groups, and view their journeys as various kinds of quests, either for authenticity, self-discovery or as rites of passage (Noy, 2004; Riley, 1988). Although most of the tourists interviewed for this study conformed to such characterizations, it is important to note that they also comprised a diverse group and certainly had personal 'baggage' that colored their experiences and interactions in very particular ways. However, despite these idiosyncrasies and differences in age, country of origin, occupation and gender, their responses to the children on the riverfront, and their desires to enter into relationships with them often revealed a range of strikingly similar patterns, and it is these patterns of response that I will analyze below.

In so doing, I will also argue that the personal relationships that tourists sought to establish with these children not only emerged as objects of consumption, but they also suggested a shift in the very *modality* of tourist consumption. The idea that tourism, like consumption in general, is organized around the production and appropriation of signs has been widely noted (Culler, 1981), and yet, within the literature, overwhelming attention has been paid to the way these signs are appropriated in and through the gaze (Bhattacharyya, 1997; Hutnyk, 1996; McGregor, 2000; Mellinger, 1994; Urry, 1990). This recurring tendency to prioritize the ocular has led to a depreciation of the highly interactive nature of much tourist consumption and travel. Not only is the gaze frequently interrupted and challenged in and through the encounters that tourists have with local people. But, as other scholars have pointed out, (Adams, 1996) and, as will be seen in this chapter, often, this is precisely what is desired. On its own, gazing provides only a partial, and for many travelers, a deeply unsatisfying mode of consumption and what is yearned for instead is the opportunity to *interact* with locals and develop relationships which make travel experiences seem more intimate, authentic, or unique.

The riverfront of Banaras

As one of the most ancient metropolises in the world, and as one of the most important pilgrimage sites for Hindus, the city of Banaras, also known as Benares, Kashi, and Varanasi, has long occupied a powerful place in national and international imaginings of India. Its status as an ultimate icon of 'the timeless, mystical East' has been most poignantly preserved through images of its famous riverfront, which meanders four miles along the crescent shaped bend of the sacred river Ganga For most of the year, when the river is low, the contiguous chain of broad landings or steps, known as *ghats*, form a cherished promenade for residents and tourists who wish to spend some time sitting, or strolling along the city's edge.

For many of the lower class and lower caste children who live near the riverfront and use the ghats as a place to bathe and play, this influx of travelers has rendered the riverfront a lucrative place to do business. Between late October to the end of March, when the tourist season is at its peak, children can be found peddling postcards and souvenirs or, offering their guiding services to foreign tourists. One of the most popular areas for these children to work, and the place where I concentrated my research, is near the Main Ghat of Dasashwamedh. The area surrounding Dasashwamedh Ghat and the bustling Godaulia Bazaar which sits atop it, have long been a central artery for foreign tourist traffic, and today, Dasashwamedh Ghat continues to be one of the most popular departure points for boat rides down the Ganga.

On an average day during the tourist season, there were usually between twenty to thirty children operating on or near the vicinity of Dasashwamedh Ghat. Selling postcards and trinkets was secondary to the objective of guiding foreign tourists for many of these children, especially the boys, who were permitted to move more freely about the city. The children usually offered to guide tourists around the city of free of charge, an offer which some tourists immediately found suspicious and others endearing. However, ultimately the children's goal was to lure these customers into different shops where they received a commission if the tourist purchased something. Thus, while the riverfront usually provided the initial space of encounter, and the place where these youngsters first found and 'wooed' (*pataana*) their customers, most of their earnings were predicated upon successfully transitioning tourists from the riverfront to the bazaar above.

For Western tourists, being on the riverfront, like being in Banaras, was often an ambivalent experience. On the one hand, as numerous scholars have noted, it is a fantastic space that locates tourists at the very center of the Romantic imaginary of India (Cohen 1998; Cohn 1996; Huberman 2005) and enables them to indulge in a range of personal and collective fantasies. The numerous tea stalls and drink stands that line the long promenade of landings also provide some of the most popular places for tourists to congregate and exchange stories and information with other travelers as well as locals. In contrast to the streets and markets above, many tourists find the riverfront to be a comparatively peaceful place which offers a space of relief from the congested urban bustle. During religious holidays and festivals, when the riverfront is besieged by thousands of pilgrims and visitors, the tranquility of the ghats gives way to a more carnivalesque atmosphere which inspires some tourists to 'let loose and be more playful,' and drives others back into the calm and safety of their guest houses. Indeed, even during more 'tranquil' times, for some tourists the comparatively open space of the ghats seems to render them even more susceptible to the unwanted advances of 'pushy salespeople' or 'curious' locals especially, as they draw near to Dasashwamedh Ghat where they are more actively pursued by a cadre of peddlers, guides, boatmen and masseurs. Tourists often said that when they were on the ghat they felt like they were being 'buzzed around like flies on shit,' or treated like 'walking dollars signs,' 'cash cows,' 'white freaks,' 'easy targets,' 'dumb foreigners' or 'oddities for Indians to make fun of.' The riverfront, and Dasashwamedh Ghat more specifically, are thus extremely complex spaces, which are marked by a recurring confrontation between locals' desires for commerce and tourists' attempts to escape it. As will be seen now, as central mediators in this conjuncture, the children who worked as peddlers and guides often elicited powerful reactions from these visitors.

The gift of chocolate

Jacqueline was in her mid-fifties and worked as a language and literature teacher in France at the Ecole Normale Superior. She was traveling with a lady friend, and it was her second visit to the city of Banaras. I was introduced to Jacqueline by Pramod, a thirteen-year-old boy on the ghat who frequently guided tourists. I was passing by while they were involved in a rather uncomfortable looking conversation; Jacqueline's face was twisted with confusion and skepticism and Pramod was smiling as though he had just been caught doing something wrong. Whether he called me over as favor or as a diversion I am still not sure but when I came up to say hello he immediately told Jacqueline that I was doing 'research' on tourists and rather boldly, insisted that she grant me an interview. Then, he quickly departed. Although somewhat bewildered by what had just transpired, Jacquline was amenable to the idea, and we set up an appointment for the next day.

During our interview, I asked Jacqueline how she had met Pramod, and as she answered, it became clearer to me why their conversation seemed so awkward when I observed them speaking the day before. As Jacqueline explained:

> J: We met Pramod one day on the ghat and we talked and we had planned a meeting for the next day, we wanted to go by boat with him and we fixed a meeting but he was not there. And I had ... because I had some chocolate, from home I brought chocolates for him because it was the only thing I had, because he was nice, he did not ask for money. Tourists in India are usually treated like walking dollar signs, but we had a nice relationship and because he wasn't there I was very disappointed because my feeling went out to him, and I got nothing back ... (in an animated and upset voice) and so he wasn't there and I ate all the chocolates because I was upset! And we met him two days after and I asked him and he told me 'I came,' but I don't think he came. So I said, 'I don't understand, we were here at the meeting point and we waited for a half an hour.' So I was disappointed because when you speak a long time with somebody and they are nice, they explain, and I understand ... because I am a tourist in India, so for me to meet Indian people is very important but for him he sees so many it doesn't matter, we need a relationship with Indian people because if you don't have a relationship it's not an interesting travel. We need Indians much more than they need us, they need our money. I think that we consume relationships, we need Indian relationships, if you go to India and you have no relationships ... why do people agree to pay somebody who is nice? It is normal they give ... but also when there is money involved you are not sure if it is something true or not, that's why it is so difficult with money, because you cannot ... so I don't know it's very difficult.

Pursuing this issue further, I then asked:

> JH: So you think that money makes it uncertain?
> J: It depends on the way it ... for example, if you, if somebody lets you feel that he wants only your money, and first money ... but if first he is nice with you, at the end, you know that he needs money

and he is nice and you want to give him . . . but immediately, it's more difficult and you don't know what he wants to give you, it's very, very difficult.

Like Jacqueline, many other tourists whom I met and spoke with also shared such feelings of uncertainty and tales of disappointment, and as is perhaps evident from the transcript above, in Jacqueline's case, these feelings were made manifest not only in what Jacqueline said, but in *how* she said it. Her speech was punctuated with emotional flair ups, deliberating pauses, and incomplete thoughts, and as we spoke, it seemed as though she was actually struggling to figure out why this encounter had left her so dismayed.

Jacqueline's remarks raise interesting questions about the kinds of expectations and desires which fueled tourists' interactions with these youngsters. More specifically, they draw attention to the ways that money, or rather requests for it, became an important signifier in these exchanges. By breaking down this narrative and examining it more closely, I hope to begin to delineate what and how tourists wanted to consume in these encounters, and I explore some of the obstacles that they faced in trying to do so.

Jacqueline's remarks move from an account of what happened, to an explanation of why it happened, to a series of broader reflections on her status as a tourist and interactions with people in India. Beginning with the first dimension, Jacqueline reported that she and her friend met Pramod on the ghat, spoke with him for a while, and then agreed to meet him the following day for a boat ride. Jacqueline arrived bearing chocolates for Pramod, however, when he failed to show up, Jacqueline devoured the sweets in a fit of disappointment.

Within the first part of her account, therefore, several interesting points and questions emerge. First of all, what was Jacqueline's *gift* of chocolates supposed to symbolize or secure? Why did she bring them to India in the first place? And, why did she want to give them to a boy whom she had just met the day before, proclaiming, that it was 'the *only* thing' she had to offer him?

It is significant, and not at all unusual, that Jacqueline brought chocolates with her to India. Guide books consistently frame India as a place for giving. At the most extreme end, they instruct tourists on how to make charitable donations, either through monetary contributions or personal service to different organizations or individuals. They also frequently advise tourists to bring small items, such as candy or pens to hand out to the children whom they encounter on their travels. However, in this case, Jacqueline's offer went beyond a mere 'hand out' and was motivated by feelings of appreciation and indebtedness. As Jacqueline remarked, Pramod 'was nice, he did not ask for money.' In other words, from Jacqueline's perspective, Pramod had already gifted her with the courtesy of *not* treating her like a tourist, or in her words, as 'a walking dollar sign' and this surprising gesture was itself significant enough to stir Jacqueline's feelings and make her want to reciprocate. However, because Jacqueline viewed money as a potential stumbling block to a 'nice relationship,' (and as an uncomfortable reminder of her status as a tourist), she required a different medium through which to return his kindness: chocolates from home. If the gift of chocolates expressed Jacqueline's feelings of gratitude, and her desires to even deepen her relationship with Pramod, her ultimate consumption of the sweets may be read as a self-consoling attempt to digest her disappointment when the reciprocity did break down, and she received 'nothing back' in return.

In the second part of her narrative, Jacqueline shifted from an account of *what* happened to an explanation of *why* it happened. From Jacqueline's viewpoint, the disappointing encounter was hardly the product of a personality clash or a casual misunderstanding. Rather, it reflected the way that she, as a Western tourist, and Pramod, as an Indian guide whose life was inundated with tourists, were differentially positioned in regards to a larger set of structural relations, interests, and antagonisms. According to Jacqueline, while tourists long to develop relationships with Indians who can make their travel experiences unique and interesting, boys like Pramod, her comments imply, seek to extract the same homogenous, substance from all of them. These differing interests and positions, Jacqueline maintained, also give rise to an asymmetry in power relations between the tourist and 'the toured.' Boys like Pramod can easily pursue another tourist if the prospects at hand do not look profitable. But as Jacqueline proposed, travelers like herself become emotionally invested in these relationships, they *'need'* them, for they not only play upon the traveler's desire to be seen as something other than a tourist, but they also provide the critical link between the tourist and his or her 'passage' to India: as Jacqueline queried, if tourists travel to India but have 'no relationships,' then what? Have they really seen or experienced the country?

Jacqueline thus identified 'the relationship' as the object of consumption and in so doing she suggested that the relationship itself functions as a *sign* of an authentic experience of India. However, unlike tangible products whose structural properties and integrity are clearly defined from the outset, or sign objects that already exist within a hierarchical code, these 'relationships,' as her remarks above make clear, represent a significantly different kind of 'object' for they can only emerge as such retrospectively. They are created in and through interactions, which require skillful performances and an apt sense of timing. Moreover, in order for them to take on the status of a sign object *they have to first be experienced as gratifying.* This was rendered clear in the last part of Jacqueline's remarks when she explained that on the one hand, 'it is normal' and perhaps inevitable, at least when one is a tourist in India, to pay for relationships, 'to pay somebody who is nice.' However, on the other hand, she pointed out that as soon as money is involved it becomes increasingly difficult for the tourist to sustain his or her fantasy of creating a 'true' relationship. At such moments, money emerges as an unsettling signifier, which discourages tourists from following their hearts and forces them to acknowledge that they are still immersed in a highly rationalized system of exchange.

If the act of payment threatened to obliterate the very object that tourists wanted to consume, how then, was this tension reconciled? How did tourists pay for something, which from their perspective, was not supposed to have a price tag on it (See Zelizer, 1994)? And, how did the children whom they encountered on the ghats facilitate this process and help them feel as though they were developing qualitatively unique 'relationships' and not just involved in generic business transactions?

In many cases, these tensions did prove insurmountable and the encounter culminated with tourists feeling utterly disenchanted and the children on the ghats complaining about 'stingy foreigners' who did not pay them enough. However, as Jacqueline's remarks also suggest there were ways of reconciling these antagonisms. Through skillful performances and a keen sense of timing, the children on the ghats could make tourists feel as though they came first: the money was not a payment demanded by the children, but rather a gift, lovingly bestowed upon them through the tourists' own initiative and feelings of gratitude and generosity. Such strategies – and they were indeed conscious ones which the youngsters on the ghat openly discussed – not only played upon the tourist's longing to be seen and treated as more than a dollar sign, but they also accommodated their desire to *remain in control* of these encounters and to *preserve the power* of being able to decide when, where, and how much they would give. As John Hutnyk has remarked in his study of low budget charity tourism in Calcutta: 'the Western visitor has the power to give and yet also fake the gift, and abandon the effort when the demand becomes too much' (Hutnyk, 1996, p. 209).

Paradoxically, therefore, while tourists longed to have 'real' relationships with these youngsters, the relationship itself required a certain amount of 'misrecognition' (Bourdieu, 1977) in order for it to develop. If, from the beginning, tourists openly acknowledged that these children wanted or needed their money it was, as Jacqueline noted, very difficult for them to invest their feelings in the encounter. As Jacqueline suggested, only 'at the end' could the tourist comfortably acknowledge this truth because by that point, the tension was resolved: the tourist *'wanted to give.'* In such cases, therefore, the production of an 'authentic' experience or relationship was not oriented around the tourist's struggle to 'get back stage' (MacCannell, 1976), have an absolutely 'spontaneous' or 'natural' interaction, or discover the 'real' motives and desires of the other, but rather, it was dependent upon the tourist's *disinclination* to even try.

What is perhaps more interesting, however, is that this kind of misrecognition not only enabled tourists to construct desirable images of these children and their relationships with them, but it also played a pivotal role in the way they constructed desirable images of themselves. In some situations, tourists could derive an immense amount of pleasure and sense of empowerment by being able to reward or punish these children with money, but many tourists did not want to acknowledge such asymmetries, or discover that they were the kind of people who would use purchasing power as a way of coercing good behavior or affection from these youngsters. Consequently, while Jacqueline may have been correct to identify the personal relationship as the object of tourist consumption, what must also be noted is that the relationship that was produced, consumed, and desired in these encounters was not just one between the tourist and the Indian child, but it was also one between the tourist and his or her self. As Baudrillard pointed out, tourists did frequently draw upon 'models' such as the benevolent and generous Western benefactor, in constructing images of themselves as certain kinds of travelers in India.

Foster children

Indeed, 'saving the children', was one of the more common roles that tourists assumed in relation to the youngsters whom they encountered on the ghats, and elsewhere in India, a phenomenon which Hutnyk has also observed in his study of low budget charity tourism in Calcutta (Hutnyk, 1996). For instance, Sara was a twenty-nine-year-old nurse from Canada who was working as volunteer at a clinic in Nepal. Sara had come to Banaras for a two week vacation to celebrate the festival of Holi and during her stay she had met and befriended three little girls who sold postcards on the ghat (Jaila, Ritthi, and Seenu). 'These girls,' she told, me, 'have totally made my stay here, I've gone to their house, I've met their parents, I've gotten a real insight into their lives!' The day before the holiday, Sara decided to take the girls shopping for new outfits. Recounting their excursion, she said:

> S: I would have preferred to spend the money on something more useful for them, but of course, every little girl wants a pretty dress! I remember how much I loved getting a new dress when I was little. When we were in the store Ritthi was petting and kissing this one dress which was ughh, very frilly and way too much like Western duds but eventually she found a different one, but I bought *salwar kurtas* for Jaila and Seenu, I just can't resist little kids in a *salwar kurta*!.

This excursion enabled Sara to revisit her own pleasant childhood memories, express her charitable good will, step into the role of the nurturing mother (or rather, Mother Theresa), and it allowed her to exercise control over these children. By taking these youngsters on this shopping spree, steering them away from the 'Western duds,' and ultimately outfitting them in traditional Indian garb, Sara was able to refashion their images in ways that she found more aesthetically pleasing and that enabled her to better sustain her own illusions of an 'authentic' India. Nor, were these girls the only ones who Sara befriended and shopped for. On the many occasions when I ran into her on the ghats, or elsewhere in town, I saw her buying treats and presents for various other children who worked on the riverfront. When I asked Sara how she had enjoyed her stay in Banaras she responded: 'It's been great, I've spent two weeks here, four hundred dollars, and now I've got about 20 foster kids!'

The shopping list

While many tourists took these children on shopping sprees when they were in Banaras, other tourists sent gifts and money to these youngsters from home. Such was the case with Marion. Marion worked as political organizer in California and was in her mid fifties. She was traveling alone but upon her arrival in Banaras she met two boys who became her guides. Recalling their introduction she said:

> M: When I stopped for a coke in the street I ran into two young men one 12 and one 15, that were just as sharp as little tacks, and after talking to them for a while they asked me if I wanted to go for a

sunset boat ride, and the price sounded right and I liked the both of them by that time and I said, 'sure, sure.' And so we went out we had a great time. At one point, I pulled out pictures me and my family to show them. I had one small picture of myself and my husband and they said, 'can I have the picture, can I have picture of you?' And then they started fighting over who was going to have the picture and I don't think they would do that if they didn't really have an interest in who I am and you know, so I wrote my name on the back and the date. They're really great kids. So at the end, I told them that I would like to see some of the sights, and that I would like them to show me around, that I would like their company to do it. So they're going to take me out again tomorrow.

As was the case with Jacqueline, in Marion's account it is also evident that it was not just the great personalities of these children that endeared them to her, but again, it was that these boys made her feel recognized as a unique person. In fact, Marion was so appreciative of the boys' gestures that after spending one afternoon with them, she had already decided to put them on her 'shopping list.' As she explained:

M: One of them, probably two of them are already on my shopping list, (laughing).
JH: What do you mean by your shopping list?
M: Well there's a couple of people ... I have one person who I'm buying binoculars for, one person who I'm going to send a maglite to, one person a Swiss army knife and you know a couple watches, and when I give my word, my word is you know, something I'm going to follow through with, and I met one nice young man in Gokarna, and I had a Swiss Army knife with me and he wanted one and I said it was a gift from my husband and I can't give away presents and he agreed with me and I said, 'well I will you send you one' ... so that's what I mean about my shopping list.

In many other places throughout our interview, Marion emphasized the importance of making good on promises and demonstrating that she was a woman of her word, but in addition to advertising these virtues and values in herself, she also made it clear that she was trying to impart them to the people whom she met on her travels. The boys would not only be the beneficiaries of presents from abroad, but from Marion's perspective they also stood to gain valuable moral lessons and interpersonal skills by following her exemplary conduct.

In terms of the present discussion though, what is more noteworthy about Marion's remarks is that Marion herself describes gifts as objects that bind people together or, to use Baudrillard's terms, are 'inseparable' from the relationships they establish, and thus 'cannot be given away.' In addition to proving her credibility, therefore, the gifting of these items provided Marion with a way of demonstrating that a relationship had been established and that she was in fact, present in these people's lives. However, once again, the point here is not just that tourists like Marion longed to establish these seemingly more authentic relationships based on symbolic exchange. It is also that the relationships themselves became important signs for tourists which enabled them to achieve a certain level of distinction (Bordieu, 1984). Like Sara and Jacqueline, Marion, also used these relationships to construct personalized travel narratives which set her apart from other tourists who merely *saw* the sights, and by the end of her trip she would have acquired a virtual tourist map of all *the people* whom she had encountered in India.

Conclusion: shopping *for* people, or shopping for *people*?

All of these examples, therefore, beg the question: Were these tourists shopping *for* people or, were they shopping for *people*? That is, were they engaged in symbolic exchange or, were they engaged in consumption? The answer, I suggest, is both. The personal relationships which tourists sought to establish through gift exchange, simultaneously became appropriated and manipulated as sign objects which enabled these visitors to elaborate more 'authentic' 'unique' and 'intimate' passages to India. On the one hand, therefore, these relationships became part of a code of differences which enabled travelers to distinguish themselves as certain kinds of consumers in India but, on the other hand, they took on symbolic significance and imbued tourists with the hope that they might be able to transcend their status as consumers, and, as Jacqueline put it, be treated as something more than 'walking dollars signs.' In other words, to return to the question posed at the outset of this chapter, 'the something extra' that tourists sought from these children, was a form of recognition that made them feel like unique and special human beings, rather than generic tourists or consumers.

By focusing on the *lived experiences* of consumption, this chapter has also demonstrated that the ways in which people, money, objects and relationships take on value within markets, particularly informal ones, cannot be assumed at the outset. First, attention must be paid to how buyers and sellers draw upon particular cultural frameworks and narratives in negotiating and interpreting their transactions. As such, throughout this chapter I have argued that we need to take seriously the meaningful distinctions that tourists made between a more personal, 'authentic' realm of symbolic exchange and a more rationalized and 'dehumanizing' sphere of consumption. For instance, I showed that as one of the more ubiquitous signs of this rationalized system of exchange, the children's requests for *money* often became deeply unsettling for tourists. But, I also demonstrated that by viewing money as a gift rather than payment, tourists were able to overcome this aversion and make their dollars 'work' towards their desired ends.

From a methodological perspective this implies that studying the lived experiences of consumption also requires studying the ways that cultural distinctions and signs are deployed and reworked in *practice*. Money, people, objects and relationships do not just take on value as instantiations of particular cultural categories that exist in some abstract and fixed system. But rather, their significance emerges through being deployed in dynamic human interactions and projects in the world (Sahlins, 1981). Thus by paying closer attention to the communicative goals and blunders that shape transactions between buyers and sellers in the marketplace, we may arrive at a more adequate understanding of the lived experiences of consumption as ongoing and contingent *process*.

Finally, turning our attention to the specific relations and contexts that shape people's experiences of consumption, does not, however, mean disregarding the larger ones with which they articulate. The challenge, as Danile Miller so aptly puts it, is to assume 'a dialectical perspective that ... proceeds by rearticulating the sundered local and global. On the one hand we observe the manner by which both individuals and groups objectify themselves and their values through their material culture and consumption acts. The aim is to reveal the humanity of this process. But this must be reattached to the study of the micro and macro projects of commerce' (Miller, 1995: 53–4). Thus, in viewing these interactions as instances of both symbolic exchange and consumption, I have attempted to render faithful the personal experiences and practices of the Western tourists whom entered into transactions with the children on the river-front of Banaras. However, I have also suggested that their very efforts to engage these youngsters in more 'personal' forms of symbolic exchange may be viewed as a response to rather than a complete transcendence of a rationalizing sphere of consumption that they found alienating and dehumanizing. In concluding therefore, I want to emphasize that from an analytic standpoint, instead of starkly opposing a more 'authentic' and personal world of symbolic exchange against a reified world of consumption, as Baudrillard (and many tourists) tended to do, it seems more productive to assume a more dialectical perspective and try to illuminate how the realm of personal, intimate exchange is never free from broader processes of rationalization, and yet also, how processes of rationalization may themselves embody traces of ambivalences and elements that may be more difficult to codify.

References

Adams, Vincanne (1996). *Tigers of the Snow and Other Virtual Sherpas* (New Jersey: Princeton University Press).

Baudrillard, Jean (1981). *For a Critique of the Political Economy of the Sign* (United States: Telos Press).

—— (1988). *The Consumer Society* (London: Sage Publications).

Bhattacharyya, Deborah (1997). 'Mediating India: An Analysis of a Guidebook,' *Annals of Tourism Research* 21(2) 371–89.

Bourdieu, Pierre (1977). *Outline of a Theory of Practice* (Cambridge: Cambridge University Press).

—— (1984). *Distinction: A Social Critique of the Judgment of Taste* (Cambridge: Harvard University Press).

Caine, W.S. (1890). *Picturesque India: A Handbook for European Travelers* (London: Routledge).

Cohen, Lawrence (1998). *No Aging in India: Alzheimer's, the Bad Family, and Other Modern Things* (Berkeley: The University of California Press).

Cohn, Bernard (1996). *Colonialism and Its Forms of Knowledge* (New Jersey: Princeton University Press).

Culler, Jonathan (1981). 'Semiotics of Tourism,' *American Journal of Semiotics*, Vol. 1. Nos 1–2, 127–40.

Huberman, Jenny (2005). 'Consuming Children: Reading the Impacts of Tourism in the City of Banaras,' *Childhood*, Vol. 12, No. 2 (London: Sage Publications).

Hutnyk, John (1996). *The Rumor of Calcutta: Tourism, Charity and the Poverty of Representation* (London: Zed Books).

Kirschenblatt-Gimblett, B (1988). *Destination Culture: Tourism, Museums, and Heritage* (Berkeley: University of California Press).

MacCannell, Dean (1976). *The Tourist: A New Theory of the Leisure Class* (London: Macmillan).

Marchant, William (1896). *In India* (transl. from the French of Andre Chervrillion) (New York: Henry Holt).

McGregor, Andrew (2000). 'Dynamic Texts and Tourist Gaze: Death, Bones and Buffalo,' *Annals of Tourism Research* 27(1) 27–50.

Mellinger, Wayne (1994). 'Toward a Critical Analysis of Tourism Representations,' *Annals of Tourism Research* 21(4) 792–811.

Miller, Daniel (1995). 'Consumption as the Vanguard of History,' *Acknowledging Consumption*. Daniel Miller (ed.) (London: Routledge) pp. 1–57.

Riley, Pamela (1988). 'Road Culture of International Long-Term Budget Travelers,' *Annals of Tourism Research*. Vol. 15. 313–28.

Noy, Chaim (2004). 'This Trip Really Changed Me: Backpacker's Naratives of Self-Change,' *Annals of Tourism Research*. Vol. 15: 315–28.

Sahlins, Marshall (1981). *Historical Metaphors and Mythical Realities* (Ann Arbor: The University of Michigan Press).

Zelizer, Viviana (1994). *Pricing the Priceless Child: The Changing Social Value of Children* (New Jersey: Princeton University Press).

—— (2005). *The Purchase of Intimacy* (New Jersey: Princeton University Press).

Part II
Blurred Boundaries Between Market and Home

4

'Pleasure from Bitterness': Shopping and Leisure in the Everyday Lives of Taiwanese Mothers

YuLing Chen
National Taiwan College of Physical Education

There is no epithet with enough precision to encompass the relationship between Taiwanese mothers and shopping in their everyday lives. For those who live in the urban environment, shopping and shopping places seem to be a natural attachment blended into women's daily life since childhood. Women of Taiwan virtually grow up within and among shopping places – from the local marketplace right next to our homes, to the department store located behind our high schools, and the street trade located in every corner on our way to every other place. Shopping is ever-present in women's life perspective – literally and symbolically – starting at the time when our mothers ask that very first question: 'Hey dear, do you want to go to marketplace with mom?'

To be sure, the traditional gender ideology intends to train women to become the primary consumers and make that identity a fundamental component of 'feminine' identity (see Pringle, 1983; McDowell, 1999). Yet, any observer of the Taiwanese social scene cannot deny that the shopping place might be the only significant space that allows women to surpass men in the public sphere where women's needs, preferences, and decisions are both seriously considered and respected (Rappaport 2000a,b, also see Underhill, 2000; Benson, 1988). Furthermore, shopping not only refers to a mere money–object exchange activity but also offers an ideal place for the life representation and social relationship a woman chooses for herself and her family. In particular, shopping has become a specially marked activity for mothers due to their constrained situation and unshirkable duty resulted from the ethic of care (Gilligan,

1984). Once a woman moves to the stage of 'settling down' that usually involves marriage and the emergence of parenthood, she is forced to confront dramatic changes in her every aspect of life, including her lifestyle and identity (Green, 1998). As her focus shifts to the care of and relations with family (see Rapoport and Rapoport, 1975), it seems 'natural' for a married woman to start to view herself from the perspective of the roles she has with respect to her relations. Finding a way to rejuvenate their spirit and replenish their emery becomes a central preoccupation for mothers living in a situation of time deprivation and limited mobility.

As many have pointed out, a mother's role is not as passive as conventionally assumed. Instead, mothers' agency is revealed through the process of the 'war' (as one interviewee put it) they had to confront on an everyday basis – it is a war of balancing their own time and activities over and against those of their children and husband (Green, 1998; Coates, 1996). In particular, mothers are able to find resources to assist their duties and dig up the possibilities to do something outside their routine (tasks) in order to achieve one purpose: prevent the damage caused by overwork. This lifestyle – occurring in almost every mother's ordinary life – endows leisure with significance because they need an efficient retreat from their daily battlefield. However, mothers' retreat is different from other people's, like many husbands and many single women, who have a clear separation between their work and non-work time segments. Moreover, it is necessary for them to stay vigilant without making any big mistakes as long as their children are present. Hence, mothers are forced to confront constraints concerning what they can and cannot do to accommodate their own needs to their daily situation. As Ms N related:

> In interviews conducted with Taiwanese mothers, I found that they are able to create new meanings from their daily routine and actively interpret them in the process of constructing a different self-representation from their everyday experience would itself seem to allow. In particular, how mothers' acknowledge the significance of leisure, originally seen as almost an impossibility within motherhood, becomes an key issue. The mothers found their leisure to be a mixed, contradictory experience as it is inseparable from their obligations. 'Ku-zhung-zhu-lo' is the term they often used to refer to the idea that a mother needs to be capable of gaining some fun from doing some harsh or weary activities because, as Mrs J put it, 'This [motherhood]is a choice among no-choice, rather than continuously complaining about your situation.'

In the context of motherhood, leisure acquires a dramatic new meaning – gaining happiness from bitterness. I found that shopping, in particular, has become a special activity for mothers because it offers a place and a context for them to acquire and claim a 'mixed leisure experience' while they are performing their domestic duties (Jansen-Verbeke, 1987; Bowlby, 1997; Maenpaa, 1997; Rappaport 2000a,b). Ms H, for example, describes how she felt when she is doing shopping in Chinese traditional market (TM) place:

> You have to go there [traditional market] frequently, you know, because I have to prepare meals for family, but I like to go there, or I should said, I enjoy going there and buying stuff ... in that place I can do lots of stuff, and buy lots of stuff, eat lots of stuff. Although I know the major purpose to go there is buying groceries for family, but it's fun!

Based on mothers' unique living situation, this ethnographically-based study asks: 'How does shopping blend in mothers' everyday life?' and 'How do mothers recognize the role of shopping in their daily routine?' As Mowl and Towner (1995) discuss, the beauty of these answers seem to hide behind the diverse meanings and applications of shopping according to different places and with respect to different performers (shoppers). In particular, if we analyze the concept of shopping from the perspective of mothers' leisure, or their hoped-for leisure, its significance will take on a new light.

For the purpose of understanding what type of meanings shopping carries in mothers' everyday practice, I examined how Taiwanese mothers practice and understand this 'mundane but pleasurable' activity by privileging mothers' daily situation through the direct exposure of their voice. Through interviews conducted with 21 Taiwanese mothers in 2003 and 2004, I came to understand how identity, geography and consumption intersect and interacted their daily lives to produce particular tactics for balancing obligation to others with personal pleasure (see Mowl and Towners, 1995). The significant point here is that shopping occurs in particular places, involving particular social geographies, which substantially affect every aspect of a woman's life. These places as well also efficiently provide mothers an opportunity to rewrite their own identity and to use a new version of self to redefine their recognition toward leisure, and thus to acquire new meanings in this restricted life sphere. In particular, how mothers' agency functions in mothers' self-determination process will be the focus in the following analysis.

Between work and leisure: traditional markets and mothers' geographies

Evidently, Taiwanese mothers' use of space relates directly to their time problem. Due to the shortage of time or to their fragmented schedule, mothers' daily spaces appear centered around particular locations. These sites can be categorized as 'must-go' places that necessitate their access on a daily basis. All other activities, obligated or non-obligated, need to be accommodated to these locations and limited to the nearby areas in order to meet their time constraints. However, in urbanized Taiwan, shopping places of various kinds exist almost everywhere, and this fact benefits mothers' constrained lives and enriches their daily space with more possibilities, both in terms of their obligation and leisure.

Thus, although mothers' space is circumscribed by the demands posed by family obligations, some know how to dig up the possibilities around local areas for themselves by using their space wisely, like Ms N, a full time mother:

> I usually ride my scooter to deliver my sons to their schools or after-school centers.... One advantage of riding a scooter is that I can stop anywhere on my way home, like some special stores along the streets, such as the traditional markets or super markets, and...oh, flower markets, I like flower markets. So I can just use the time period between my sons' classes and do such kind of things instead of going home, browse a little bit, and have little fun by myself.

Those 'on the way' shopping places, especially the traditional markets [discussed below], turn out to play a very crucial position in those mothers' daily lives because of the advantage of accessibility. Mothers' daily routine can be tense, and the issue of their time shortage always presents a problem. In this context, both professional, working mothers and full-time mothers feel the requirement to stick to their major route based on their daily plan.

The accessibility makes mothers feel that shopping at those nearby marketplaces is an 'easier' thing to do. Ms H, a career woman with two kids, expressed this tendency when she talked about her daily schedule in terms of her geographic constraints:

> Basically, my daily routine is a triangle – my home, kids' place [i.e. school], and my office. I have no time to go far away from this triangle, and everything should be accomplished within the nearby areas

of this triangle. Like, I just told you I will use my lunch time to go shopping, and the market I usually go is right behind my office, only 2 minutes away, so it is easy for me just to go there to have some lunch and pick up some groceries for my household.

Here, a mother's geography is phrased in terms of a social geometry where 'the triangle' almost seems to encapsulate Mrs H's workaday life as it forms the practical boundary to her physical movement as a woman and mother.

Almost every mother I spoke with acknowledged the traditional market as the most important place among all shopping places. In addition to the 'easy come easy go' feature, a traditional market is also a decidedly 'feminine' place centering on motherhood. The primary goods carried in traditional markets are foods (meats, fresh vegetables, fruits, and deli), and the primary customers are those responsible for the cooking in households – married women and mothers. On the basis of traditional images, the groceries (foods) vended in traditional markets have been viewed as 'fresher' and 'cheaper' than at other shopping places.

This supremacy of product compensates the deficiency of the poor environment making it the biggest attraction of traditional markets. Market vendors carry non-grocery merchandise as well in order to extend their business to mothers such as women's clothes/cosmetics, children's clothes and related things, kitchen accessories, etc. The quality of that merchandise is not as upscale as in department stores or specialty stores, the price is considerably lower. This point grabs mothers' attention since they have different consideration then other social groups:

> There is lots of stuff there, like me, I will buy some comfortable wear there with a very cheap price, you know, a housewife does not need fancy clothes. So, if I see something good there, I'll buy it. Sometimes I will buy shoes, slippers, you know, I don't have extra time to go to department stores, so if I see something good in traditional market, I'll buy, if I don't expect something too fancy. (Ms C)

As I mentioned before, mothers reveal a particular, culturally inflected tendency in the ways they re-identify their daily experience via the self-negotiation between work and leisure – _Ku-zhung-zhu-lo_, gaining happiness from bitterness. In other words, these women are able to transform the experience of work or obligation into the feeling of pleasure or enjoyment. The marketplace in this sense becomes an ideal space for this transformation process. Based on the 'easy come easy go' and feminine-oriented characteristics, the traditional market – although still duty-oriented – can also transform into an extraordinary place for mothers. In this context, traditional markets have taken on a veil of a special role – places capable of providing something more than instrumental shopping for women and offering a context where mothers' identity can be seen as shifting from a passive task performer to an active leisure participant.

For example, a sense of enjoyment and pleasure emerges from mothers' voices:

> I *love* to go different markets. Every time, when I deliver my kid to his school, I will stop by there, use a short period of time to buy groceries, then I can browse around, look at some new stuff, talk to vendors asking about some recipes, try on some apparel, and of course, eating. *At a TM, you don't need to worry about your image, you can even eat while you are walking...* [laughing]. (Ms W)

Not having to 'worry about your image' – i.e. not feeling that one is under the gaze of others – promotes the sense of gratification among mothers and further makes women feel delightful because 'this place is made for me':

> *I love TMs to death.* It is hard to find a place that takes care for our (mothers) needs only. If a TM only carries foods and groceries, I won't choose it. For me, buying daily groceries is the last thing in a shopping trip at a TM, and basically, I believe, for almost every mother, the reason for spending so much time in TM is not buying food; instead, they are *browsing* and *looking around*, or trying something new, or for me, of course, eating ... ha ha. (Ms H)

That is true, traditional markets, like markets in general, can be places that offer its customers fun in addition to merchandise as Prus and Dawson (1991) put it. A market can be a 'playful place' for women thanks to its abundance, introducing a source of novelty into their mundane routine.

Mothers, in addition, understand the traditional market as a magical place with cultural meanings. It is particularly suited to endow mothers with the feeling of 'freedom.' As Ms S states:

> For me, the TM is such a *magical place*. It carries a lot of traditional stuff, can you believe that TMs still have my favor snacks when I was

a child? And, it got new stuff too, so I like goofing around, looking around, seeing something old and something new. If I have enough time, I can be there more than 2 hours. 100 bucks can buy lots of things, who wouldn't love it?

From these narratives, shopping at traditional markets turns out to be a fun experience for mothers, and this type of place has become a magical wonderland in mothers' ordinary lives, albeit a fleeting one. This 'magic,' however, is tied directly to women's practical, gendered experience and must be understood in the context of the women's own explanation of the meanings of leisure they experience. If women were unable to negotiate the meanings of their frivolous obligations associated with motherhood, or if women were not be able to believe they are entitled to gain pleasurable enjoyment in this restricted life span, it would be impossible for the traditional market to transform from an obligation-oriented place to a leisure-oriented wonderland.

Through the work of women's self-determination, even the most ordinary place can create a magic – that is, a transformative context – in mothers' mundane lives. They can browse, pick, choose very freely within their time limit, then pick-up and go to their next stop. Progressively, this type of shopping place – the 'on the way' playground – has become a must-have element within mothers' daily schedule.

Hypermarkets: a playground for all of us

The traditional market, as we have seen, fulfills several kinds and levels of needs and desires for mothers in terms of their weekday or work week lives. On weekends when the children are not attending school and neither parent goes to the office, another shopping place and experience offers opportunities to enfold domestic tasks into pleasurable activities:

> Every Saturday, or sometimes during weekdays, like the time after dinner, we (the whole family) will drive to Carrefour to buy some stuff.
>
> [What will you usually buy in Carrefour[1]?]
>
> Everything, depends on what we lack.... You can find everything there, and the price is ... um ... okay, of course it is not as cheap as stuff in TM, but I won't go to two different places for a couple of bucks, you know? (Ms N)

As Ms N pointed out, hypermarkets, the big-size and one-stop shopping place, gradually gain its significance in Taiwan mothers' shopping schedule since 1990s. Hypermarkets (HM) are usually located in a multifloored building with plenty of parking lots included to solve the urbanization space issue. In terms of merchandise, a hypermarket is combination of many different kinds of shopping places. In addition to offering the same foods and groceries as traditional markets, a hypermarket extends its service to retailing household appliances, clothes, housewares, children's merchandise, books, and other leisure-related merchandises. In other words, this is a 'everything under one roof' shopping place, similar to many so-called 'mega-stores' in the USA. At some level, this shopping place is like a department store that carries varied merchandise, only shifting focus from lifestyle, the fancy display, and upscale products. Rather, the emphasis of a hypermarket is on people's mundane needs rather than conspicuous consumption. Similar to the 'on the way' shopping places, a hypermarket usually targets common customers with daily interest. However, different from 'on the way' shopping places, hypermarket shopping holds a special spot in mothers' weekend schedule because access of hypermarkets is not as 'easy come easy go' as the TM:

> If I want to go Carrefour, I got better to ask my husband to drive me there because I always buy a lot of stuff in one shopping trip. I don't have to go there very often, but every time I go, I buy a lot. (Ms L)

Although hypermarket shopping has been viewed as a fundamental shopping place in mothers' daily lives, it has different meanings from shopping at traditional markets. From the perspective of daily necessities, including perishable foods, hypermarkets obviously provide a more ideal and convenient one-stop shopping place for mothers. Yet, in terms of foods, traditional markets still has its irreplaceable reputation for the freshness of seafood and meat, and the most importantly, the low price and different merchandise on a daily basis. Additionally, compared to traditional markets' focus on motherhood, hypermarkets tend to provide a more family-oriented space:

> It is different, two different places. The former [traditional market] is more traditional, and it is more ... um ... bustling, and freer. I don't need to wear my makeup, and I can even wear my slippers ... (laughing). But hypermarket is bigger and a little bit formal. It is very convenient, of course, and it is more modern, and friendlier to kids. (Ms Q)

With the reality of tightened and fragmented mothers' schedules, accomplishing tasks quickly and efficiently is their big concern:

> ... that's why I go to Da-Mei-Chia[2] because I can get everything there in one shopping trip. Every Saturday, I will use a period of time to go there and buy everything I need, like milk, yogurts, some fruits, and if I ran out of veggies, I will buy some veggies there too. (Ms A)

Hypermarkets have grown in popularity among mothers, due to their one-stop convenience which helps save time and energy. Additionally, the variety of goods and the clean environment a hypermarket offers provides more functions than mere grocery shopping. The enclosed environment and shopping carts allow mothers to feel that shopping with kids is not that difficult to control:

> I go to the traditional market by myself, but I prefer to go hypermarkets with my kids because of the environmental issue, you know, I can just put them in the shopping cart with the stuff we bought. Of course they are really annoying, but at least, I don't need to ask my husband to stay at home and watch them, that is impossible. Rather, I can bring them with me. So I can go there to shop anytime because we (her kids and she) are more mobile. (Ms L.)

It is not surprising that my conversational partners use 'we' – she, her husband and children – in their narratives of shopping trips. Compared to traditional markets' 'feminine' flavor and focus on motherhood, the hypermarket is rather a family shopping place because every family member can find their own spot there.

> It is quite ideal. The environment is good, clean and safe, and we go there together, so my husband can help me watch kids while I shop in the food area. Usually, my husband will bring my kids to look around, play something, I don't know exactly, but they stay in the books department and the music/video section a lot. I know they are there, so I just go ahead to buy my groceries first, then come back to find them. (Ms E)

This fact adds on a dramatic impact to the hypermarket's potential to become a family-oriented leisure place, especially on weekends. Although mothers still have to perform some 'obligation shopping' there, they also have an opportunity to browse, and more importantly, have fun *with their family*, while maintaining the coordination of tasks under the woman's control. From interviewees' descriptions, hypermarkets have become a usual place for family leisure, as it is not as strictly a gendered space as the traditional market. Their spouses do not resist this kind of shopping place and men (fathers) show more interests in appearing in such a place along with their children and wives. The burden in this way is lessened on the woman.

Mothers profoundly understand this advantage and constructively use it as an efficient way to manage family leisure. Ms H provides interesting comments:

> If you ask about our family leisure, let me tell you, it is very simple. Except for some kids' place, my family usually goes to different HMs if we are available to do that. Why? It is simple, I like buying foods, my husband likes to watch and test some exercise equipments, and my twins like to read. So, it is impossible for us to go to all those different places, then we go to hypermarkets, one place fulfills everybody's needs at one time. Isn't that simple?

As women themselves tell us, both traditional markets and hyper-markets serve an instrumental purpose. Still, each shopping place has a different charisma and character to attract mothers for different purposes and at different times of the week and day. The traditional market, doubtlessly, is the most significant daily place besides mothers' private sphere. Mothers buy fresh foods there, have fun browsing, enjoy the capricious goods, and most importantly, this place makes them feel happy and liberated without worrying about their dress, hairdo, social class, and money. Compared to the traditional market's intimacy and closeness to women, hypermarkets attempt to attract mothers' and other family members' attention by providing a big, easy-to-control, convenient, and fun surrounding able to satisfy 'everybody's interest.' The dimension of leisure, especially family leisure, can be represented by their family-oriented slogans – 'your best neighbor.'[3] This emphasis allows hypermarkets to become significant for family leisure while it simultaneously provides mothers with a chance to perceive themselves as ordinary consumers rather than domestic job performers.

Between a mother and a woman: department stores and women's self-representation

Being a mother is never an easy task in any culture. The tightness of women's time, resulting from obligations to perform multi-functional roles of caregivers impacts women's daily lives seriously and further affects the way they identify themselves in the context of family. However, being a mother does not mean a mother is a married women's only role. What if sometimes mothers do not want to recognize themselves as bounded to their family at all times? Indeed, my conversational partners revealed an eagerness for their personal freedom that could allow them to enjoy something not only belonging to the category of 'mothers':

> It's tiring, you know. being a mother has to stay alert all the time since you never know what will happen in the next second, and you need to battle with so much tiny and frivolous things. You'll feel restricted and exhausted, and gradually become an old, yellow-face-women[4] and forgot I am still an educated, highly professional, and modern woman in my working place. This is sad. (Ms M)

From this description we can understand that being mother is the most important role in many women's belief. Yet, being a mother does not mean a woman is obligated to only have this identity and disregard other identities she already had or she planed to create. In contrast to affiliated leisure that focuses on family relationship management (Henderson et al., 1989, 1996), women see another form of leisure as 'required' for daily life – i.e. the notion of 'Me time,' emerged from conversational partners' voices:

> It is really good to have some extra time to sit down, even for a short period of time. But it is really good to have that moment without yelling at kids or cleaning stuff. Sometimes even I don't want to talk since I am too exhausted and all I want to do is sit there, feel I am still alive, and enjoy the quietness. (Ms J)

As some researches pointed out, the 'quietness' here does not mean the real silence of her surroundings; instead, it implies a peaceful state of mind that can provide a mother with a moment to re-focus on herself (including her feeling and needs) again without worrying about some frivolous stuff that occupies most of her time. Except for 'doing nothing' or 'relaxing' (Henderson and Bialeschki, 1991; Freysinger, 1988; Russell, 2002), my interviewees revealed a tendency of utilizing this period of time as a chance to positively develop or enjoy something they like or to be whoever they want to be, rather than remain restricted in the role of motherhood. Those identities can be reflected by the activities they chose to perform in their me-time.

For example, Ms P chooses to be a professional shopper that enables herself to have the feeling of control:

> I love the feeling of controlling your money. I think while I am shopping, it is the only time that I feel I have the total control of everything.

For these mothers, 'me-time' is not only limited to providing women with a feeling of pleasure or relaxation. It also offers women a good site to extend their identity and enrich the meanings of motherhood. Compared to family leisure, 'me-time' carries more active, self-determinate purpose, including the backlash of their restricted identity and the entitlement of better treatment:

> I think, I should treat myself better. I treat anybody else better than myself. I didn't realize this fact until I got my second child because enough is enough. Before, I devoted every minute to take care of kids, but from now on I think I should leave more time for myself and go out to do something I enjoy or like, such as shopping ... (Ms N)

In this context, shopping has become a common 'me-time' strategy employed by Taiwanese mothers to re-identify their motherhood, and it is necessary to mention the other kind of shopping place – department stores (DS) – because this shopping place plays a very significant role in how mothers understand themselves:

> Everything in department stores is different, you *feel* different, even if you found similar or the same thing in other market places before, when you see that thing displayed on a delicate shelf, it is different. Of course, the price is a big difference ... ha ha, do you understand what I mean? (Ms P)

Unlike the ordinary monotony of other shopping places, department stores offer a style of shopping that opposes previously addressed shopping places in terms of purpose, atmosphere, environment, and consumers. Indeed, what a department store offers is everything but ordinary.

Similar to the USA, department stores symbolize the modernization of a city, and target the customers who seek a 'Happy New Life – quality life, delicate life, and tasteful life.'[5] In other words, the department store targets those willing to spend for something outside the routine, and it usually excessively praises the idea of the refined, luxury, and exquisite living style. Unlike other shopping places that present themselves as welcoming most anyone, a department store mostly targets the consumers able and willing to afford more tasteful and expensive commodities.

In essence a department store is a place for conspicuous consumption – above and beyond shopping styles.

> Going to a department store is not as easy as going to traditional markets, you know? I need to *dress up* a little bit, of course I won't dress too much since I am more casual. But at least I need to ware *make up* and something more formal than casual, you know? Otherwise, the service representatives are all very snobbish, they will look down on you if you ... um ... appear as a person from a rural area. (Ms F)

'Not ordinary' is the first characteristic that differentiates a department store from other shopping places, including the daily life perspective. The need of 'dressing up' or 'putting on make up' implies a different persona women play in this public consumption place, where the social judgments are involved in shaping women's and their families' social image. Different from the private sphere or traditional markets that are full of mundane, routine, and ordinary sense, a department store is a spectacle and modern place, that provides a place to be gazed at and at the same time with its consumers becoming the objects of being gazed at themselves (McDowell, 1999; Winship, 2000). It is a place of demonstration set up by commodities and consumers. In this context, shopping in department stores gives mothers a novel and extraordinary experience, and further allows mothers fully concentrate on themselves.

Shopping alone in such a 'wonderful' (i.e. literally, full of wonder) setting provides mothers the feeling of freedom which is hard to achieve in their daily routine:

> If I have chance to go there alone, I will feel ... um ... *feel free to look at what I like.* For example, I like crafts, and you know DS always carries lots of delicate crafts there, and I really like to go there alone, take my time, and look around. It is good to concentrate on myself, you know? (Ms W)

Although mothers express high interest in shopping alone in department stores, sometimes it is difficult to separate mothers from the restriction caused by the ethic of care (Gilligan, 1993). Similar to hypermarkets, department stores provide an ideal place for family leisure because of its multifunctional floors carrying different merchandise for different age groups. The department store is another form of 'everything under one roof,' but in a fancier, more luxurious and extravagant way. Over and above basic merchandise, such as women's apparel/cosmetics, clothes, children's department, teenagers' department, sports goods, leisure goods, and other luxury commodities, it also includes small-scale supermarkets, a bakery, bookstores, music stores, playgrounds/game zones (for kids and teens separately), and most importantly – formal restaurants and food courts. The variety of offerings and departments makes this kind of shopping place attractive for all, and particularly for families.

Based on my interviews, although shopping in department stores is not a everyday destination because the 'refined,' 'delicate,' and 'upscale' tendency is somewhat deviant from the mothers' perspective, mothers still sometimes express that they will go to department stores 'sometimes' to experience a feeling different from their ordinary lives. Instead of buying, most mothers reveal their interest in 'feeling' and 'browsing.' In Mrs U's words, their purpose may be purely to enjoy the surroundings and feeling young and unique again:

> You know, as a housewife I rarely have an opportunity to put on a beautiful dress and wear a make-up, sometimes I just feel I've become a 'yellow-face-woman,' you see what I mean? So sometimes I will go department stores either alone or with other sisters-in-law, have a cup of coffee at Starbucks,' look around, and buy some cosmetics or fancy stuff. It is nice to feel I am still able to do such things. (Ms U)

Or, when they feel they should treat themselves better, they might arrange a lavish shopping spree for themselves in order to reward their hard work:

> You know men, they are so stupid for buying stuff, so I prefer to use his money and buy something for myself if I feel I should do so. Like my birthday, Valentine's Day, or anytime I feel I should buy something good to reward myself. Haha, you know, I always very stingy when it comes to myself, and when I have chance, I will buy something good for me without any hesitation. (Ms A)

Naturally, more or less, mothers will buy something during their shopping trips, and usually spend a lot of time buying things for their children.

Similarly to what they do in other shopping places, it is difficult for a mother to divorce herself from motherhood during her shopping trip because she always mixes herself and others, thus making even the purpose of shopping usually for gaining a 'sense of self,' as Peiss points out (1986, p. 7). However, the point is simply to buy something: purchasing something for themselves or for other family members is not a big matter. Instead, what counts is the feeling of being connected with the outside world, seeing something new, gathering some information, having the feeling of control (money-wise), enjoying the environment, and most importantly, acquiring the sense of freedom by identifying themselves as a confident women, not constrained mothers:

> Shopping is amazing, you know, no matter where you shop or what you actually buy, you'll feel happy, because this activity is able to make you feel free, feel surprised, and feel connected to the world. It also can help me to update myself, and allow me to have a chance to get out of my house and become pretty and modern again ... (Ms E)

I shop, therefore I am

In mothers' mundane schedules, each day has different types of shopping involved in their routine. For a career mother, Monday to Friday is most hectic since she needs to determine how to use her restricted time efficiently. Under such time constraints, a career mom might go shopping at 'on the way shopping places' during her 'breaks,' such as lunchtime or shortly before dinner. If she has time, she may browse around for a while, and try to come up with a fun activity in the rare opportunity for relaxation. On weekends, she may spend longer time in traditional markets buying primary groceries for one week. Or, she will go to a nearby hypermarket with her family. A department store might serve as a destination for dining out on a Saturday night for herself and her family to spend fun time together and giving her possibilities for browsing around a little bit with her child. From time to time, she can pre-arrange some 'me-time' for herself in order to go to a department store alone to look for something new, enjoy being alone, or reward herself with little fancy gifts.

The crucial task for a full time mother is penetrating the barricade set up by their fragmented time and composed of felt requirements of 'intensive mothering' (Hays, 1996). Traditional markets or other 'on the way' market places will be an everyday place. When they deliver their children to school in the morning, they go to a local traditional market, buy fresh fish and veggies, and browse around, finding something attracting their attention, spending on something for family. In the afternoon, a mother may go to a nearby special market, such as flowers/plants market, for her own interest on her way to pick up the children. On occasion, if she has enough time, she can go to department stores too. Then before dinnertime, she might go to a local evening market again to search for cooking materials or delicious deli for dinner. After dinner, she and her family may go to nearby hypermarkets for family shopping if no special plan was determined in advance. Additionally, on weekends, she might plan dinning out in a nice restaurant. Sometimes she and her family will go to department stores and have family fun there since each family can find their favor spot.

So, what is shopping in mothers' everyday lives? What makes shopping places unique from other type of places? The answer depends on how we approach the concept of shopping and how we identify the role of performers. We have to understand the meaning of shopping could be a very monotonous activity, yet, the meaning of shopping could be varied, multi-dimensional, and cultural also, especially when we respect the self-determination process of shoppers and their subjective interpretation toward their daily situation. If we examine the idea of shopping without attending to women's agency or their ability to negotiate with constraints, shopping indeed appears to be extremely task-oriented for most of time.

Through the work of women's own agency, mothers are capable of developing their leisure possibilities and further extend the meanings of shopping. Obviously, shopping has become a leisure place after women's negotiation with their daily restrictions. It is a resistance to the reality; meanwhile, it is the re-claiming of their self-control, as Henderson (1991) said:

> ... if women believe that they are entitled to leisure, it may be useful to describe within a feminist framework how women can empower themselves and transform their lives through leisure. (p. 62)

According to the women I interviewed, shopping as an activity which encompasses the dimension of leisure thereby transforms mothers' restricted situations. Shopping, in other words can and does can empower women (Hine, 2002) *in particular contexts and in particular ways*, especially for those who have to battle with everlasting constraints resulting from love and an ethic of care. A few interviewees spent quite lot of time complaining about the structural constraints (Crawford *et al.*, 1991) they encountered in their everyday routines They also stated how they appreciated the possibilities provided by different shopping places that allow them to attain a feeling of control, even if transient and context bound.

From the interviews we discover that mothers are able to acquire the sense of power and further achieve higher self-respect via the gratification and benefits produced by shopping experience – particularly in terms of the use of time, space, money and identity. In terms of the use of time, the on-the-way shopping places such as traditional markets enable mothers to accomplish domestic jobs and experience enjoyment in a short, discrete periods of time; in terms of space, the characteristics of easy-come-easy-go and 'everything under one roof' enable mothers to efficiently control and extend their daily space without exerting undo much effort; in terms of money, shopping in their lives facilitates the ability to experience the *pleasure of control* in the process of spending and decision making, even when the explicit purpose of shopping is oftentimes instrumental. For an example, shopping surely provides mothers the sense of victory that implies 'being powerful':

> Bargaining is funny, you know, I have a price in you mind, and the seller has a price in his mind, then, we have to achieve a compromise. It is so fun. I got to tell you, not every woman can bargain. This ability is something to be proud of, you know, oh, the sense of victory ... ha ha ... (Ms U)

Additionally, in terms of identity, shopping helps hard-working mothers attain the feeling of being respected or spoiled due to the feminine-oriented atmosphere managed by many shopping places. In such places, mothers are active explores who can discover something attracting and bring it into their family, rather than being passive purchasing agents restricted by their shopping lists. The victory of their discovery has been demonstrated in every corner of their houses, such as their children's mugs, clothes, the dinning sets, and the woodcrafts hung on the wall. Those things do not only symbolize products, but also the love behind it when mothers pay attention and use their time to pick them up in a shopping place. A mother is also usually a quick learner who pays attention to new information and new goods in order to absorb new knowledge about the 'outside world' (compared to a mother's routine) from this process. This merit disputes the traditional image of 'passive consumers' – only spending and buying – and give women the ability to keep influencing the development of the shopping place according to their needs (Underhill, 2000).

Shopping places, as we have seen, have the potential to serve an efficient site for mothers to resist the identity of being an 'ordinary mom.' What the interviewees chose to resist is not 'being a mom,' instead, for many of them, the identity they refused to accept was the restricted living conditions and the unpleasant social expectation accompanying assumed expectations of Taiwanese motherhood – i.e. the limited mobility, the fragmented schedules, and most importantly, the ethic of care that ties them to the traditional image of 'good moms,' and 'good wives.' They too issue with the imposed imperative which emphasizes the virtue of sacrifice (c.f. Miller 1998). In this context and in these ways, shopping gives women a way out of being constrained and further provides mothers with a place to invent or discover opportunities for leisure – for self-enjoyment.

Ms M's sweet memory recalls some fun experiences of her childhood, helping her to make her own shopping trips to be 'a little girl's shopping' instead of mothers' duty:

> I grew up there [traditional market]; I used to go there with my mom when I was young. Now I am a mom, and I think traditional market is the only place that retains all my child memory with my mom ... (laughing). (Ms M)

Shopping also creates the feeling of 'among the people,' a sense of belonging, that makes mothers experience friendship in shopping places:

> Traditional market is really crowded, and amazingly, I don't hate that. Instead, I have a feeling, *'I am one of them'*, you know, I don't know how to describe it, but the experience is totally different from being alone. I like it, I like to hear some noise that is not from my kids, haha, am I mean? Actually, I think I enjoy an environment that is not ... um ... home. It feels like finally you got a chance to talk to somebody else.

> [You mean, who?]

> Well, not exactly you 'talk' to somebody else, but you can have some.. communication with vendors or other moms ... am I silly? ... ha ha. (Ms M)

The sense of belonging derived from women's talk and mutual connection in marketplace is similar to Coates' (1996) study that regards
women's friendship as a resistance through the form of leisure. Coates
argues that mothers' friendship, built up by their 'talk' while they are
taking care of children, offers women a very good site to feel connections
and gain the sense of belonging that positively contributes mothers'
reconstruction of self-image. Thus, shopping serves similar functions.
Through the feeling of belonging constituted by sharing, interactions
and conversations among mothers as well as with other people (e.g.
vendors) in traditional markets, women are able to use a positive attitude to treat the identity of 'shopping agents' and acquire enjoyment
and gratification from it.

In addition, mothers seem to enjoy the shopping environment co-
produced by goods, consumers, and sellers. During a shopping trip,
whether it belongs to mundane shopping or other luxury shopping in
department stores, the possibilities of 'browsing,' 'looking around,' and
'finding out something new' provided by different shopping places, such
as traditional markets or hypermarkets, allow mothers to resist the separation between their daily routine and 'outside world,' and further obtain
the happiness from this update and feeling of connection. This perspective surely brings a positive influence in mothers' monotone life style:

> I just want to go out, look around, see what's going on in our
> surrounding, and make sure I can still update myself. (Ms Q.)

At this sense, a mother is not only a mother; she is also an active explorer,
an aggressive learner, an independent consumer, and most importantly,
a woman who can obtain the sense of self and define their experience –
on their own.

Through the presentation of goods, the space setup, the social interaction in different shopping spaces, and the process of how women's
demands affect those places, shopping is a cultural activity – a cultural consumption – which not only reflects mothers' daily reality but
also reveals and constructs their identity through their relation to other
people. The traditional image of consumption, such as 'extravagance,'
'waste,' and 'no contribution' are not logical for them since this activity
has already become an important part of mothers' daily life, tight and
inseparable: 'Nobody can take over this job for me, and I won't expect
them can do that, besides, I somehow enjoy it a lot' (Ms H).

These mothers do not care whether this activity is degraded in other
people's eyes, they are not afraid to go to a dirty marketplace in order to

get fresher food materials, and they have no interest in knowing what kind of symbolism that can possibly imply. In the end, *Ku-zhung-zhu-lo* is a tactic in an overall strategy of creating a good life for all. For them, the accomplishment is gaining the most positive attitude for themselves. Seeing their families happy – enjoying the food they bought, wearing the clothing they picked out and having fun in shopping places they go together – this is the real focus in mothers' everyday lives.

Notes

1. A famous chain hypermarket. Please see www.Carrefour.com for more information.
2. A nearby hypermarket of Ms A's house.
3. The slogan used by a chain hypermarkets, Da-Ma-Chia, in 2004.
4. 'Yellow-face-woman', is a Chinese slang to describe a woman who does not dress or maintain herself, and then allows herself become ugly and lack of elegance.
5. The slogan used by Shin-Kong Mitshkoshi department stores. See www.skm.com.tw for more details.

References

Bensou, S. (1988) *Counter Culture*. Urbana, IL: University of Illinois Press.
Bowlby, R. (1997) 'Supermarket Futures,' in P. Falk and C. Campbell (eds), *The Shopping Experience*. London: Sage.
Coates, J. (1996) *Women Talk*. Oxford: Blackwell.
Crawford, D., Jackson, E. and Godbey, G. (1991) 'A Hierarchical Model of Leisure Constraints, *Leisure Sciences*, 9, 119–27.
Freysinger, V. J. (1988) *'The Meaning of Leisure in Middle Adulthood: Gender Differences and Changes since Young Adulthood,'* unpublished doctoral dissertation, University of Wisconsin at Madison, Madison, WI.
Freysinger, V. J. and Flannery, D. (1992) 'Women's leisure: Affiliation, Self-Determination, Empowerment and Resistance?,' *Society and Leisure* 15(1): 303–22.
Gilligan, C. (1993) [1982] *In a Different Voice*. Cambridge, MA: Harvard University Press.
Green, E. (1998) 'Women Doing Friendship: An Analysis of Women's Leisure as a Site of Identity, Constructive Empowerment and Resistance.' Leisure Studies, 17, 171–8.
Hays, S. (1996) *The Cultural Contradictions of Motherhood*. New Haven, CT: Yale University Press.
Henderson, K. A. (1991) *Dimensions of Choice: A Qualitative Approach to Recreation, Parks, and Leisure Research*. State College, PA: Venture.
Henderson, K. A. (1996) 'One Size Doesn't Fit All: The Meanings of Women's Leisure,' *Journal of Leisure Research* 28(3): 139–54.

Henderson, K. A., Bialeschki, D. M., Shaw, S. M. and Freysinger, V. J. (1989) *A Leisure of One's Own: A Feminist Perspective on Women's Leisure*. State College, PA: Venture Publishing.

Henderson, K. A., Bialeschki, D. M., Shaw, S. M. and Freysinger, V. J. (1996) *Both Gains and Gaps: Feminist Perspectives on Women's Leisure*. State College, PA:Venture Publishing.

Henderson, K. A. and Bialeschki, D. M. (1991) 'A Sense of Entitlement to Leisure as Constraint and Empowerment for Women,' *Leisure Studies* 13: 51–65.

Henderson, K. A. and Rannell, J. S. (1988) 'Farm Women and the Meaning of Work and Leisure: An Oral History Perspective,' *Leisure Sciences* 10: 41–50.

Hine, T. (2002) *'I Want That!': How We All Became Shoppers*. New York: Harper-Collins.

Jansen-Verbeke, M. (1987) 'Women, Shopping and Leisure,' *Leisure Studies* 6: 71–86.

Maenpaa, P. and Lehtanen, T. (1994) 'Shopping in the East Centre Mall.' In P. Falk and C. Campbell (eds), The Shopping Experience (pp. 136–65). London: Sage.

McDowell, L. (1999) *Gender, Identity and Place: Understanding Feminist Geographies*. Minneapolis, MN: University of Minnesota Press.

Miller, D. (1998) *A Theory of Shopping*. New York: Cornell University Press.

Mowl, G. and Towner, J. (1995) 'Women, Gender, Leisure and Place: Toward a More Humanistic Geography of Women's Leisure,' *Leisure Studies* 14: 102–16.

Peiss, K. (1986) *Cheap Amusement*. Philadelphia: Temple University Press.

Pringle, R. (1983) *Women and Consumer Capitalism: Women, Social Welfare and the State of Australia*. Sydney, Australia: Allen and Unwin.

Prus, R. and Dawson, L. (1991) 'Shop Til You Drop: Shopping as Recreational and Laborious Activity,' *Canadian Journal Sociology* 16(2): 145–64.

Rapoport, R. and Rapoport, R. N. (1975) *Leisure and the Family Life Cycle*. London: Routledge and Kegan Paul.

Rappaport, E. D. (2000a) 'A New Era of Shopping: The Promotion of Women's Pleasure in London's West End, 1909–1914,' in J. Scanlon (ed.) *The Gender and Consumer Culture Reader*, pp. 30–47. New York: New York University Press.

Rappaport, E. D. (2000b) *Shopping for Pleasure*. Princeton, NJ: Princeton University Press.

Russell, R. V. (2002) *Pastimes: The Context of Contemporary Leisure*. Champaign, IL: Sagamore Publishing.

Underhill, P. (2000) 'What Women Want,' *Interiors* 159 (11): 33–6.

Winship, J. (2000) 'New Disciplines for Women and the Rise of the Chain Store in the 1930s,' in M. Andrews and M. Talbot (eds.), *All the World and Her Husband*, pp. 23–45. London and New York: Cassell.

5

'Attention, Shoppers – Family Being Constructed on Aisle Six!': Grocery Shopping and the Accomplishment of Family[1]

Jan Phillips
University of Southern Maine/Lewiston-Auburn College

Trading recipes with family members. Scanning the newspaper and clipping food coupons from store supplements. Making a grocery list. Deciding who will do the shopping. Noticing a billboard ad for a store's fresh produce on the way to get enough gas to drive to that store. Remembering a newscast about the dangers of food additives. Placing an apple from New Zealand in the cart. Negotiating snack purchases with the oldest of the kids. Allowing a younger child, sitting in the grocery cart, to eat a free cookie from the in-store bakery while the shopping gets done. Managing the emotions of a child's temper tantrum at the checkout lane. Noticing that the person first in line is (also) using food stamps. Unloading the groceries and putting them in specific places. Fixing and serving a meal from the food just purchased, then cleaning the dishes. Baking a cake for a family member, with the kids helping. Making a payment on the refrigerator. Weighing whether the family can afford a new microwave.

We think of grocery shopping as common, fairly straightforward commercial activity: we shop, we purchase, we survive another briefly lived encounter with the marketplace that brings us, and often accompanying family members, into direct contact with the world of largely edible goods. Look closer, however, and we see a familiar social practice through which people make particular sorts of meaning and identity. In fact, grocery shopping is first and foremost an opportunity to *accomplish* or *enact* family through the routine, recurring work of consumption. Children and adults together become not merely social persons but social relationships through this commercial activity, their deliberation over the processes, items, and agency involved in food provisioning helping to construct and reaffirm the essence of family itself. As such, grocery shopping is a longer string of consumption interactions than merely setting foot in a store, and woven through those interactions, alongside any expression of nutritional desire, are the ways family participants (children, youth, and adults alike) construct, challenge, and reconstitute their most intimate relations.

Drawing upon research conducted during 2005–2006 using in-store observation, interviews with consumers and grocery store employees, and content analysis of consumption diaries kept by college students, this work explores the ways Americans give meaning to family identity and dynamics as they plan for, acquire, use, and ultimately dispose of grocery food stuffs and other household items. A highly gendered practice where women often carry special emotional and experiential responsibility, grocery shopping is also the earliest shopping experience for many, one in which a majority of children make their first purchasing requests and in-store purchases (McNeal, 1999). Grocery shopping therefore stands as a key socio-emotional site in which to observe adults and children engaging one another in cultural practice, especially so as they socially construct themselves into family members and consumers. At the same time, to study grocery shopping and food provisioning generally is to witness particularly fertile generational enactment, which shapes and is shaped by consumption practices even as adults and children together constitute themselves as 'consuming families.'

'Doing' family by way of personal grocery shopping

My professional interest in grocery shopping began several years ago, with a family trip to the supermarket that turned into what Hochschild (2003: 16) terms a 'magnified moment' (a metaphorically and insightfully rich episode that yields insight into the social construction of reality). As my then twelve-year-old son and I moved from one profusely stocked aisle to the next, what had seemed ordinary parent and child bleating over which foods would go into the cart suddenly escalated into a frustrated engagement over how many different cookies to buy. Finally, he explained that he had to have the *right* cookies to trade in the lunchroom, as the kids he most wanted to eat with expected good food trading. This, I thought, is what Veblen (1961), were he still alive, might call '*trophy* purchasing' in order to be a player in the informal economy of school (and therefore about my child's status and self-esteem in light of corporate branding). From that realization we could move to working out a compromise: he got enough of what he wanted to demonstrate social exchange (i.e. give-and-take) credibility to peers, but agreed to forgo other items in favor of my advocacy for healthier options.

I used this experience the next week in teaching consumption and children's peer identity issues. Presenting it in that light received knowing looks from my mostly non-traditional aged students; they could fit it to readings on childhood peer relations and relate it to their own peer-pleasing consumption, if not that of their children. But the slow fuse of understanding didn't really ignite until weeks later, when I finally understood that the episode wasn't only about a social dance among peers. It was just as much about the dance my son and I were doing, one in which a seemingly small moment permitted us to construct and reaffirm some essence of our family through consumption practices. There in the store, we adjudged what our family did and didn't value, played out decision-making, used the opportunity to teach/learn about when and what to share, as well as undertake what Hochschild (1983) terms emotion work (in this case, how and why to share), and covered it all with two generations working through issues of gaining and displaying human agency. Trophy purchase or not, we were 'doing' family by way of the cookie jar.

After all, our son's birth didn't mean that we immediately emerged fully formed as a family; it was more that through everyday routines and rituals, and thus the enactment of our most micro-political selves, we continually reconstituted ourselves as family. And far from being one-directional, the exchange worked both ways. That day in the grocery store my son made sure I acknowledged what was important to him as my child and family member about navigating consumptive peer culture, in the process giving him credit for a savvy assessment of commodities. By the same token, I asked that we deliberate our household's relation to the larger world of commodities and cultural capital, in ways that reaffirmed our 'family-ness' and my 'adultness.' Ellen Seiter (1993: 212) might argue that we were engaged in a 'covert' control embedded in the sort of social-ization favored by middle-class parents ('positive reinforcement, joint decision making, and "talking feelings out,"' is how she phrases it), but to leave it at that diminishes the reciprocity of engagement and enabling.

Moreover, my son and I together were 'doing' a particular kind of fam-ily, and conveying it to others and ourselves: we are a family which can comfortably afford to feed numerous members, which not only recog-nizes but actively encourages child-specific (and branded) consumption, which makes food core to education and training, and which can shop collaboratively because we are generally in agreement over our needs and wants. There is no need to romanticize the engagement or remove it from the larger picture. The familial identity we accomplished on that occasion was harmonious, but sometimes it can be fragile or contentious; often it is linked to specific places (home, stores, traveling in the car, eating out), and always it relates to a larger social structural context.

In this particular instance, for example, our interaction focused upon retail food items, a portion of the commodity market very successfully shaped by a multinational food industry. The full range of food commodities my son and I might bicker over admittedly is determined by that food industry, which, as Marion Nestle (2002: 22) tells us, in the U.S. alone accounts for 13 per cent of the gross national product, employs 17 per cent of the labor force, and spends US$33 billion a year on advertising and promotion. It is little wonder Americans spend US$800 billion a year on food and drink (Nestle, 2002: 11), much of it snack food, and equally unsurprising that a great majority of these purchases involve the influence of children. Marketers, in fact, have long respected the agency of kids far more than social scientists (see Cook, 2004), defining children by the late 1990s as 'an irresistible marketing opportunity' with a total influence on purchase decisions approaching half a trillion dollars! (Nestle, 2002: 178, 176).

Even more, our family is what the US Department of Agriculture refers to as 'food secure' (that is, we consistently get enough food to remain active and healthy), unlike a majority of households with below-poverty incomes (Nestle, 2002: 174). Should we desire snack foods, we have the resources to obtain them when and where we want (and to make them simply one part of a sufficient overall diet). We aren't limited to our neighborhood market, where the selection of foodstuffs is relatively low and the prices are high. We can drive, as we did on this occasion, to a suburban supermarket. Once there, we can choose from an enormous number of food goods brought daily from around the world, and pay for it all using a checking or credit card account (as opposed to suffering the constraints of too little available money or food stamps). When we return home, refrigeration and freezers await our purchases, and we don't have to worry that the power to run them might be a casualty to this month's rent or conditions of war. A host of inequalities, some socioeconomic and others socio-geographic, differentiates our consumption horizon.

In that light, compare our interchange with an exchange about food witnessed by Elizabeth Chin in *Purchasing Power*, her 2001 account of poor black children's consumer culture in inner-city New Haven, Connecticut. Arriving for an impromptu visit at the home of one of her ethnographic informants, Chin finds ten-year-old Tionna interacting with Celia, her grandmother. Both live with Tionna's great-grandmother Ella in what amounts to a separate household that more and more is isolated to their small room. As Chin (2001: 65) describes it, there is 'some tension between Celia and Tionna on the one hand and Ella on the other, especially regarding the day-to-day tasks of raising Tionna and maintaining the house.' As a consequence, no one volunteers to clean and at least for the moment everyone seems to have given up cooking, none of the three wanting to be saddled cleaning or cooking for the other two. The family rarely eats together and tensions have led to something of a partitioning of both space and food. Hence, the following:

> Tionna spied a glazed donut lying on a paper napkin on top of the bureau. "Ma, is that your donut?" Tionna asked her grandmother. "Yes," Celia answered, and Tionna intoned, "I want one..." "Well, they're your grandmother's donuts," Celia said (Tionna often calls her grandmother "Ma" and her great-grandmother "Grandma"). "You have to ask her if you can have one." Either Tionna did not want to ask or Celia decided she did not need the whole donut because she quickly called Tionna back and told her she could eat half. "I won't be able to eat the whole thing, anyway," she said gruffly. (Chin, 2001: 65)

The outcome sounds familiar, an adult 'giving in' to the entreaty of a child for food. Yet, upon closer inspection, we see that Tionna's pleading begins with a query about property rights within the family and then rapidly moves to a call for the obligations of parenthood, pulling her grandmother into negotiation over caring for and sharing with her granddaughter. Unlike middle-class households, where children's embrace of consumer items can be a form of resistance to the child-centered parent (Seiter, 1993: 234), consumption requests by Tionna are first and foremost an insistence on connection. They may come within a social geography conspicuously more constrained than that of the middle-class (notice how we move quickly from store to bureau, bypassing kitchen and refrigerator altogether), but they are nonetheless just as effective in etching family dynamics as the insistence of my son.

Consuming families, constructing families: the theoretical view

In advancing a perspective that privileges children and adults engaging in family enactments over consumption, the sort of thing illustrated by my son and I or Tionna and her grandmother, I join an ongoing debate about fluidity and change in family arrangements – and about how to capture that change when we study contemporary household consumption. Like a growing number of observers, I argue that focus must shift from some singularly fixed, 'true' essence of either family or consumption to the importance of interactively constructed consumptive practices for everyday family life. In order to do so, I suggest that we must shift our thinking in another way, beyond acknowledging children as standing diminutively alongside adults to seeing them as actual co-constructors of consumption practices and thus family itself.

The very idea that families are populated by reflexive, constructive social actors of any age is the product of an era when choices about how to live and relate to others (especially in 'Western' or 'Northern' societies) less and less seem to follow set paths of living. When we no longer face orderly and predictable ('standard') biographies, particularly of the sort previously fixed by rigid work and kinship expectations (Giddens, 1992), more and more we must fashion, as Ulrich Beck (1992: 135) puts it, 'do-it-yourself biographies.' We do not do so in isolation, however, for the give-and-take of social life remains a foundational means by which we assemble and manage identity; it is the site of indispensable identity work. After all, everyday life must be achieved and in large measure continuously performed through 'often routine, sometimes impressive but always ongoing, recurring social and collective work' (Laz, 2003: 506). Thus, the self *in relationship with others* is also continuously accomplished.

Accordingly, some students of family have begun insisting that we shift from conceptualizing and studying family as 'a thing-like object' to envisioning it as an active process (see Morgan, 1996, 1999; Silva and Smart 1999; and Naples, 2001). David Morgan (1999), for example, urges researchers to focus on family *practices* in order to highlight how active, fluid, open to diverse interpretation yet socially grounded our everyday taken-for-granted worlds really are. Importantly, he defines as practices not only the actual activities done by and linked to families, but also rhetorical narratives used to make sense of such activities. In fact, he says, routine talk about family obligations, duties, constraints, and burdens can be a very significant form of 'family practice' (Morgan, 1999: 29), especially when family members interject into the families they live *with* a ghost image, the idealized, normative families of myth and ritual that they live *by* (Gillis, 1997). Of course, we cannot assume that family practices of any sort will bring forth only smiling faces; work underway by Margaret Nelson reminds us that constraint, control, raw power, and exclusion also taint relevant practices. Still, whatever face, it is not that we learn about the form family takes from examining family living; in this rendering it is rather that practices themselves actually constitute family. Family is therefore 'less of a noun and more of an adjective or, possibly, a verb' (Morgan, 1999: 16). Or, as Silva and Smart (1999: 11) put it even more succinctly, families 'are' what families 'do.'

Certainly, a significant portion of what families 'do' is *ordinary consumption* – that is, the routine, repetitive, often unnoticed or taken-for-granted but nonetheless continuously interactive and interpretive practices of consumption (Grownow and Warde, 2001). And among such practices, hardly anything is more commonplace than food provisioning. In fact, food cultivation, shopping, preparing, feeding, eating, and cleaning up are so insistently mundane that we may forget to notice they are also about sharing resources, carrying out responsibilities and obligations, and creating a network of relations – often in the name of women's caring (DeVault, 1991), kin devotion and sacrificial love (Miller, 1998), or household intimacy and distance (Weiss, 1996). Indeed, something much more transformative than shopping, cooking, and cleaning up happens here, for through provisioning activities and the sense we make of them we 'quite literally produce family life from day to day' (DeVault, 1991: 13).

Provisioning practices that underscore the importance of *discussing, negotiating, even problematizing* family consumption, for instance, help us construct particular sorts of family relationships; alternatively, when the same or other provisioning practices remind us how the welfare state or mass media reach directly into our most intimate activities, we construct not only families but family as an institution (Halkier, 2001: 26, 28). In any case, studying family provisioning practices cannot rest primarily upon studying goods and services themselves – nor, for that matter, overarching orientations toward goods and services (Bourdieu's 'habitus'), symbolic values read into goods and services (signs and status), or taught knowledge about goods and services (socialization). Instead, to truly understand families and their constructive consumption behaviors, focus must rest on countless everyday consumption interchanges, the *mutually constitutive* practices between family members. It is here 'where the action is' (Best, 1998: 208), here where acceptance and belonging, together with difference, defiance, and exclusion get produced as normative enterprise shapes the most familiar of social arrangements.

How curious, then, that largely missing from the accumulating accounts of food provisioning are truly co-constitutive practices by anyone in the household who isn't adult! Admittedly, children and youth earn mention across these studies; yet, more often than not, their inclusion comes as a secondary being, frequently bothersome at that, who generates for adults one more task to be squeezed in before dinner, one more outburst to be quelled during grocery shopping, one more set of preferences to work around, or one more diminutive being to properly socialize. In this manner, children are assumed to be merely passive recipients of culture still 'preparing for life,' a stance that creates a wide generational gulf. This is doubly ironic, given the recent explosion of writings in the field of childhood studies, where observers have discovered that children move actively, desirously, and self-referentially through daily life as competent social actors and even consumers (James *et al.*, 1990; Buckingham, 2000; Chin, 2001).

Therefore, the analysis which follows avoids granting the agency involved in consumption only to adults, choosing to focus instead on the way adults and children actually interact as they carry out food provisioning. I suggest that when we take this approach, we see adults and children anticipate, collaborate, and not infrequently problematize family relations and meanings through consumption practices. Examining how adults and children together do such things as make shopping lists, anticipate when they will need to share meals with relations, buy snacks, hold one another accountable for purchases, and even negotiate the use of store carts begins to correct the problem not only of the 'missing child' but also of the missing child-adult interaction in consumption analysis (Cook, 2006; Martens *et al.*, 2004).

Grocery shopping practices

Planning and anticipating

As DeVault (1991) notes, planning is essential to provisioning, which means that grocery shopping begins long before the cart is filled, sometimes far from the store itself. Analogously, the sort of family we desire to construct is also anticipated. Listen, for example, as 'Mandy' (all names are pseudonyms), a 29-year-old mother of two, describes her anticipatory consumption practices:

> After moving out of bed in the morning, I walk to the shower to get cleaned up for the upcoming day. As I stand in the hot water, I make a mental note how low the shampoo is getting, how much soap is left. As I step out of the shower, I observe how the toilet paper and laundry soap are getting lower. Each step I take around the bathroom adds another item to the grocery list.

Entering into the kitchen allows me to memorize more items that appear to be running out. The list begins to get longer and longer every step I take around the house. Between personal items, cleaning items, food, and gardening supplies, the list I make becomes harder to remember.

Though she offers her description in first person, as if only she moves through the house trying to remember what is needed, Mandy's words are tinged with the family talk of duties and obligation around two-generation household consumption. She interweaves provisioning *work* (inventorying, making a list) with getting up and showering, then adds, 'Being a mother and a wife gives me sole responsibility to make sure these items don't run out before new ones are in the house to replace them....' In an instant, she genders provisioning practices, essentializing them as *women's* work, by causally linking them to family roles – intergenerational first, and then marital (though, in fact, she and her long-time partner and co-parent have not yet married). Anticipatory consumption talk has effortlessly turned into family-construction talk, each realm helping compose the other.

Elsewhere, anticipatory consumption practices (re)construct families as multi-generational. Children and adults together contribute to list-making, for instance, perhaps discussing which store coupons to use or recipes to prepare, maybe across more than one household as well as generation – sister-to-sister, say, or mother-to-adult daughter or son. When asked what determines the items she buys, Nissa (a 24-year-old single mother with a 4-year-old son) immediately answers coupons, then corrects herself to say they don't entirely determine her shopping because she's 'very into' long-used recipes from family (including from the paternal great-grandfather and grandmother of her son), and finally mentions her sister's two-generation household, with whom she is very close:

My sister and her fiancé bought a house. I live on the first floor, they live on the second. So I am *so used* to her and her children.... If I buy – , I buy the little mini bottles of water for my son, I usually buy an extra package because her kids come in and take our food. So I'm so used to planning. Like, I know if I'm gonna make, like, pasta or something I have to buy enough of that to feed my sister and her kids 'cause she's gonna know that I'm making that and she's going to be at my house.

The phrase 'take our food' seems at first to turn Nissa's provisioning toward defensive household and generational boundary work around kin property rights, but the tone of her voice together with her frequent smile and laughter suggest a more pleasurable construction of sisterhood. Further questioning reveals that a second sister watches her son one night a week, frequently staying the weekend. Special food is often bought for this sister as well as Nissa's mother, who also regularly visits. Nissa estimates that perhaps half of any month she and her son share food with family members. Clearly, even when only she is preparing to grocery shop, more extended family affiliations are anticipated.

Collaborating

Accomplishment of family starts with anticipatory consumption and continues into shopping for and using or disposing of grocery items. At any of these points, consumption practices can feel collaborative or mutually devised, thus constructing a more inclusive family identity. Holly, a 37-year-old wife and mother of two, speaks of a trip to the grocery story as 'a way for me to connect with my family emotionally,' explaining

> I buy snacks that my children have requested and always receive an 'I love you Mom' upon their discovery of the purchase. Meal planning and purchasing items to make my husband's favorite meal (stuffed shells) is a form of relationship building for us.

Annoyed at the 'morality lessons' she gets from others who judge her '[p]urchasing of anything high in fat, cholesterol, trans fat, sugar, or calories . . . as a form of bad parenting,' Holly places more value on the family she believes collaboratively accomplished than any possible devalued family relationship others might construct.

Similarly, Susan (age 36 and a mother of two teenage boys) paints her family's ritualized consumption of food and drinks as collaborative, noting its role in the accomplishment of inter-and intra-generational relationships:

> We [she and her husband] have coffee in the morning, coffee in the afternoon, and tea at night before bed. We [she and her sons] have muffins on one weekend morning when my husband is on his "long weekend" (a once a month occurrence), and [the whole family has] chips and soda when he finishes the night shift on a Friday (another once a month occurrence). These are frequent, recurring events and taken individually, they are not particularly loaded. The significance, I suppose, lies in the repetition and in the fact that we're creating, with food, a shared family calendar of sorts.

As Holly and Susan demonstrate, children need not actually go grocery shopping to play a role in both collaborative consumption and family construction. (Indeed, it may be easier for adults to persuade themselves their families are collaborative when children are not along.) Nevertheless, previous research reveals that children 'influence' a wide variety of purchase and use decisions (Foxman *et al.*, 1989). At the same time, adults remain eager to purchase *for* children in what might be termed a preemptive attempt to construct collaborative family relationships. Wendy, a 22-year-old single female, describes talking with a mother whose very young child uttered as its first words 'buy it' while shopping. 'She then went on to explain how she had to buy the item,' reports Wendy, 'because she was scared her daughter would be disappointed that her mother did not respond to her saying her first words.'

Negotiating, resisting and problematizing

Sometimes grocery shopping and provisioning feature agency that is not all collaborative. For example, it turns out children are capable negotiators and resistors who can problematize not just consumption but adult insistence on defining family relationships and meaning as well. In some cases resistance is silent but overt, as in the example of two mother–daughter pairs encountered one after the other in a single supermarket observation. In the first case an adolescent daughter follows nearly exactly in the footsteps of her mother, talking on her cell phone; not far behind, a second, similarly-aged daughter does more or less the same while text-messaging with both thumbs. No words are exchanged between mother and daughter in either instance. The result is nuanced consumptive bargaining between adults and children, while still very much contesting imposed family performance.

Contrast that with a description from another student's field notes. As a woman and her three-year-old daughter shop for Halloween candy, we see the child receive endless normative messages and adeptly deliver a return effect:

> The mother asked her daughter to pick out some candy as a special treat. It became quite a process, however. The daughter insisted upon buying some sort of "goo" designed specifically for decorating cakes, much to her mom's dismay. This was not the kind of treat that the mother had in mind and she asked her daughter to put it back. In this respect, the mother was teaching the little girl that even though the candy that mom had in mind was probably no more healthy, the

cake decorating candy had only one purpose and that was for cakes. This appeared to make little sense to the daughter.

The girl puts up little verbal argument but continues to take her time searching for the 'right' candy, thus bringing about a consumption labor slowdown. Her mother, hoping to speed things up, makes a deal that her daughter can get what she wants at the checkout. As mother consumptively insists and child equally firmly resists, they establish a formula for joint family decision-making that calls to mind Barrie Thorne's (1993: 3) oft-quoted observation that 'children act, resist, rework, and create; they influence adults as well as being influenced by them.'

Annette Lareau (2003: 2) maintains that joint decision-making is a 'hallmark' of middle-class families, a part of the enrichment and 'robust sense of entitlement' cultivated in children of that class, but children's consumptive resistance actually crosses class lines. After admitting that the dinner table can be 'a place of conflict' with her son, Beth, a 28-year-old single mother, says this about their interaction around food provisioning: 'I am a single parent, and though I try to make healthy meals, there are many nights when we are eating frozen foods or pizza.' Hardly middle class, Beth tries to outweigh the familial limits imposed by being a single parent (with which she starts her sentence) by mutually-agreed upon food consumption.

Nor does the presence of two parents lessen consumption and family-construction contest, as shown by the words of Melissa, a 26-year-old mother of four:

> My eight-year-old, who carefully scrapes off the oats sprinkled on top of the bar, clearly misses the health appeal of the Nutri-Grain bar. I no longer buy sugared cereal for my home but every once in a while a box makes its way onto the shelves thanks to sympathetic dad who thinks it's O.K. once in a while. What amazes me the most about these mishaps is that the healthy cereal normally provided is immediately shunned and not another bite is consumed until every last bit of the sugar-laden box of breakfast crud has been consumed.

What is most striking here is that Melissa's carefully chosen words obliquely reveal how grocery shopping and its extension back into the home shape the practices and emotions of 'doing family.' Boxes inadvertently appear on the shelves when 'mishaps' occur (a way in family talk of redirecting criticism from the families we live *with*?), a co-parent is treated as a 'sympathetic dad' (thereby reinforcing the families we live *by*, since dads who are present are valued more by society than dads who are absent), and children in the family misapprehend or shun commodities as proxies for the values or behaviors of their parents. Plainly, the use of branded goods becomes a resource for consumption and also for the ways we contest 'doing' family. (Since children in the US are unavoidably born into a world of branding, they learn early just how much a resource for consumption practices it is. One student told of her 18-month-old niece asking for a new 'nuk,' at the grocery store and then vehemently rejecting any pacifiers that didn't carry what turned out to be the Nuk brand name).

Finally, consider the place of the cart in grocery shopping negotiation and resistance. Though grocery carts of an endless variety legitimize the presence of young children in the often dramatically 'themed' (Gottdiener, 2001) 'pseudo-public' spaces of consumption, carts remain a highly compressed, adult-enforced 'geography of consumption' (Mansvelt, 2005). In contrast to the profoundly *sensual* and *symbolic* adult experience of grocery shopping, young children are confined, frequently by store mandate, to the noticeably more attenuated experience of grocery carts. As a consequence, grocery carts are for the youngest of consumers what store counters and shelves are for adults – as John Fiske puts it, 'the furniture of capitalism' (quoted in Chin, 2001: 112). No surprise then that a considerable portion of adult–child grocery interaction centers on getting into, staying in, or getting out of the cart. Adults, in fact, devote almost as much time and energy to cart behavior as to shopping proper.

And what do kids do in response? Interviews and supermarket observations suggest they are anything but passive. Occasionally if they can walk they pad beside an adult-sized cart or wander in and out of carts earmarked for children; less often they stand in their seats to view or converse with other patrons. Mostly, they find ways to claim as their own what amounts to enforced seat time, as evidenced in this excerpt from my field notes:

> A man and woman move slowly along the supermarket aisle, the child with them (their young son?) repeatedly hopping in and out of the miniature car the man is pushing next to the regular cart the woman pushes. It is mid-afternoon on Super Bowl Sunday. The woman stops, asking, "Oh wait, do we need cereal or anything?" Soon she is asking the boy if he likes particular cereals. No answer. Now the man tries a different tack: "Cory, put these in the cart for me." He lifts the boy into the regular cart, to which the boy immediately says, "Want to get

out!" No, it's not safe, the man tells him. Now the boy is reaching for goods in the cart, the biggest and most brightly packaged grabbing his attention. "Take your hands off. You're going to get cuts," says the man, quickly adding aloud to himself while not looking toward the woman, "I gotta get outta here."

Notice that this child insists (successfully) that the adults remain child-centered throughout this consumption excursion. Meanwhile, the fact they are shopping at this particular time suggests both that the two adults work and that the preeminently masculine culture of the day has been renegotiated in favor of family consumption (although the male adult may be on the verge of using the child's behavior to revisit the emotion work he's being asked to do).

Nissa, the single mom discussed earlier, is equally familiar with the negotiations of cart time, and she and her son have developed a number of interactive strategies to keep him engaged with consuming itself while riding in the cart: he is allowed to choose five items a trip for himself, usually deciding on the items before they get to the store, and he knows he can lose these items if he accumulates three 'strikes' for misbehaviors; mother and son frequently start in the toy section, though they often don't purchase anything there, plus they commonly spend extended time 'visiting' the lobsters; like many children accompanying parents to the store, her son snacks on one or two selected food stuffs (cheese sticks, for example) as they shop; and most of the time she pushes the cart firmly down the middle of the aisles while keeping up a constant stream of verbal exchanges with her four-year-old son about which items to buy and how to place them in the cart. Notice how these strategies additionally help them maintain at least the appearance of an idealized family, something especially important for single-parent, gay and lesbian, adoptive, special needs, and other families. As Nissa puts it, having talked on an earlier occasion about wanting to be seen as a 'good' parent and now turning to the available discourse of avoiding children's consumption misbehavior in public, 'Yes, we *all* bribe our children 'cause none of us want that child that's screaming in the grocery store.' Plainly, the idealized family of myth and ritual is also under construction here.

Conclusion

Perhaps we shouldn't be surprised that in 1955, when *Life* magazine published an issue on *food* in the United States, it chose for its cover a picture of a mother pushing her young child in a supermarket cart surrounded by 'mass luxury' goods (Humphery, 1998: 63). Half-a-century later, adults and children in the US and increasingly elsewhere in the world continue to be preoccupied with what the metonymic grocery cart represents for the ways we might provision foodstuffs. Though grocery store offerings are not the only things humans consume and though, in an age of relative food abundance in many industrialized societies, food may no longer seem to carry the gravity it once did, activities involved in securing, preparing, serving, and using food retain considerable life-sustaining importance around the globe (Mintz, 1993).

That said, social *interactions* necessary for carrying out food provisioning also remain vitally important. At the very least, this is a set of practices that couples market and family, allowing us to intimately navigate the hierarchies and boundaries, as well as the freedoms and pleasures of everyday life. Here, not only adults and not only children, but *both together* can across time demonstrate themselves active, skilled creators and users of commodity culture. As a result, the marketplace comes to seem an expansive and unfolding lived experience, something more than merely buying things. At the same time, real people undertaking such consumption bring to life more active, 'practiced' and changeable families from their unfolding market experience. If we aren't exactly *what* we consume, then surely we are *how* we consume.

To be sure, adult-child interactions around consumption in the United States do not happen on some 'frictionless plain' but rather under at least the perceived constraints of generational hierarchy and contemporary capitalism. Kinship can impact how we plan our grocery shopping or with whom we undertake it. Age and health may affect something as basic as how many goods we carry home from the market. The need to juggle the 'second shift' (Hochschild, 1989), diminished state support of low-income households, and the expectation that women carry responsibility for emotional as well as domestic labor in families all combine to force shopping in some places rather than others, at certain times rather than others, with the ultimate purchase of some items rather than others.

Just the same, constituting family through consumptive interaction between adults and children still requires everyday activity and narrative accountings – still requires, in other words, practices helping to construct family that need not be overloaded toward adults. This view posits that grocery shopping, together with other more or less ordinary consumption practices like watching television, toy shopping, scrapbooking, and playing children's league soccer are consumption arenas in which we can watch children and adults actively collaborate and negotiate with, as well as resist one another. It also suggests a host of other ordinary practices whose study might help us better understand how family gets 'done' – bedtime storytelling and reading, picnicking, helping (or not) with homework, and mowing the lawn or gardening come quickly to mind. All these practices suggest, in the end, a very different approach to the study of family – as something recurring yet dynamic that gets created, maintained, challenged and transformed not in a millennium but in minute moments every day.

Note

1. I am very grateful to Dan Cook, Rebecca Herzig, Jan Hitchcock, and Hsin-yi Lu for professional encouragement and helpful criticism. My special thanks to Emily Kane, who truly has helped get this manuscript born; and to Dennis Grafflin and Calder Phillips-Grafflin, who have helped me analyze family consumption even as we live it.

References

Beck, U. (1992) *Risk Society: Towards a New Modernity.* London: Sage.

Best, J. (1998) 'Too Much Fun: Toys as Social Problems and the Interpretation of Culture,' *Symbolic Interaction*, 21(2): 197–212.

Buckingham, D. (2000) *After the Death of Childhood: Growing Up in the Age of Electronic Media.* Cambridge: Polity Press.

Chin, E. (2001) *Purchasing Power: Black Kids and American Consumer Culture.* Minneapolis, MN: University of Minnesota Press.

Cook, D. T. (2004) *The Commodification of Childhood: The Children's Clothing Industry and the Rise of the Child Consumer.* Durham, NC: Duke University Press.

Cook, D. T. (2006) 'The Missing Child in Consumption Theory', Plenary lecture at Child and Teen Consumption 2006 – Copenhagen. 2nd International Conference on Pluridisciplinary Perspectives on Child and Teen Consumption. Copenhagen Business School, Denmark, 27–28, April 2006.

DeVault, M. (1991) *Feeding the Family: The Social Organization of Caring as Gendered Work.* Chicago: University of Chicago Press.

Foxman, E. R., Tansuhaj, P. S. and Ekstrom, K. M. (1989) 'Family Members' Perceptions of Adolescents' Influence in Family Decision Making', *Journal of Consumer Research* 15(4): 482–91.

Giddens, A. (1992) *The Transformation of Intimacy: Sexuality, Love and Eroticism in Modern Societies.* Stanford, CA: Stanford University Press.

Gillis, J. (1997) *World of Their Own Making: Myth, Ritual, and the Quest for Family Values.* Cambridge, MA: Harvard University Press.

Gottdiener, M. (2001) *The Theming of America: American Dreams, Media Fantasies, and Themed Environments.* 2nd edn. Boulder, CO: Westview Press.

Gronow, J. and Warde, A. (eds) (2001) *Ordinary Consumption.* London: Routledge.

Halkier, B. (2001) 'Routinisation or reflexivity? Consumers and Normative Claims for Environmental Consideration,' in J. Gronow and A. Warde (eds), *Ordinary Consumption*, pp. 25–44. London: Routledge.

Hochschild, A. (1983) *The Managed Heart: Commercialization of Human Feeling.* Berkeley: University of California Press.

Hochschild, A. (2003) *The Commercialization of Intimate Life: Notes from Home and Work.* Berkeley: University of California Press.

Hochschild, A. with Machung, A. (1989) *The Second Shift.* New York: Avon.

Humphery, K. (1998) *Shelf Life: Supermarkets and the Changing Cultures of Consumption.* Cambridge: Cambridge University Press.

James, A., Jenks, C. and Prout, A. (eds) (1990) *Theorizing Childhood.* New York: Teacher's College Press.

Lareau, A. (2003) *Unequal Childhoods: Class, Race, and Family Life.* Berkeley: University of California Press.

Laz, C. (2003) 'Age Embodied', *Journal of Aging Studies*, 17: 503–19.

McNeal, J. (1999) *The Kids Market: Myths and Realities.* Ithaca, NY: Paramount Market Publishing.

Mansvelt, J. (2005) *Geographies of Consumption.* London: Sage.

Martens, L, Southerton, D. and Scott, S. (2004) 'Bringing Children (and Parents) into the Sociology of Consumption: Towards a Theoretical and Empirical Agenda,' *Journal of Consumer Culture*, 4(2): 155–82.

Miller, D. (1998) *A Theory of Shopping.* Ithaca, NY: Cornell University Press.

Mintz, S. (1993) 'The Changing Roles of Food in the Study of Consumption', in J. Brewer and R. Porter (eds), *Consumption and the World of Goods*, pp. 261–73. London: Routledge.

Morgan, D. H. J. (1996) *Family Connections: An Introduction to Family Studies.* Cambridge: Polity Press.

Morgan, D. H. J. (1999) 'Risk and Family Practices: Accounting for Change and Fluidity in Family Life', in E. Silva and C. Smart (eds), *The New Family?*, pp. 13–30. London: Sage.

Naples, N. (2001) 'A Member of the Funeral: An Introspective Ethnography', in M. Bernstein and R. Reimann (eds), *Queer Families, Queer Politics: Challenging Culture and the State*, pp. 21–43. New York: Columbia University Press.

Nestle, M. (2002) *Food Politics: How the Food Industry Influences Nutrition and Health.* Berkeley: University of California Press.

Seiter, E. (1993) *Sold Separately: Mothers and Children in Consumer Culture.* New Brunswick, NJ: Rutgers University Press.

Silva, E. and Smart, C. (eds) (1999) *The New Family?* London: Sage.

Thorne, B. (1993) *Gender Play: Girls and Boys in School.* New Brunswick, NJ: Rutgers University Press.

Veblen, T. B. (1961 [1899]) *The Theory of the Leisure Class.* New York: Random House.

Weiss, B. (1996) *The Making and Unmaking of the Haya Lived World: Consumption, Commoditization, and Everyday Practice.* Durham, NC: Duke University Press.

West, C. and Zimmerman, D. (1987) 'Doing Gender,' *Gender & Society*, 1(2): 125–51.

Part III
Transgressions and
Interstitial Spaces

6
Spreading Like a Dis/ease?: Afro-Jamaican Higglers and the Dynamics of Race/Color,[1] Class and Gender

Winnifred R. Brown-Glaude
Rutgers University

Most cities in developing and developed countries contain dual and interrelated economies: formal and informal. Socially formed meanings of markets and market activities in each of these economies vary often privileging formal markets, as more 'legitimate,' over informal markets. This essay examines the meanings of one particular market and market activity – higglering – in the informal economy of Jamaica. Higglering is a Jamaican term that denotes the informal economic activity of small-scale street vending dating back to the days of slavery, and is dominated by black, lower class Jamaican women. Higglering is generally perceived as a low status, illegitimate or illegal occupation among many Jamaicans, and higglers have been constructed as deviants in the public imagination. Richard Burton (1997) argues, for instance, that the higgler is 'regarded with ambivalence by the wider society: admired for her "manlike" autonomy and assertiveness, she is also derided on account of her often invasive physical presence, her loud dress, and her even louder demeanor and language' (Burton 1997: 164). Lisa Douglass (1992: 36) adds that the higgler is perceived as 'a comical character, a caricature of a woman' in Jamaican society.

Why are higglers and their market activities perceived as such? Are these representations simply attributed to the informal status of these women's work? How do these meanings affect the ways in which higglers experience their informal market activities? I explore these questions by deconstructing public representations of higglers and their work to expose intersectional hierarchies of race/color, class and gender that inform those meanings. To do this, I examine newspaper articles and letters to the editor published from 1985 to 2005 in two of Jamaica's popular newspapers: the *Daily Gleaner* and *Jamaica Observer*.[2] These news articles addressed, among many issues, tensions between the Jamaican government, the formal economic business community, uptown city residents and higglers over the removal of these informal market activities and workers from city streets. I turn to these resources in order to gain insights into ways in which higglering and higglers are publicly imagined because these representations serve as a backdrop to the lived experiences of these informal economic activities. Utilizing an interpretive content analysis as my research method, I identify a series of themes and theoretical insights that illuminate popular conceptions of higglers as illegitimate, undisciplined, indecent, and a threat to the well being of Jamaican society. My reading of these articles also generates insights into the social organization of public space in the city of Kingston. I also include in this essay the voices of some higglers – market women and informal commercial importers (ICIs) – who were interviewed in my larger study[3] to offer a glimpse of ways in which these women view their experiences in this context.

I demonstrate that conflicts between higglers, the formal economic business community, uptown city residents and the state over the use of public space in the city reveal the creation and contestation of racial markers as well as gender and class boundaries. There is an ideology of *social pollution* embedded in public narratives regarding the use of public space by higglers – an ideology that is intimately connected to deep rooted race/color, class and gender divisions that have long been a part of Jamaica's social and political fabric. I argue that constructed meanings around higglering and higglers are not simply attributed to the informal status of this market activity. Instead, they reveal attempts by those in power to reproduce a presumed social and spatial order shaped by race/color, class and gender divisions in a context of acute economic challenges and social instability. In these attempts higglers and their market activities are characterized as 'pollutants' or 'disease' that disrupt or contaminate an established order. By examining these public representations, this essay illuminates the racialized, classed and gendered contexts of inclusion and exclusion in which a particular market activity is imagined and experienced.

Theoretical framework

Examining public discourses in the context of special instances can shed light on lived experiences, because as I will show, these discourses feed into the practices of everyday commercial life. Further, to understand markets as lived experiences there are certain factors that must be taken into consideration. Firstly, we must understand those lived experiences as embodied (Shilling 2005; Howson 2004). Understanding lived experiences as such helps prevent the researcher from thinking about them in abstraction and, instead, concretize those experiences within the social–economic–geographical contexts in which they take place. Secondly, understanding these experiences as embodied involves us paying close attention to those bodies to ask, 'Who *are* these economic actors?' 'What *kinds* of bodies are we talking about?' This approach makes central the question of difference and encourages the researcher to recognize that these are racialized, classed, and gendered bodies that are positioned within societies in complex ways. Here the concept of, what I'm calling, *embodied intersectionality* plays a critical role. It is through the lens of embodied intersectionality that one recognizes the 'multi-textured' characteristic of our bodies. By this I mean, our bodies are embedded in multiple, intersecting hierarchies of power–race, ethnicity, nation, class, gender, sexuality, etc. – and are lived and read through frames that reflect these dimensions. Our bodies also act in ways that re/produce[4] and/or contest those multiple hierarchies of power. Bodies, then, are complex, multidimensional sites and subjects of struggle (Shilling 2005).

Thirdly, we must understand that those embodied experiences are spatialized, that is, they are located both physically and conceptually in social space. In the case of higglering, these embodied experiences are located in the city of a developing nation – a city that has experienced, among many challenges, economic decline, urban density, violence, high unemployment, urban decay, and spatial segregation shaped by race/color and class (Weis 2004; Wyss and White 2004; Portes *et al.* 1994; Huber and Stephens 1992; Clarke and Howard 1999; Clarke 1975). Cities, however, are not simply material landscapes that are fixed in time and space; they are also symbolic spaces – spaces of the imagination. The ways in which cities are imagined have real consequences on how city spaces (and the bodies that navigate them) are organized, managed and ordered (Bridge and Watson 2000; Watson 2000). The struggles between higglers, the formal business community, uptown city residents and the state, I contend, reveal this relationship between 'city imaginaries' (Bridge and Watson 2002) and the spatial organization of Kingston. My interest, however, is to tease out the racialized/colored, classed and gendered dimensions of those imaginaries, and show how they are re/produced and negotiated through various struggles over city space.

Cities and markets: constructed and produced

Understanding cities as both physical and imagined helps illuminate ways in which 'differences are constructed in, and themselves construct, city life and space' (Bridge and Watson 2000: 507). Urban theorists have demonstrated over the years that one of the many features of city spaces is its high population density and the likelihood of encounters with difference. These differences help shape and are shaped by social relations in/and city spaces (Fincher and Jacobs, 1998). Sophie Watson (2000) adds

> Space is both produced and consumed within relations of difference where women and black people are often at the bottom of the pile. And these differences, in part, are a product of the social imaginary, which classes these categories of people as subordinate (Watson 2000: 103).

City spaces are infused with complex operations of power and, as such, an analysis of the city must take into account 'how networks of power differentiate space unequally, or how the social imaginary is translated into spatial hierarchies within which the city becomes socially polarized and fragmented' (Watson 2000: 103–4). I argue, in addition, that power is not only evidenced in the ways in which difference and hierarchies are re/produced in city spaces; it is also evidenced in the ways in which those hierarchies are contested, negotiated and/or transformed through the uses of those spaces by various bodies.

As I examine the conflicts between higglers, the formal economic business community, uptown residents and the state, I discuss ways in which difference is imagined, re/produced, and contested in the city of Kingston. To do this, the urban landscape in which higgelring occurs becomes the site upon which the mapping and contestation of social boundaries of race/color, class and gender are disclosed. In her analysis of how public space in urban society becomes semiotically encoded and interpreted reality, Setha Low (1996) makes a clear distinction between what she calls the 'social production of space' and the 'social construction of space.'

> The social production of space includes all those factors – social, economic, ideological, and technological – the intended goal of which is the physical creation of the material setting ... the social construction of space is the actual transformation of space-through people's social exchanges, memories, images, and daily use of the material

setting-into scenes and actions that convey symbolic meaning (Low 1996: 861-2).

Here, Low's distinction between the social production of space and the social construction of space is quite useful in understanding the battles presently being waged between higglers, the business community, uptown residents and the state. Their struggles over the use of public urban space reveal a transformation (through contestation) of a physical setting into an arena for the contestation of symbolic space. In this context race/color, class and gender relations are re/produced and contested in a physical urban setting for economic and ideological reasons.

One of the distinctive features of the city of Kingston is its division both physically and conceptually into uptown and downtown. This division is in large part the result of class and race/color based social and spatial polarization in the 1960s and 1970s in response to high population density following an explosive rural to urban migration trend (Portes *et al.*, 1994; Clarke 1975). This race/color and class spatial polarization resulted in the configuration of the city into what Portes *et al.* (1994) describe as an 'upside down ice cream cone' where the predominantly poor black masses of Jamaicans are concentrated in downtown Kingston while the small brown and white elites are concentrated uptown.

Although migration patterns have changed since the 1970s and satellite cities have developed to relieve Kingston somewhat from its population density, those uptown/downtown distinctions have largely remained. Brown and white elites remain over-represented in uptown residential and business areas in Kingston, and although pockets of poor housing settlements are located uptown, black working class/poor Jamaicans continue to dominate downtown. Moreover, uptown/downtown distinctions are used among Kingstonians to indicate one's social standing where 'uptown' is associated with the brown or white upper/middle classes, and 'downtown' with poor blacks. Because of this, to belong 'uptown' or 'downtown' signifies one's membership in a certain racial/color/class group. When one is identified as an 'uptown lady,' for example, there are certain expectations that follow, i.e. that person is a brown middle/upper class woman who performs a middle class construction of femininity (Ulysse 1999; Douglass 1992). I return to this point below.

The social production of space, then, involves a geographical location and its meanings (uptown/downtown distinctions on the physical landscape of the city). The social construction of space involves those symbolic interpretations that emerge out of the everyday *use* of a physical setting. It is the symbolic construction, identification and performance of one's social standing, which can be – but not necessarily –[5] tied to their physical location. The social construction of space also involves the delineation of boundaries (social and spatial) that emerge through people's everyday practices, particularly through their struggles over the use of that physical location. It is in these practices where we find the distribution of social honor leading to the reproduction of what Max Weber (1993) calls a status order. What this suggests is that urban landscapes are not blank places upon which everyday practices simply unfold; these landscapes shape, and are shaped by, those practices and imaginaries in various ways.

In many practices of boundary creation and the reproduction of a status order, we can find ideas of pollution, disease and dirt that are used to signify anomalies in an existing system. As Mary Douglas (2002) argues in her classical text, *Purity and Danger*, dirt is 'matter out of place,'

> It implies two conditions: a set of ordered relations and a contravention of that order. Dirt then, is never a unique isolated event. Where there is dirt there is a system. Dirt is the by-product of a systematic ordering and classification of matter, in so far as ordering involves rejecting inappropriate elements (Douglas 2002: 44).

Ideas of dirt often legitimize the expulsion or containment of anomalies, which if successful, fortifies existing boundaries and re/produces a preferred social and spatial order. Over the last few decades the business of higglering and higglers have often been associated with pollution, dirt and disease. It is essential, then, that we examine these representations and responses to them for they reveal a presumed social and spatial order in Jamaica that is racialized, classed and gendered.

The 'problem' of higglering

After Jamaica gained its independence from Britain in 1962, political and economic power was transferred from a white (British) elite to a brown elite. This brown elite, which is made up of people of mixed heritage and ethnic minorities such as Jews, Lebanese and Chinese, remained in power up until 1992 when P.J. Patterson became the first self-identified 'black' Prime Minister. Today, a budding black professional class controls the political process in Jamaica, but the brown elite continues to control the economy and enjoy local economic wealth (Robotham 2000).

Like many Caribbean and Latin American nations Jamaica, since Independence, has pursued an economic development model that has, in effect, entrenched the economy further in a dependent relationship in the global market (Portes *et al.* 1994; Huber and Stephens 1992). The devastating effects of structural adjustment policies that have undermined previous solutions to urbanization and economic development, reduced government employment, weakened the purchasing power of local wages, and drastically curtailed public services, health and welfare programs, have produced incredible hardships for Jamaicans, especially the poor. On the other hand, the elite and traditional middle classes have fared better. These groups have managed to maintain their privileged positions in society and have, in fact, expanded in spite of structural adjustment (Clarke and Howard 2006: 109–14).

Over the years the economy has contracted under pressures of increasing debt, both foreign and domestic. To manage this debt more than half of the national budget has been earmarked for debt servicing. In fact, in the 2004/2005 fiscal year debt servicing consumed roughly 70 per cent of the national budget.[6] One of the outcomes of Jamaica's debt problems is the drastic reduction of formal sector jobs resulting in high unemployment rates hovering around 10–11 per cent. This situation is particularly difficult for Jamaican women who in 2006 experienced twice the level of unemployment (13 per cent) in comparison to men (6.9 per cent).[7] What we find, then, is since Independence there has been a rapid expansion of the informal economy of Jamaica as the formal economy contracts. As a response to deteriorating economic conditions, limited formal employment options, and their primary responsibilities of supporting their households many Jamaican women turn to the informal economy, particularly street vending. Today half of Kingston's male labor force and more than half of the female labor force consist of informal workers (Clarke and Howard 2006: 110).

As the informal economy expands the formal business community and uptown city residents express anxieties over the presence of higglers on the streets of Kingston, and each year a struggle ensues among these groups over the use of city space. When we examine these tensions we see that public perceptions of higglers are fraught with contradictions. On one hand, higglers are admired for their ability to survive in the face of great adversity; they are thought to exemplify the strength and resilience of Jamaicans. On the other hand, higglers are scorned for their presumed indiscipline and vulgarity. These perceptions often fuel public debates that call for the government to contain the ever-expanding informal economy, particularly the business of higglering. Efforts by the state to restrict the activities of higglers include the use of agencies like the Kingston and St Andrew Corporation (KSAC) and the Metropolitan Parks and Market (MPM),[8] along with local police to relocate them from the streets to designated market places. These attempts of intervention sometimes result in the destruction of higglers' property and their means of generating income.

Although struggles over city space occur at various moments throughout the year, they tend to intensify around Christmas – the busiest shopping season of the year. In an editorial entitled 'The drama of Christmas Vending' published in the *Daily Gleaner* on December 10, 2003, Peter Espeut argues that the Christmas trade is so lucrative that profits made in this season can carry the business sector, financially, through most of the following year. So much money is to be made at Christmas, he asserts, that each year it 'draws every higgler and would-be higgler on to the streets and sidewalks of every city and every town in Jamaica to get a piece of the action' (Espeut, 2003). He adds that some Jamaicans who have migrated abroad would return to Jamaica at Christmas to sell on the streets. Indeed, the informal economy – higglering in particular – presents a real source of competition to formal economic businesses, especially during this season.

Public discourses on higglering reveal, on one level, anxieties by the business community over the economic competition higglering creates. In these discourses, social and spatial boundaries between formal/ informal, legitimacy and illegitimacy are created that preserve the privileged positions of formal sector businesses in Jamaica's weakened economy. These boundaries are also supported by many uptown city residents and are re/produced in their discourses around higglering in the city. A close examination of these discourses, however, suggest that those boundary constructions do not simply reinforce formal/informal economic divisions, but they also re/produce and reinforce racialized, classed and gendered boundaries of exclusion and inclusion that are mapped upon, and negotiated by bodies in city space.

Higglers vs formal businesses

The articles in the *Daily Gleaner* and *Jamaica Observer* revealed various narratives of higglers getting 'out of control' and 'taking over' city streets and sidewalks. Higglers were also imagined as public nuisances and an unfair threat to legitimate businesses. An article published on December 28, 1999, for example, described the practice of street vending[9] as old as civilization itself but that a major problem is 'its unfair threat to store-based businesses' ('Vending: The Bigger Picture,' *Daily Gleaner,* 28 December 1999). This 'unfair threat' includes triggering a decline in the profits of formal economic businesses. For instance, on December 18, 1999 Michael Ammar Jr, Vice President of the Jamaica Chamber of Commerce at the time, and a prominent member of Jamaica's brown elite, told the *Daily Gleaner* that stores that were blocked by higglers (who would sell on the sidewalks in front of them) reported a 30 per cent drop in their business, and that their customers complained of jostling to get in and out of them. He added that in order for the downtown business district to be restored,[10] the 'problem of illegal vending' must be addressed.

I think it is fair to say that the private sector has done more than its fair share to try to restore downtown Kingston. However, without the rule of law and order, our investments are all at risk ('Sellers squabble over space,' *Daily Gleaner,* 18 December 1999).

In this and other narratives higglers are associated with lawlessness and disorder. What exactly is being dis-*ordered* by higglers? The activities of higglers signify the disruption of a spatialized economic *order* that has been firmly in place since the colonial era (Clarke 1975) – an economic order that secures greater access to economic resources for formal businesses in a weakened economy. These formal businesses are dominated by Jamaica's brown elites who currently control the economy.

Higglers are aware of this racialized/colored economic order and their less privileged positions within it. In my larger study, for example, higglers were asked to identify the numbers of people from various racial/colored groups, particularly Chinese, whites and browns, whom they have observed engaged in higglering. In response, one market woman stated, 'I haven't seen any Chinese women higglering, *they are mostly in the shops*. I haven't seen any whites either, *they are mostly in the clothes business* (emphasis added)' (Market Woman #1, 19 February 2001, personal communication). This market woman's response was supported by an ICI, who stated, 'Chinese people *get the breaks*, they get the shops (emphasis added)' (ICI #25, February 16, 2001, personal communication). In this response the ICI not only identified a racialized/colored division of the economy but also insinuated that she was in a disadvantaged position *vis-à-vis* the Chinese.

Other higglers gave similar responses such as the Chinese, browns and/or whites 'sell in stores that's rented'; 'they own the stores'; 'they have their own business enterprises.' One market woman explicitly stated that the Chinese do not sell at her worksite because of the 'location.' The location she was referring to was the public market at Papine in uptown Kingston, a market that has historically been occupied by working class/poor black women. These responses signify the presence of a racialized/colored and class division of the economy where Chinese, browns and white Jamaicans – members of the elite – are relegated to more privileged segments (as formal sector store owners) and are not found higglering, whereas working class/poor black women tend to be relegated to the informal sector and are likely to be found higglering. While this is no surprise, the movements of higglers' multi-textured bodies, when read in this broader spatialized context, take on greater significance. On one level, their movements into more exclusive spaces in the economy suggest a transgression, consciously or unconsciously, of this racialized/colored and classed economic order on city space. The public responds to these transgressions by admonishing higglers for 'disrupting' law and order in the city.

The disorder to the business world signified by higglers extends to the city as a whole where their 'undisciplined' bodies pose a threat to general city life. An editorial in the *Daily Gleaner* (2 December 2003) in support of the removal of higglers from the streets described their presence as 'hold[ing] the city of Kingston ransom for yet another Christmas season.' It applauded the KSAC's attempts to enforce a set of rules on higglers in order to create 'civil order' while allowing them to sell in designated areas. It was expected, however, that higglers would protest their removal, and these protests were perceived as indicative of their indiscipline. The editorial asserted, '. . . the *infection* of indiscipline is beginning to spread among the vendors (emphasis added),' but expressed its support of the Mayor to take a 'zero-tolerance' stance against them. Describing higglering as 'a subset of squatting,' which had gotten out of hand, the editorial declared,

> Many vendors are much more affluent than they make out to avoid paying taxes on their profits. Their wholesale capturing of the streets of downtown Kingston is an affront to law and order and a stop must be put to it once and for all. This will call for a mix of force and tact but unless the authorities prevail the city will fall victim to incremental chaos ('Vendors must obey the rules,' *Daily Gleaner*, 2 December 2003).

Here, the social imaginary of the city as an 'ordered' space is revealed – an 'order' that socially and spatially fragments city space to contain the 'infection' of undesirables.

Historically, downtown Kingston was polarized in such a way where black lower class Jamaicans were relegated to West Kingston (contributing to a concentration of racialized poverty and unemployment in this area) and formal businesses were relegated to the East (Clarke 1975). Higglers, however, have actively transformed the downtown city space expanding it, particularly the streets, into a site of economic opportunities for larger numbers of Jamaicans, especially the poor. The presumably 'infectious indiscipline' of higglers, then, signifies their refusal to passively use city space in accordance with established rules created by authorities and supported by those social groups who benefit from those rules – especially those from the well off classes (many of whom have investments in the downtown area).

What interest me about these narratives are the ways in which the city becomes a metaphor for the economy through which the boundaries of legitimate vs. illegitimate, lawful vs. lawless and perhaps more importantly, formal vs informal are constructed. The expansion of the informal economy is evidenced on city space through the proliferation of street vendors, and their presence is thought to signify urban and, by extension, economic decay. Concerns about the 'capture' of city streets by higglers merge with concerns about their competition in the economy. To create 'order' on city space, then, is to create 'order' in the economy, that is, to contain the informal economy and its social pollution, consequently removing the competition it creates for formal businesses.

In these narratives the formal economy occupies a privileged position, as it is associated with – and indeed defines – legitimacy and lawfulness. Yet, the formal economy is described as vulnerable in relation to the informal economy due to the 'unfair' practices of 'illegitimate' businesses. The city (and the economy) is perceived as under siege by higglers who 'infect' the space with 'indiscipline' causing 'civil disorder'. A sense of fairness denied the law abiding citizen, i.e. formal business owners, is implied in these narratives, which raises questions around the government's ability to effectively protect its citizens, enforce law and order in the city, and resuscitate a failing economy. These questions are especially significant given the government's diminishing role in the economy as part of IMF imposed structural adjustment policies and its adoption of a neo-liberal economic framework that minimizes its power, factors which have contributed to a loss of confidence in the government in the minds of many citizens.

There are, however, interesting racial/color, gender and class dimensions at work in these narratives as well. Working class/poor black Jamaican women dominate the business of higglering. The public discourse describes their presence on the streets, and in economically viable spaces in downtown Kingston as contaminating or disrupting an economic order that privileges formal sector businesses dominated by the brown elite. The public maps social pathologies onto these black, working class/poor female bodies and cast them as threatening an established social and economic order. In these narratives disruptions of city space by black poor female bodies symbolize anomalies in the established racialized/colored economy. In other words, higglers' bodies are 'out of place' (Douglas 2002). The narratives, then, create a sense of moral panic and help legitimize the government's control, and sometimes, violent removal of these workers from city streets. If these removal efforts are successful black, working class/poor female bodies are kept 'in their place' and the established (racialized/color, classed and gendered) economic order is fortified.

These removal efforts, when successful, benefit formal businesses. For instance, a news article in the *Jamaica Observer* in 21 December 2003 reported that formal businesses, especially those uptown, were doing better than those located downtown during the Christmas season. Informal businesses, particularly higglering, were the least successful as a result, in large part, of relocation efforts and heavy policing by the state. The article reads,

> But while some businesses in the downtown shopping area also reported brisk sales, vendors, recently removed from the shopping districts and sidewalks, say their source of income has all but dried up. 'We a suffer down here, from them move us off the streets we a dead fi hungry like dog.'[11] A licensed higgler in the Buck Town vendors arcade on Peters Lane said ('Uptown businesses outdoing downtown.' *Jamaica Observer*, 21 December 2003).

In the meanwhile, storeowner Michael Ammar Senior reported that the removal of higglers had enhanced his business. 'Business is not bad. Better access to the sidewalk brought back some of our old time customers who are happy to know they can return downtown' ('Uptown businesses outdoing downtown,' *Jamaica Observer*, 21 December 2003). It is very likely that the 'old time customers' Ammar is referring to are uptowners, since black working class/poor customers have already been shopping downtown in significant numbers where prices are more affordable. With the help of local police formal businesses are protected from competition with higglers, and is able to capture a lion's share of the profits earned in this lucrative shopping season.

What is also illuminated in these public narratives is the relationship between 'city imaginaries' (Bridge and Watson 2002) and the spatial organization of Kingston. In a capitalist economy most informal economic businesses are marginalized as evidenced in their concealment from public view, and from government records. Although street vending in Jamaica is not concealed from public view, its marginalization is evidenced in the treatment of higglers and the relegation of these micro-enterprises to markets located outside of the central business district and in areas that are not conducive to good business.

Higglers feel this marginalization in their day-to-day work experience. In my interviews, all 45 higglers reported that the government was unsupportive of them. But even more telling is the sense among most that higglers do not receive the respect they deserve. Three market women described the squalid conditions of the market in which they work as evidence of this lack of respect. One stated, for instance, 'the market is dirty, if we talk, the head of the market don't like it. We get no support from the government. The market want to look after and the government don't do anything' (Market Woman #17, 14 July 2001, personal communication). It was quite common to see piles of garbage, puddles of mud and to experience foul stenches in the air when you entered these markets as opposed to the Plazas. The state of the market, along with the unsanitary conditions of the bathroom facilities, was a common complaint among the market women who intimated that I would not encounter these conditions at the Plazas. An older market woman argued, for instance, 'There is no security here in the market and the sanitary conditions are nasty. No, we don't get the same respect as the Plazas' (Market Woman #1, 19 February 2001, personal communication). In this way, socially polluting higglers are both symbolically and spatially 'put in place' by being relegated to the filthy places of the city.

These sentiments were echoed by the ICIs. One ICI remarked, for instance, that the 'government believe higglers are the low-low class of people' (ICI #29, 14 June 2001, personal communication). Another ICI stated, that higglers get no respect, because 'you are not looked upon as a business person' (ICI #42, 17 July 2001, personal communication). One ICI described being targeted by customs and having to pay unfair duties. She stated, 'Higglers get no respect. Customs handle you bad. You have to pay high duties. They just treat you bad' (ICI #38, 28 June 2001, personal communication). This ICI compared her treatment to formal sector business people, particularly Syrian/Lebanese (racialized as brown), who she believed receive better treatment. Like the market women, the idea of preferential treatment for formal businesses in the

Plazas was also common among the ICIs. One ICI stated, for instance, 'we don't get the same respect as the people in the Plaza. The people in the Plaza don't feel you are capable, they feel they are better to run their business' (ICI #37, 22 June 2001 personal communication). Another ICI remarked, 'Mr Ammar's buyers don't get the same treatment like ICIs and higglers' (ICI #29, 14 June 2001, personal communication).

Although the higglers in my study viewed their businesses as a source of great pride, since it helped them support their families and gain a sense of independence, higglering was also a source of pain because of the differential treatment and disrespect they believe they receive in comparison to formal businesses. In some ways, many higglers felt betrayed. One ICI remarked,

> We don't get respect again like we used to. In the 1980s when big businesses left, vendors stayed here and kept the country going, but we don't get respect now. Jamaica encourage foreign business and not encourage vendors. They encourage the Chinese and other foreigners over vendors. Chinese sell what the vendors sell and undercut their profits. I wonder if the Chinese pay duties? (ICI #36, 19 June 2001, personal communication).

In spite of this sense of this betrayal among many, higglers continue on with their businesses, partly out of necessity but also out of pride in their work.

Higglers have challenged their marginalization by refusing to remain in the markets and continuing to sell on the streets. They have used various strategies of resistance ranging from engaging in a 'cat and mouse' game with local authorities to direct confrontations with the police and business owners. In December 2001, for instance, an article in the *Daily Gleaner* reported that despite the KSAC's 'zero-tolerance' approaches towards higglers 'street vending in the commercial district remain as hectic as ever with a few new twists' (Clarke, Petulia. 'Cat-and-mouse game downtown Kingston – Vendors remain determined to cash in on Xmas sales,' *Daily Gleaner*, 6 December 2001). Higglers, determined to profit from the busy Christmas season, remained constantly mobile, moving from one street to the next, to avoid getting caught by the authorities. Some higglers have also hired 'watchmen' to alert them of approaching authorities so that they can clear the streets before they arrived. Most higglers' view the streets as safer and most profitable locations to conduct their businesses, and so they sell there in spite of the risks.

Higglers have also engaged in direct confrontations with local authorities and business people. For instance, In December 2003, the *Jamaica
Observer* reported that higglers chanting 'No vendors! No stores!' gathered in front of the KSAC and stormed businesses in major shopping
areas, forcing many to pull down their shutters ('Vendors Protest .... But
KSAC vows not to back down,' *Jamaica Observer*, 9 December 2003). In
another protest a few years earlier, higglers marched onto formal business
stores downtown, drew down their shutters and shouted 'if we caan sell,
then nobody will sell'[12] forcing local authorities and businesses to negotiate with them for space to sell. In both instances, higglers challenged
attempts to push them out of economically viable spaces by simply
using their bodies either to avoid detection by authorities or directly
confronting them. Here, the multi-textured bodies of higglers purposely
create disorder instead of being or embodying disorder. Instead of passively accepting their marginalization higglers use their bodies to actively
contest it and, at times, are successful in their struggles – although
temporarily.

Higglers vs uptown residents

In addition to formal businesses, local residents are constructed as victims of higglering in the public discourse. On 16 November 1986 Dawn
Ritch, a popular columnist of the *Daily Gleaner* (and member of the
brown elite), published an article titled 'No Such Thing as a Happy Higgler: They are spreading like a disease into every residential area' where
she bemoaned the encroachment of higglers into uptown residential
areas. She asserted,

> They've oppressed and endangered the environment, and the coun-
> try's public health standard. They are spreading like a disease into
> every residential area, and will continue until stopped. What was once
> quaint is now a morass of indiscipline because higglers want to make
> money but don't display the responsibility that usually comes with
> earning it. Higglers are just too bright for their own good. And I don't
> believe in appeasing them because there is no such thing as a happy
> higgler (Ritch 1986: A6).

Ritch's use of the metaphor 'disease' speaks volumes to the ways in
which higglers are imagined. Social pathologies again are mapped onto
black poor female bodies of higglers' who are figured as contami-
nants. Their movements into uptown residential areas signify 'dis/ease'

since long established patterns of racialized/color and classed residential segregation (Clarke and Howard 1999; Portes *et al.* 1994), are challenged.

Ronald Sundstrom (2003) reminds us that 'when we sort people by categories, we do so spatially; with race come racialized spaces' (Sundstrom 2003: 92). He insists that we must take seriously the relationship between social space and human categories since 'who we are is bound up with place ...' (Sundstrom 2003: 92). As I mentioned earlier, among Kingstonians, 'uptown' (like downtown) is not simply a geographic identifier, it also signifies one's social standing. The social standing of the brown elite is bound up with uptown residential space. Higglers' presence uptown, then, not only disrupts spatial boundaries but also can potentially change the meaning of 'uptown' space and jeopardize the social standing of browns. To put it bluntly, if 'uptown' is now dominated by poor black female bodies (that signify social pathology and degradation in the public imagination) then that can potentially change the meaning of 'uptown' and impact the social standing of brown residents. On Ritch's view the presence of these predominantly black, working class/poor higglers in previously restricted uptown areas signifies a contamination that must be removed so that social order (racialized/color/classed residential segregation) is restored and, I might add, the social standing of the brown elite is protected.

It is important to note that many uptown residents purchase locally grown produce from market women, especially on Saturday mornings.[13] This was evidenced at the Papine Market in uptown Kingston where I conducted my research. But these spaces and workers are spatially contained. With the deterioration of the Jamaican economy and the expansion of the informal economy, however, informal business spaces are expanding and privileged spaces of the brown elite are not easily insulated. Higglers, then, take up *too much space* in the minds of many uptowners, as these black women move into previously restricted areas in search for new customers.

The themes of contamination and the construction of higglers as public nuisances are evidenced in other letters to the *Daily Gleaner*. For example, in a letter to the editor published on 26 March 2000 entitled 'The Making of a Slum,' John H. Williams, a resident from the primarily upper-middle class, uptown Kingston 8 area, described what he considered the 'deteriorating condition of Manor Park.'

Manor Park should be a prime and pristine residential area. It is now deteriorating into a "slum." At the foot of [Stony Hill] which was once a large green common area is now taken over by higglers, taxis, and an assorted bunch of idlers who have now turned the once lovely green area into a filthy wasteland ('The Making of a Slum,' *Daily Gleaner: Letter*, 26 March, 2000).

He described bus sheds being 'taken over by higglers and idlers making the pedestrians and buses fight for space in the middle of the road.' He added that the Constant Spring market, where higglers sell, was an eyesore,

> Its ghoulish shoddy ambience contributes greatly to the general chaka chaka[14] of Manor Park. This entity is completely out of place and should be removed ('The Making of a Slum,' *Daily Gleaner: Letter*, 26 March 2000).

He goes on to describe formal businesses in Manor Park as needing to be 'relocated or moved back so that the roadways can be widened.' The general breakdown, he says, 'makes the place look like a growing holocaust and creates traffic jams even on Sundays' ('The Making of a Slum,' *Daily Gleaner: Letter*, 26 March 2000).

What interests me about this letter is Williams' suggestion to remove the Constant Spring market and for that matter, higglers, because they are 'out of place' and yet formal economic businesses are to be 'relocated or moved back.' Higglering is not perceived as suitable for that upper-middle class area, even if they conduct their business in the designated marketplace. Here, Williams has a definite idea about what is appropriate for that particular geographical area. His concern is not simply the aesthetics of Manor Park but the social meanings attributed to this upper-middle class area, that is, what *kind* of place it is and what *kind* of people live there. Williams description of Manor park's deterioration as its being 'taken over' by higglers, idlers and taxis carries subtle racial and class meanings since these activities are dominated by the black poor. The use of the term 'slum' operates similarly. Like the terms 'ghetto' or 'urban neighborhoods' in the US context, 'slums' represent the social and spatial location of the black poor (Sundstrom 2003). By claiming that Manor Park was deteriorating into a slum and associating higglers with filth and waste, and a source of this deterioration, Williams uses race/color and class symbols to generate a sense of moral panic among Jamaicans, particularly uptown residents.

Williams also used gender symbols against class and race/color. He asked, 'What kind of country is this where higglers and idlers easily capture every inch of space? Where is the town planning department, the security forces, the KSAC, the Member of Parliament? Are all these paid entities afraid or impotent?' ('The Making of a Slum,' *Daily Gleaner: Letter*, 26 March 2000). Williams questioning of the impotence of government agencies is a means by which he challenged structures of masculinist power identifying its inability to control the poor in general, poor black women in particular. What, for instance, would 'potency' mean? Here it seems that potency would mean not only protecting law-abiding citizens by controlling the black poor and women, but also having the power to restore a presumed social and spatial order structured by race/color, class and gender.

The use of gender symbols against class and race/color is also evidenced in public constructions of the Jamaican 'lady' and 'woman,' and the placement of higglers among the latter. In her study on the Jamaican white elite, Lisa Douglass (1992) makes a clear distinction between public constructions of a Jamaican 'lady' and a 'woman.' She argues,

> A lady is educated and refined. She exudes femininity in all her attributes, from her diminutive size and unobtrusive manner, to her high heels and exquisite grooming, to her soft voice and careful diction.... She does not use vulgar language or even patois... (Douglass 1992: 75).

Higglers do not fit into a middle class construction of 'ladies.' Higglering occurs in the public sphere, particularly in the streets, a space that has traditionally been imagined and often practiced as masculine. According to Douglass, not only is the street the domain of men, it is also the domain of lower-class 'women.' An uptown 'lady' would not venture out into the streets without her car or unaccompanied. The work site of higglers, then, always already frames how these women are perceived. Ladies don't higgle in the streets.

Another important characteristic in the construction of a Jamaican 'lady', Douglass argues, is its association with race/color and class where 'ladies' are generally understood as middle and upper class brown women. Higglers do not fit into this ideal of femininity. These predominantly working class/poor, dark-skinned women are stereotyped in the public discourse as loud, aggressive 'black women' who are vulgar, unruly and, basically, unfeminine. The construction of the Jamaican 'lady,' then, excludes working class/poor black women, including higglers.

An example of the construction of higglers as 'women' is evidenced in an editorial published in 10 August 1986 where Morris Cargill, a white Jamaican male suggested that modern higglers were the result of 'selective breeding.' He ridiculed these women by describing their bodies as follows:

> I suggested at the start of this piece that the modern higgler has been the result of selective breeding. To begin with, few seem to weigh less than 250 lbs. They are also a special shape, sticking out back and front simultaneously; huge protruding bottoms and equally huge tops, both of which they use as battering rams ('On Higglers,' *Daily Gleaner*, Editorial, 10 August 1986).

Cargill's construction of higglers goes against middle class definitions of a lady that are determined by, among many things, her diminutive size. His claim that higglers use their 'huge' breasts as 'battering rams' speaks to the higgler's perceived obtrusive manner, which also makes her unfeminine since 'ladies' are socialized to take up as little space with their bodies as possible. Higglers, then, in their practices and presences make space as much as they 'take up space.' In addition to disrupting the commercial and social–urban order, their racialized, out of place bodies also disrupt classed gender arrangements and assumptions.

Cargill's invocation of dark-skinned women with huge breasts and protruding bottoms battering unsuspecting bystanders relies on a background stereotypical image of the black mammy figure. We see this image reproduced in various artistic representations of the higgler. Her head is wrapped. Her breasts are large. And her bottom protrudes. But most importantly, she is represented as asexual; her body is not to be desired. In fact, Cargill writes that it is 'worse still [to] have [a higgler] run up against you and you soon know that there is no soft flabby fat there, but solid muscle ...' ('On Higglers,' *Daily Gleaner*, Editorial, 10 August 1986). He likens the higgler to Russian weightlifters who do what they do 'because they happen to be built like that in the first place.' As he writes in a 1999 editorial, under the subheading 'Bras with Cement,' 'in the case of the higglers these cleavages are not for sex but for storage' ('Bleaching, etc.,' *Daily Gleaner*, Editorial, 29 July 1999). To be sure, the image of the black mammy-as-higgler serves Cargill's purpose to justify their removal from public view, and this justification trades on a host of racist associations that inform Jamaica's more general public discourse.

In response to Cargill's editorial, members of the uptown Higglers Association demanded an apology from the author. Mrs Williams-Edwards, president of the Association described Cargill's statement as 'an insult to all women, not just higglers' ('Higglers blast Cargill article as "an insult to all women"', *Daily Gleaner*, 15 August 1986) and defended higglers who, on her view, were the 'backbone of the society' and major contributors to the Jamaican economy. Taking exception to the label 'higgler,' Williams-Edwards suggested that higglers use the term 'vendor' as a way of managing the stigma through a process of redefinition and disassociation. In my interviews, only 8 out of 45 women identified themselves as higglers. Additionally many of these women, especially those who sold in designated markets uptown, performed a certain conception of femininity in their interactions with customers (they spoke softly, didn't call out to passers by, they refrained from speaking patois, etc.). In fact, these higglers called my attention to their reserved behaviors to demonstrate their rejection of the negative image in the public discourse. In spite of these stigma management techniques, however, the terms higgler and vendor are used interchangeably in the public discourse and the stigma associated with the term 'higglering' is transferred to 'street vending.'

Conclusion

All of the articles suggest that the activities of higglering and their conflicts with the state, uptown residents, and formal businesses reveal how the social imaginary (as evidenced in the public discourse) is translated into spatial hierarchies that polarizes and fragments the city of Kingston. Using a theoretical lens of 'embodied intersectionality' I show that these spatial hierarchies are racialized/colored, classed and gendered, and the conflicts reveal ways in which networks of power are re/produced, negotiated and/or challenged. The physical presence of higglers are conceptualized as having a 'polluting' effect on middle and upper class areas because, among many things, their black bodies make poverty visible. Moreover, their bodies are mobile and, as such, established social and spatial boundaries are tested and made vulnerable simply by the movements of these working class/poor black women into previously restricted areas. The conflicts between higglers, the state, city residents and formal businesses, then, reveal challenges to those long established social and spatial boundaries, and attempts to fortify them. At the heart of these conflicts is the question of 'order': who is 'out of order' and who wants to, and is able to, maintain 'order.' The concept of order, deployed in public discourses in this way, reveals hegemonic notions of social space and place.

The case of Afro-Jamaican higglers suggest that to understand markets as lived experiences it is essential that we not limit our investigations solely to economic factors but also examine social–ideological ones, particularly the ways in which constructions of race/color and gender are infused in them as indicative of disorder and pollution. Embodied intersectionality helps tease out these multiple dimensions of power by focusing on the multi-textured bodies of actors and the broader social and economic contexts in which they work. An examination of social and economic factors are essential in this framework because as Max Weber (1993) tells us,

"Economically conditioned" power is not, of course, identical with "power" as such. On the contrary, the emergence of economic power may be *the consequence of power existing on other grounds* (Weber, in Lemert, 1993: 126, emphasis added).

Here, Weber identifies structures of power as interrelated, and his insight is especially significant in the context of Jamaica, given its high correlation of class status and race/color in that society. This approach offers a more in-depth assessment of the lived experiences of markets by exposing complex and, sometimes, subtle obstacles that may shape and constrain those experiences.

In contracting urban economies, particularly in developing countries, competition for 'scarce benefits and spoils' intensifies as local elites vie to maintain their privileged positions, and the poor struggles to earn a living. To manage this competition, differences among various groups are magnified and mechanisms of inclusion and exclusion are developed. In these processes of inclusion and exclusion categories of race/color and gender are given greater meaning and work with class (and other categories of inequality) to organize bodies and structure contexts in which market (including informal market) activities occur. Colin Clarke and David Howard (2006) argued that in Jamaica 'the elite and traditional middle class largely managed to maintain their positions in urban society, despite the contraction of the economy' (Clarke and Howard 2006: 114). Of course, there are multiple factors that can account for their success including quality educational opportunities, and greater access to high-income jobs and housing. But to what extent is success also attributed to these groups' ability to secure (with support from the government) privileged positions in the economy by containing informal workers? To what extent are uptown residents able to secure access to more privileged residential areas by excluding those deemed less desirable? To what extent are the economic successes of the elite and traditional middle classes intertwined with the re/production of racial/color hierarchies that are used to legitimize and protect their privileged positions in the economy and society? While these questions are not answered in this essay, the case of Afro-Jamaican higglers suggests that a singular focus on economic factors only scratches the surface of our understanding of their lived experiences.

In his elaboration of the history of struggles between higglers and formal businesses over city space, Peter Espeut (2003) asserts,

> This script has played out – with a few variations – over many decades. A comedy or tragedy? It is almost the archetype of class struggle – between the rich and the poor, between the poor and the power-less, between the merchants and the higglers, between the formal and the informal sector. It demonstrates how the powerful can amass the forces of the state to act in their interests; and it shows the ability of the Jamaican underclass to struggle and survive in the face of great adversity' ('The Drama of Christmas Vending,' *Daily Gleaner*, 10 December 2003).

Espeut described this drama as a class struggle. However, using the lens of embodied intersectionality I show that the lived experiences of higglering reveal a complex web of power that go beyond informal/formal divisions. Indeed, they illuminate racialized/colored, classed and gendered contexts of inclusion and exclusion that working class/poor, black women in Jamaica grapple with as they struggle 'fi mek a sale'[15] and thereby dis/ease the everyday order.

Notes

1. I use the term race/color because in Jamaica skin color – white, brown, black – are often used to identify racial differences. As opposed to US context where a person of light brown complexion would be identified as 'black' due to the history of the 'one drop rule,' in Jamaica, this person likely to be identified as 'brown.' Of course, these categories are all socially constructed. In Jamaica, there is a high correlation of class and color – a product of its colonial history – where groups located at the top of class structure are predominantly white and brown; those located in the middle classes are predominantly brown and those at the bottom of the class structure are predominantly black. What we find, then, is generally a three-tiered racialized class system consisting of a predominantly white upper class, a brown middle class and the black poor.
2. *The Jamaica Gleaner* (the oldest extant newspaper in Jamaica) and *Jamaica Observer* (launched in 1993) are two are Jamaica's most popular newspapers that are widely circulated on the island. In this essay I analyzed 57 articles from both newspapers over a 20-year period. These articles were published either in the feature section, editorial section, letters to the editor or, if the

topic was on vendor protests, were cover stories. Articles published from 1998 onwards were accessed electronically. Articles published prior to 1998 were collected by the author from the University of the West Indies (Mona campus, Jamaica) Library. The limitation with this sample is that it only includes articles and letters to the editor that were registered with 'higgler' or 'vendor' as one of their topics. Out of the total sample of news articles, 9 were feature articles that highlighted either one special higgler or market; the remaining 48 articles discussed higglering as a 'problem.' Out of this number (N = 48), 38 articles discussed (in varying degrees) efforts to remove higglers/vendors from the Kingston metropolitan area, while the remaining 10 articles discussed these efforts in other cities on the island.

3. This is part of my larger working manuscript entitled *Dis/orderly Women: Bodies, Public Space and Representations of Higglers in Jamaica*. During my fieldwork from 2000 to 2001, forty-five higglers were interviewed. Twenty-three of these women were 'traditional' higglers or Market Women who specialize in the sale of locally grown produce. This traditional type of higglering has been a significant part of the Jamaican economy since slavery. The remaining 22 women were Informal Commercial Importers (ICIs) who are considered 'modern' higglers who specialize in the sale of foreign goods and clothing. This type of higglering is considered 'modern' because of its emergence in the Jamaican economy around the 1970's as opposed to traditional higglering. Both groups of higglers are perceived as deviant in the Jamaican public imagination although there are subtle intra-group variations in the ways in which they are represented. These variations are teased out in the larger project.

4. I borrow this term from Cecilia Green to connote the simultaneous production and reproduction of categories of difference. See Green, Cecilia. 'Gender, race and class in the social economy of the English-speaking Caribbean'. *Social and Economic Studies* 44, 2/3 (1995): 65–102.

5. One can be identified as belonging 'downtown' without actually living there. So those who live in poor communities in the uptown areas are often not associated with 'uptown living'; their behaviors and lifestyles are more likely associated with 'downtown.' Here then 'downtown' is associated with social standing.

6. On 1 April 2004 Dr Omar Davies, Finance minister of Jamaica, announced the 2004/2005 national budget. A significant portion of this budget was slated to debt servicing amounting to approximately 70 cents to every dollar. See for example, '330B Budget: most of increase to finance debt,' *Jamaica Gleaner*, 1 April 2004 (on-line edition); 'Budgeting for debt,' *Jamaica Gleaner*, 2 April 2004 (on-line edition).

7. These are October 2006 estimates. See the Statistical Institute of Jamaica (STATIN): Main Labour Force Indicators, 2004–2006. http://www.statinja. com/stats.html#2. Accessed 1 March 2007. Also, for an in depth analysis of the plight of poor Jamaicans, see Brenda Wyss and Marceline White. June 2004. 'The Effects of Trade Liberalization on Jamaica's Poor: An Analysis of Agriculture and Services,' Report by the Women's Edge Coalition and CAFRA.

8. These are government agencies responsible for the beautification and maintenance of parks and city streets; the operation of markets; public cleansing and sanitation. The KSAC is also responsible for the redevelopment of

downtown Kingston in the efforts to transform it from its current deteriorating state into a modernized financial sector.

9. In the news articles, I found the terms higglering/higgler and street vending/vendor used interchangeably. Much of this is due to attempts by higglers to rename themselves in their efforts to avoid the stigma associated this type of work (I return to this point later.). I use the term 'higgler' however to draw attention to the stigma associated with this work and its continued effects on the lived experiences of these workers. This is an issue that is not adequately addressed in the literature on higglering in Jamaica.

10. Over the last several decades efforts have been made to redevelop downtown Kingston and transform it into the financial capital of Jamaica and the wider Caribbean. These efforts have met various obstacles over the years, and although some development has occurred, downtown Kingston has a long way to go to reach its full potential.

11. 'We are suffering down here, from the time they removed us off the streets we are dying of hunger like a dog.'

12. 'If we can't sell, then nobody will sell.'

13. And yet they are not chastised in the public discourse. This exemplifies the ambivalence that Jamaicans feel towards higglers as Richard Burton described. Higglers, particularly market women, are recognized for their important roles in distributing local produce from rural to urban areas and making them available to Kingstonians at affordable prices.

14. The phrase 'chaka chaka' can be translated as chaotic.

15. To make a sale.

References

Bridge, Gary and Sophie Watson. (eds) 2000. *A Companion to the City*. Oxford: Malden Mass., Blackwell.

Burton, Richard D.E. 1997. *Afro-Creole: Power, Opposition and Play in the Caribbean*. Ithaca and London: Cornell University Press.

——. 1999. 'Bleaching, etc.,' *The Jamaica Gleaner (on-line)*, Editorial, 29 July Retrieved May 6, 2001. http://www.jamaica-gleaner.com/gleaner/19990729/index.html

Cargill, Morris. 1986. 'On Higglers,' *The Jamaica Gleaner*, editorial, August 10: 3.

Clarke, Colin and David Howard. 2006. 'Contradictory socio-economic consequences of structural adjustment in Kingston, Jamaica,' *The Geographical Journal*, Vol. 172(2): 106–29.

——. 1999. 'Colour, race and space: residential segregation in Kingston, Jamaica, in the late colonial period,' *Caribbean Geography*, 10(1): 4–18.

Clarke, Colin. 1975. *Kingston, Jamaica: Urban Development and Social Change, 1692–1962*. Berkeley: University of California Press.

Clarke, Petulia. 2001. 'Cat-and-mouse game downtown Kingston – Vendors remain determined to cash in on Xmas sales,' *Jamaica Gleaner (on-line)*, 6 December. Retrieved 16 April 2006. http://www.jamaica-gleaner.com/gleaner/20011206/news/news2.html

Douglass, Lisa. 1992. *The Power of Sentiment*. Boulder: West view Press

Douglas, Mary. 2002. *Purity and Danger: An Analysis of Concepts of Pollution and Taboo*. NY: Routledge.

Espeut, Peter. 'The Drama of Christmas Vending,' *Jamaica Gleaner (on-line)*, 10 December 2003. Retrieved 16 April 2006. http://www.jamaicagleaner.com/gleaner/20031210/cleisure/cleisure3.html

Fincher, Ruth and Jane M. Jacobs (eds). 1998. *Cities of Difference*. New York: The Guilford Press.

Green, Cecilia. 1995. 'Gender, race and class in the social economy of the English-speaking Caribbean,' *Social and Economic Studies*, 44 (2/3): 65–102.

Howson, Alexandra. 2004. *The Body in Society: An Introduction*. Cambridge: Polity Press.

Higglers blast Cargill article as 'an insult to all women,' *The Jamaica Gleaner*, 15 August 1986, p.1.

Huber, Evelyn and John D. Stephens. 1992. 'Changing Development Models in Small Communities: The Case of Jamaica from the 1950's to the 1990's,' *Studies in Comparative International Development*, Vol. 27 (3): 57–93.

Lemert, Charles. 1993. *Social Theory: The Multicultural and Classic Readings*. Boulder, CO: Westview Press.

Low, Setha M. 1996. 'Spatializing Culture: The Social Production and Social Construction of public space in Costa Rica,' *American Ethnologist*, 23, (4): 861–80.

Portes, Alejandro, Jose Itzigsohn and Carlos Dore-Cabral. 1994. *Latin American Research Review*, Vol. 29 (2): 3–35.

Ritch, Dawn. 'No Such Thing as a Happy Higgler: They are spreading like a disease into every residential area,' *The Sunday Gleaner*, editorial, 16 November 1986. p. A6

Robotham, Don. 2000. 'Blackening the Nation: The Travails of a Black Bourgeoisie in a Globalized World,' *Identities*, 7 (1): 1–37.

'Sellers squabble over space', *The Jamaica Gleaner* 18 December 1999. Retrieved 28 May 2002. http://www.go.jamaica.com/gleaner/19991218/f1.html

Shilling, Chris. 2005. *The Body in Culture, Technology and Society*. London: Sage Publications.

Sundstrom, Ronald. 2003. 'Race and place: social space in the production of human kinds,' *Philosophy and Geography*, 6, n.1: 83–95.

Ulysse, Gina. 1999. 'Uptown Ladies and Downtown Women: Female Represen-tations of Class and Color in Jamaica,' In Jean Muteba Rahier (ed.). *Representations of Blackness and the Performance of Identities*. Westport, Ct: Bergen and Garvey.

'Vending: The Bigger Picture,' *The Jamaica Gleaner (on-line)*, 28 December 1999. Retrieved 4 April 2002. http://www.go.jamaica.com/gleaner/19991228/c1.html.

'Vendors must obey the rules,' *Jamaica Gleaner*, 2 December 2003. Retrieved 16 April 2006 http://www.jamaica-gleaner.com/gleaner/20031202/cleisure/cleisure1.html

'Vendors Protest ... But KSAC vows not to back down,' *The Jamaica Observer*. Retrieved 16 April 2006. 9 December 2003. http://www.jamaicaobserver.com/news/html/20031208t230000-0500_52825_obs_vendors_protest_.asp

Watson, Sophie. April 2000. 'Bodies, Gender, Cities,' *City*, Vol. 4 (1): 101–5.

Weber, Max. 'Class Status and Party,' in Charles Lemert. 1993. *Social Theory: The Multicultural and Classic Readings*. Boulder, CO West view Press.

Weis, Tony. October 2004. 'Restructuring and Redundancy: The Impacts and Illogic of Neoliberal Agricultural Reforms in Jamaica,' *Journal of Agrarian Change*, Vol. 4 No. 4: 461–91.

Williams, John. A. 'The Making of a Slum,' *The Jamaica Gleaner: Letter (on-line)* 26 March 2000. http://www.jamaica-gleaner.com/gleaner/20000326/index.html

Wyss, Brenda and Marceline White. June 2004. 'The Effects of Trade Liberalization on Jamaica's Poor: An Analysis of Agriculture and Services,' Report by the Women's Edge Coalition and CAFRA. Accessed on-line at http://www.eldis.org/static/DOC16084.htm

7

'The Flow of Words and the Flow of Value': Illegal Behavior, Social Identity and Marketplace Experiences in Turin, Italy

Giovanni Semi
University of Milan

> So the tumult of the marketplace is largely a tumult of words.
>
> Clifford Geertz (1979: 202).

Introduction

Being insulted, teased or mocked is a normal interactional style in the open-air market of Porta Palazzo in Turin, northwestern Italy. It is a place where one can expect easily to get back home with a bag full of cheap vegetables and a head full of questions about what went on when all the vendors were laughing at you during your last haggle.

Besides the act of exchange, the general frame that shapes a market (and a marketplace) is that of openness and freedom. Historians, anthropologists, sociologists, economists have long underlined these aspects (Kapchan, 2001). I consider Freedom by a double social process: the one that allows everyone the chance to perform his or her identity during the exchange, which is an interactional freedom (de La Pradelle 2006), and the one that makes the marketplace an open space for potentially everybody, which is an institutional freedom (Berthoud 1992).

I propose to investigate the social construction of a marketplace as a public space where the framing of the exchange relationship occurs in a limited and liminal situation, namely the unlicensed selling of goods. The presence of unlicensed selling practices shows both the role of institutions in the control of economic activities and the strategies adopted by social actors to carry out their own activities in accordance with or in spite of the institutions. Conceiving a marketplace as a public space requires not only a description of the inner aspects that make it as it is but also a precise elucidation of the forces that create a market as a public space. It isn't simply a matter of neoclassical encounters in real life but of the institutional framing of the same space and the attribution of meaning to such encounters by social actors. Public institutions, private actors, individuals, urban legacies and many other forces work daily to create and maintain marketplaces as institutions with the features described above. These, to quote Goffman, act as 'principals of organisation' in the framing of events (1974: 10).

I was part too of the framing during my fieldwork, and still are through these lines, while during 2002 and 2003 I spent my days strolling around the alleys as a customer, or sitting behind a stall as I was personally involved in the selling of mint, plastic handbags and newspapers. The research was part of my PhD research based on multicultural gatherings in the inner-city neighborhood of Porta Palazzo, Turin, the aim of which is to highlight how immigration was changing the urban space of Turin in the 1990s (cfr Carter 1997).

The area

Turin, a city in northwestern Italy, boasts the biggest open-air marketplace in Europe, 'Porta Palazzo,' which has occupied a big square near the town center since 1837. It is still considered the great regional exchange site for both Piedmont (the northwestern region of Italy) and Savoie (the southeastern region of France). Porta Palazzo market (Figure 7.1) occupies piazza della Repubblica every morning from Monday to Friday and for the whole of Saturday, the day when one can observe nearly 100,000 people strolling through the alleys in search of various goods such as food, clothing, furnishings and more (cfr. Black 2006). Divided into sections according to the type of goods for sale, the market features four covered areas which host various stalls, and many other open-air areas filled with a succession of stalls by which the customers pass. Just about anything is for sale in this immense area designed to foster exchanges of all kinds – from locally-produced food to imported produce, from clothing to décor as well as 'side' exchanges and sales of labor and illegal goods such as drugs.

The exchange

Exchange is the economic and therefore social activity which precedes 'the market,' which, in turn, can be seen as a mechanism of social organization for the exchange. Market activity incorporates something beyond

Figure 7.1 Porta Palazzo's square and the open-air marketplace [courtesy of Giovanni Fontana]

the simple exchange of goods for money. In all market activities, social relations arise which are situationally dependent upon the invisible, but vital commodity of trust.

The function of trust is mainly to reduce the so-called 'transaction costs' (North, 1994), namely those costs, such as information, which weigh on the exchange. Patrons often do not know where the goods being exchanged actually come from, what their original value was, and if they will fulfil their envisaged function. And on one can be sure, especially at the beginning of a transactional relationship, if the vendor will behave as expected. All of this uncertainty increases the cost of the transaction, and trust lessens this 'weighting.' Trust, however, varies in importance depending on whether we are engaged in a transaction in the formal, informal or illegal market. The formal market represents an institutional guarantee for both buyer and seller that the exchange will take place in conditions that both deem proper – namely the presence of the stalls, vendors behind them and their behaviors, price tags and the general 'suspension of doubt' over the fact that this might not be the kind of market we were expecting. As Linda Seligmann points out that 'stall control . . . is one of the most controversial and politicized aspects of marketing' (2000: 29). In a sense this is the domain of the political economy of the legal marketplace. Throughout the square on a daily basis there are opportunities for exchange and it is necessary to acknowledge the informal and illegal exchanges in order to offer a comprehensive perspective of the setting. While the formal market is what occupies the square during the day from Monday to Saturday and operates according to City Council regulations (i.e. possession of a licence, payment of taxes, obligations to the customer, observance of rules of health and hygiene and so forth), the informal market represents everything that lies between the formal sector and the illegal sector (Portes, 1995: 428).

Two different reasons must be accounted for the inclusion of the informal marketplace in the overall description of this paper: one ideographical and the other theoretical. Ideographically speaking, one cannot avoid accounting for informal economic and social relations in a formal marketplace such as Porta Palazzo's one. In the shared historical memory and in the daily practices of the turinees, this space is one in which the institutional level always deals with the non conventional, where the tactics of urban survival (de Certeau 1988) have their own legitimacy. Porta Palazzo is the prototypical space of informality of Turin. Nonetheless the two, formal and informal, are deeply interwined as we will see in the next pages but they still remain different and requires an analytic distinction. This distinction is a theoretical one: beside of being nominalistic, to introduce the dimension of informality is to recognize a distinct sphere of daily activities, the so-called 'unregulated' one. As Alejandro Portes rightly pointed out regarding migrants activities, 'for some immigrants, the informal economy is a means of survival in a strange social environment; for others, it is a vehicle for rapid economic ascent. For still others, it is a way of reconciling economic needs with culturally defined obligations' (1995: 30). The Porta Palazzo's marketplace is the migrant's marketplace *par excellence*, as the next pages will show.

Dealing with uncertainty: cooperation and conflict

The formal market possesses a series of elements that guarantee its validity and legitimacy, such as stalls, labels and price tags, the type of interaction that goes on and the approach of the vendors. When walking around the market, one feels confident and reassured that behind the marketplace there is a formal kind of organization, like the general markets where goods are bought wholesale. In informal markets, the stall is a wooden crate that anyone could get hold of and fill with goods they want to sell. There are no prices shown and it is therefore obligatory to interact with the vendor to find out what is for sale and how much it costs. Moreover, if the transaction does not proceed to the satisfaction of both parties, there is no 'third party' entity to act as guarantee. All in all, while the formal market offers a high level of predictability and certainty, the opposite can be said of the informal kind. Informal markets, however, offer several things which are not found in their more formal counterparts: the prices are usually considerably lower, the goods offered are hard to find elsewhere, and perhaps the emotional investment and enjoyment to be had from conversing with the vendor. For present purposes, the most relevant reason is the second: the young foreigners, mostly Moroccans, working in this sector, are not in competition with the formal market because they sell goods which are not on sale elsewhere in the square.

The best day for business is Saturday, as is the case for all markets, except maybe for illegal drugs, which is characterized by greater continuity and is not influenced to any great extent by the pattern of the working week. Saturday is the day when the highest numbers of buyers and sellers are present, and thus when the best business is done. From 7 am, when the older customers shop, to 7 pm, when the late-comers, workers and families show up, the square is a hive of activity.

Sa'id and the other mint sellers arrive around 10 am. They spend evenings concluding the purchase of mint, coriander and wormwood which arrives directly from Morocco on Wednesday afternoons. Issam and his peers wait until the bazaars in the surrounding areas open in the morning to buy their plastic bags and telephone cards to sell in the square (Semi 2006). Moustapha, a good friend of Issam's, spends the morning preparing boiled eggs, milky coffee and *harira*[1] to sell in the square.

The earliest arrivals bag the best spots, and Sa'id always manages to station himself as near as possible to the entrance of the fruit and vegetable market to profit from the flow of people passing through on their way to the tram stop, or towards the Tettoia dell'Orologio building to continue with their purchases. The others arrive gradually, forming a line alongside the vans parked by the market. The stocks of mint and piles of plastic shopping bags are hidden inside the Iveco, Ford or Renault trucks, vans and minivans, with the tacit agreement of the regular traders. What is actually displayed is a quantity which can be sold there and then, what they can afford to do away with or what they can allow to be seized by the police or traffic wardens during frequent raids. Their stalls are made

Figure 7.2   Mint-sellers [photo by Giovanni Semi]

of two wooden crates, one set upright and the other balanced on top per-pendicular to the bottom one, containing bunches of mint (Figure 7.2). If the police pass through, the stall/crates can easily be lifted away, so the stall-holders can hide behind the vans until the police have gone and they can come out and start selling again.

The police

The police play a vital role both in the daily life of the market and in the analytical distinction between informal and illegal. When I first began my research work, between July and October 2002, it was pretty much business as usual for this informal market: it was tolerated and the police passed through for the sake of appearances and to convey to the public that the market was a safe place, that it was monitored. I was there as a plastic handbag seller, at the stall held by my friend Issam who found funny enough to let me work for him. 'You're a Moroccan now,' he said laughing, as he stared at me offering bags for the strollers. I was also a relevant friend, since I was the only one with a white face and a 'white' paper of citizenship within the informal marketplace. The strategic use of my condition was twofold, I could stay as the quarrels between police and vendors started and be a useful translator in the intercultural communication that occurs during economic exchanges and other events.

For instance, there were intense hissed communications between the police officers and traffic wardens and the vendors, with phrases like, 'Come on, get a move on, you know you can't stay here,' 'Come on, what did we say? At least don't do it here in front of us' and so forth. The informal stall-holders went along with this game, which however was starting to get risky: some called the traffic warden or police officer by name, some mimed starting a scuffle or an argument. Sometimes the police even instigated the joke. For a while I was able to sell the local newspaper *La Stampa* for Peppe, originally from Casablanca. My 'work colleagues' were a couple of Italian receivers of stolen goods, one from Sicily and one from the Calabria region, and a small number of telephone card sellers. On one such occasion, a mixed patrol of policemen and traffic wardens came out of the building behind us. One of the traffic wardens came out first, taking us all by surprise and exclaimed:

Warden: BOO!!!
We all jumped and remained momentarily startled, before he added:
Warden: I had you going there!
And everyone burst out laughing while the patrol headed over towards the telephone card sellers, who were already off. In any case humor and jokes are the order of the day. At one point, while father and son (the son of the Sicilian sometimes worked with his father) went off to look at a mobile phone with a supplier, the Calabrian caught my eye, winked and made the classic hand gesture indicating dodgy goods! (fieldnote 24 September 2002)

The police have detailed knowledge of the layout of the 'irregular' activities in the square, and depending on the period, orders from above or the need to restore balance or assert personal status, the officers modify the public implementation of their powers.

As for the 'handling' of illegal vendors, after this initial phase of negotiated conflict, in parallel with the closure of the deadlines to regularize immigrants in the autumn of 2002, and a number of media campaigns against the black market, there was a harsher, more widespread form of conflict.

> ... I went to see Sa'id and Issam ..., but I had only just got there when I saw two policemen and two traffic wardens intimidating Sa'id as he was working. They were explaining that things had changed and that the next time they would throw away his things, and the time after that they would seize his stocks. Sa'id, red-faced with fear, was laughing nervously and trying to bargain with the 'Sicilian', the nickname for the darker-complexioned policeman who was threatening him (Issam later said of this policeman, 'He's a bastard'). He was touching the policeman's arm, smiling and trying to negotiate in his halting Italian, to play it down, but the 'Sicilian' wasn't playing ball. In the meantime the other three had formed a semi-circle around them to keep out prying eyes. The old women who passed by hissed things like, 'It's about time', and, 'Let's hope they leave now'. And Issam disappeared round the corner with his plastic shopping bags. While I was speaking to him, the 'Sicilian' approached us too, and shouted, 'We're warning you. Now we'll be throwing it all away, the system is changing!' (fieldnote 12 September 2002)

Following on from this encounter, the form of control and relations arising followed a cyclical pattern: at times stricter, and often violent, with some lenient interludes. It is easy to point to the purely violent aspect of social control, but its implementation is so fragmentary and changeable that its main characteristic is uncertainty: there is no way of predicting how traffic wardens, police and customs officers will behave, and this only has the effect of increasing the uncertain nature already present in the exchange process of informal trade.

Exchange, joking and conflict in the market

We have looked at one of the most important aspects in the context of informal trading, namely relations with the forces of law and order. So keeping a careful eye on what is going on around him, the vendor thus waits for his customer to approach. We have seen that in this exchange it is necessary to facilitate interaction and the transaction on the one hand by offering reassurances about the product and its reliability, and on the other convincing the customer that there is nothing to fear from dealing with a foreign 'black market' vendor.

Lively banter goes on throughout the market and the 'spiel' of the sellers is an essential part of the exchange – part of the 'colorful' character of this world. In the fruit and vegetable market, which has its own rules compared to those of other markets, double entendres, puns and conflicts masked by words are a widespread, accepted way of establishing social relations[2] (Sarnelli 2003). In order to be able to buy their zucchini for less, the middle-class ladies of Turin know that they may be gently mocked: 'Zucchini for the ladies! Ladies get your zucchini here!'. This phrase, addressed to a genteel, elderly Turin lady, is just one example of the teasing sexual innuendo bandied around at the market, like, 'Come and get it, you know you want it . . . tomato!'. Then there is the old fruit seller shouting, 'One bag for a Euro, two bags for two Euros,' poking fun at her colleagues who mark down their prices to encourage clients to buy larger quantities.

Considering that teasing is little more than a ritualized form of conflict (see Bateson 1972), at times the masked conflict and joking can lead to genuine disputes, which from time to time escalate into offensive insults or even physical fights. It is a fine line:

> In front of one stall there is a growing argument between a vendor, his wife and a client. He has a strong southern-Italy accent, his wife a marked northern one, while the customer has a firm but soft voice with a northern accent too. The conflict has arisen because of something the customer has done: without thinking she has propped her bags of shopping on the stall where she made her last purchase, risking squashing the vegetables beneath. The stall-holder has started to complain and instead of accepting the criticism the woman has answered back, giving rise to increasingly heated tones.
> Vendor – Ok ok [taking a theatrical bow] please excuse me, you are absolutely right!
> Customer – [in a low voice] There was no need for that tone of voice . . .
> Vendor – [who moves away and then comes back, entering and leaving the space of the interaction] No, because you're ruining all my stock!
> Wife of vendor – [raising her voice and taking on a marked Piedmontese accent, almost teasingly] Yeah, because you with your two little

zucchini are ruining loads of mine!
Customer – [red in the face, mutters something incomprehensible about the tone of voice they are using]
Vendor – [who once more goes away and comes back again] You'd better clear off, before I tell you to fuck off!
All around, the general hubbub that had preceded the conflict suddenly falls silent, and the customer moves away quickly, enabling the vendor to have the final say without any comeback.
Vendor – Well fuck her, though who'd want to!
At this point the vendor meets my gaze to elicit the sympathy of his other customers. I pretend to put my bags down on his stall and, there is general relieved laughter all round. (field note: 3.7.02)

The use of linguistic and paralinguistic codes, physical presence and the use of the body lent specific form to this conflict. The mockery of the first pretend bow was then followed by the vendor's unsettling strategy of leaving and returning to the space of the conflict. Each time he returned to the scene, he appeared to do so with renewed vigor, as if by leaving he had gathered strength and fresh motivation. At the same time the accusers doubled up, as did arguments used against the customer, who was not only accused of ruining the goods but also of being of little interest in terms of business, almost a charity case ('you with your two little zucchini are ruining loads of mine!'). The conclusion of the interaction was very violent, completely overturning the conventions of the relationship. The client, who was initially protesting about the tone of voice used against her, was responded to with symbolic violence of a sexual nature, which forced her to flee.

Violence, which for some is part of the 'colorful' character of the market, is an integral part of the regular market and in any case represents a form of conflict management rather than a random, episodic, 'blind' attack. A few meters further on, in the mint sellers' domain, most of these practices for handling conflict cease to apply. Most of the joking goes on between vendors and all do their utmost not to harass the customers, to be courteous. Sometimes the jokiness comes to the fore, such as when this Senegalese telephone card seller, Omar was involved in this almost theatrical sketch with a Moroccan, Sa'id, one of the mint sellers:

Sa'id: Go on Omar, camarade, tell them what our mint is like
Omar: Mint? You sell mint? Oh, that ...
Sa'id: Yes ... this ...
Omar: Mint from Khouribga! Yes, ladies and gentlemen (shouting),

here we have mint from Khouribga, full of phosphates! (fieldnote 15
November 2002)

The humor lies in the fact that Omar remembers that the Khouribga
area produces sulphur and not mint, but Sa'id comes from there, and as
for the customer, it is unlikely that he or she knows what is produced
in that region, so there is a margin of play between the sellers in the
organization of a gathering such as the market exchange. A gathering,
following Goffman, that needs a real 'teamwork' to produce a representation (Goffman 1959, 1969), and these sellers apparently had something
of a practiced relation in this manner.

In most cases, however, the important thing is to set the customer's
mind at rest and compensate for the lack of reciprocal trust with effective
intercultural communications. This regards above all sales to people not
from the same area as the vendor. Sa'id calls, '*Mint, na'na, erba buena,
ci-ci,*' to the flow of South Americans, Chinese, Italians and Moroccans,
addresses the Senegalese '*camarade*' and the infrequent distinguished-
looking Italian customers crossing the area as '*Doctor.*' Spoken language,
the ability to lend a genuine text to the goods being exchanged, is vital,
even, as Geertz sustained, 'the flow of words and the flow of values are
not two separate things, but two aspects of the same thing' (1979: 199).

Issam smiles and winks, Youssef gesticulates and thanks his customers
over and over: the sellers always try to pick out the best bunch of mint
and never complain if they are given a 'big' banknote, and have to give
back a lot of change (with the risk of being paid with a forged note, as I
observed on a couple of occasions). This politeness clashes, at time very
evidently, both with the stereotypical image of the young, insolent Turin
Moroccan, and with the many misunderstandings that may arise. In
many cases there is no mutual comprehension, and a few words may be
enough to block the interaction, in what Robin Wagner-Pacifici dubbed
a *standoff*, 'a frozen moment, where the mechanisms and proceses of
social interaction have ceased to function in their usual predictable and
elastic way' (2000: 5).

Joking, conflict and work at the market intermingle in different, ever-
changing forms and ways. Take Youssef-Peppe's stall. The naturalization
of the name 'Youssef', translated into Italian as 'Giuseppe,' and shortened
to 'Peppe,' illustrates one way in which diversity is incorporated, but
alone this does not do justice to the multicultural nature of the situation
that Youssef, Francesco and their customers operate in. The element that
transforms this scene of interaction into something which then leads to
other social relations is the participants' willingness to make humorous

use of their differences and transform them into a terrain of encounter and contrast through joking, simulated conflict, banter. Francesco does not hide the fact that he has always been a 'small-time crook', and is now a receiver of stolen goods. He dispenses good advice to the drug addicts who come to sell him car radios, video cassettes, DVDs or other goods obtained from shoplifting or burglary:

> The drug addicts are addressed by name and also given advice. One in particular is told by Francesco to 'eat something now and then, with all that shit you take your body needs all the help it can get!'. The response is a whispered, 'Yes'. (fieldnote 24.9.2002)

He also jokes with the Nigerian *mamans* (madams) who come to buy condoms, pretending to think they are for personal use and not for their charges: 'But how many are you using? You're old, watch out!'. He is always acting out little numbers with the people he meets, and these provide an opportunity for further exchanges and social relations.

Youssef-Peppe sells his newspapers just two meters away. He has a loyal clientele of old ladies who buy *La Stampa* from him: 'Even though I could buy it round the corner from my house, I prefer to get it from him because he's so polite,' one of them explained. He speaks in a strong Piedmontese accent, repeats the word 'signora' ad infinitum and goes overboard with old-fashioned gallantries and courtesy. He is a practising, devout Muslim and always uses this fact to build bridges with his customers. At the end of the day, as he always points out, Allah is the same for Muslims and Christians, just as both observe many moral precepts. So what do a devout Muslim and an ageing Italian crook have in common? The area of play:

> Youssef – Francesco, tell Giovanni about your wife!
> Francesco – No, I couldn't . . . what would he think of me Peppe? He's a good boy . . .
> Y – Go on signor Francesco, tell him . . . (and he laughs and watches me)
> So Francesco starts telling me about his sex life with his wife, as an old person, and the time he fell asleep while having sex and was woken by his wife punching him . . .
> F – That's the way it is. Things like that never used to happen to me . . .
> Y – That's enough signor Francesco, signor Giovanni is not interested in that . . . .
> F – And why not? He wants to know everything. . . .

Y – What do you want to tell him? That you've been a crook all your life?

F – That's enough Peppe! What's the problem with that?

Y – What about God? He knows what you're up to

F – God? Of course he knows! And the Virgin Mary knows too, that I'm a wheeler-dealer, but they still love me... they know I'm a good worker!

Y – Ok, let's make up, give me a kiss.

F – What? Kiss you? I'm not some kind of poof like you Muslims! Crooked, but not bent!

Y – Signor Francesco! What will signor Giovanni be thinking!

F – He knows I'm joking. But you're not getting a kiss. (fieldnote 23 July 2002)

The banter, role reversals and making a feature out of their diversity are part of the rules of the game, as the participants constantly make a play of falling out and making up. Here play is clearly a meta-communication, as described by Bateson (1972). Physically and verbally, Youssef and Francesco spend their mornings mocking themselves, their role and their presence in the square showing that the focus of their play is not in it's content. This interplay of relations makes the description of characters who come across as 'loveable rogues' more complex: they are on the wrong side of the law, but possess an aura of mystery and humor that is often part of the representation of Porta Palazzo's marketplace. The link between marketplaces and dramaturgy is embedded in vendors' behavior, in their public performance of jokes. But the violence that these characters, like Francesco and his Sicilian 'colleague' may adopt is difficult to shrug off simply with a joke. The shifting from a Batesonian play frame into a set of precise acts is then part of the representation.

For instance, when one of them is engaged in a deal to purchase gold or silver that the immigrants go to sell in exchange for cash, the exchange is not always humorous. Sometimes the neediness of the foreign seller who is giving away family heirlooms to survive is not always used ironically by the buyers. Francesco himself is capable of humiliating a would-be seller in order to get a better price, of saying that there is no market for the goods in question, or forcing the issue by pretending to break off negotiations: '20 Euros, take it or leave it!'. The faces of those who have come to this market, women, often Moroccan, who hope that a smile will bring them even just 5 Euros more, and the firm, unyielding expression of Francesco are not sights you easily forget. Then of course Francesco himself is capable of mocking the colleague who has gone off to one side with a drug addict to negotiate over the purchase of a car radio, and turn to me, wink and perform the hand gesture used to indicate a dodgy deal, as if to distance himself from that type of activity. Joking and humor are not just a light-hearted way of looking at life and coping with the unpredictability of things; they are also a strategy, one of the relational approaches offered by the context and the reciprocal ability to use it and give it a meaning. Alongside these behaviors, which offer valuable insight into certain social relations, there are also other equally meaningful practices.

From informal to illegal: temporal dimensions of market behavior

Throughout most of the time I spent doing field work, a transition occurred when from around 4 am and sometimes up to midnight during the long summer days, the regular market makes the changes from working day to the period dedicated to taking down the stalls, cleaning the square and putting everything away. Once their work is over the regular vendors load their remaining stock and their scales into their vans and depart to unload them in the areas of the city they came from at the first light of day. Their 'irregular' colleagues also leave, some to neighborhood garrets, and some to the many bars in the ghetto district for a bite to eat before returning to the square in the early afternoon. They usually bring the same goods they have been selling in the morning, and take up position in a particular area of the square, under the shelter which is the morning site for the vendors of household goods from steel coffeemakers to plastic trash cans. Some of them always work in the same spot: some of the telephone card sellers who also spend the long mornings discreetly stationed at one end or the other of the shelter selling their 'Lion' or 'Tim' cards. Others, like the mint sellers, who spend the morning on the edge of the fruit and vegetable market, move along a few meters.

The passing trade for this small afternoon market comprises public transport users heading to and from the stop beside the shelter, or those passing through by car, or by those who come on purpose to buy bread or mint. There is hardly any casual trade, customers drawn into the atmosphere of the market who decide to indulge in an unexpected interaction and buy a product they had probably not thought of buying before. Most of these potential morning customers are Italian, and in their absence the informal market in the afternoon suffers a down turn and changes radically. Not only do the Italians not come; if they do, they belong to one of two breeds: drug users or plain clothes policemen who thus help drag the informal market down into a spiral of illegality, with heavy social consequences.

We have seen that the goods for sale do not change. This statement is true with one important exception, namely the arrival of small-scale marijuana dealers who every so often come to use this market, to blend in or more simply to get new clients. The illegal narcotics market, from Class A drugs like heroin and cocaine, to lighter drugs is just a few meters away. The 'weed' market is concentrated in a street adjacent to the market and is subject to a particular form of police control: it is periodically suppressed then periodically resumed. The effect of this police action is something like landing a punch in a bowl of water: dispersion towards the outlying areas and transfer of the old trade and social relations to new areas. Then slowly the water comes back and everything goes back to how it was before. When there were campaigns against small-scale drug dealing, the effect was to shift trade into outlying areas. One of these was the informal market area, which thus underwent a change in rules to accommodate this influx of small-scale dealers. This 'contamination' is only possible in the afternoon, when the narcotics market comes to life and takes over more of the square, determining the first major change in the relational framework in question.

A second important factor regards the clientele. We have already talked about the absence of Italians, so who is left? Foreigners, obviously, but to be more precise, not all foreigners. Not only do the bold Italian mint buyers disappear, but also the Romanians, Albanians, Chinese and South Americans – basically all those who have no reason to come to piazza della Repubblica in the afternoon, thus depriving the young informal vendors their usual clientele. In the afternoon the marketplace is frequented by Moroccans, plus some rare passing trade and a few marginal characters such as the old lady mentioned at the beginning of this paragraph. The informal market rapidly boils down to one ethnicity and the range of intercultural exchanges is limited to that with drug addicts and small-time users of recreational drugs.

To sum up, there are three changes which alter the status of the informal market due to time of day: Italians and foreigners are entirely replaced by Moroccan clients, and fragments of the adjacent illegal drugs market are added to the mix, bringing its own clients and relational approach. Even the policemen, as I have attempted to describe, who often attempt a form of communication in the morning, have a change of attitude (despite being the self-same policemen or traffic wardens who were present a few hours previously), and take on the role of force of law and order, repressing illegal conduct. In short, the market goes from informal to illegal, and the former is incorporated into the latter.

How behavior changes

Mohammad 'Mineur' is a slight man. He looks like a boy and this is why his friends jokingly call him 'minor'. Also from Khouribga, with a few cousins here in Piedmont, he is an illegal immigrant working on the margins of Porta Palazzo. He sells pre-paid telephone cards, one of the most widespread activities among the area's illegal immigrants waiting to regularize their status. One August evening, 'mineur' told me about how he had managed to pull off a fast one: the police had come across him selling a piece of 'hash' to an Italian client. When the client saw the police car he disappeared, but he had already paid for the goods, so little Mohammad managed to keep the money and the goods, making a bit of a profit. He spoke a little English and we began a strange conversation in Italian, Arabic and English. We managed to engage in this conversation because things are much more drawn out than in the morning. There are few customers, and they almost all show up between 6 and 9 pm, when the immigrants who work in the various building sites and factories around the city return to Porta Palazzo. The market represents a kind of service economy for these people: they can get hold of the bare essentials needed to eat and drink something and contact their families abroad. In the long intervals between customers, joking, playing around and avoiding the police are the only activities I witnessed, but these go on in a completely different way compared to the morning. The police, as we have seen, have an entirely different attitude.

Wednesday 9 pm, I went down to the square to see what was going on in the informal market. The 'Sicilian' and the other policemen were surveying the shelter, and there were only a few Moroccans around. The one on crutches was there so I stopped to speak to him. Basically, in line with what they had said, the police had effectively enforced a clamp-down. For the last week they had not been permitting black market sales during the day, or the presence of the market during the evening. But looking around I could see that everyone was there. Sa'id, for example, was watching to see when the police were going to leave, as were Issam and the others. When Sa'id saw me he made a move towards me but the 'Sicilian' intervened: 'Go away, do you hear me? Get lost!'. And he made him leave, guilty of frequenting an area that is off-limits to illegal immigrants. So Sa'id headed towards the bus and tried to get on, but the 'Sicilian' followed him and pulled him by the sleeve and the arm and said, 'Not by bus, you're not allowed -, on your on two feet, get it?'. (fieldnote 9 October 2002)

These minor abuses of power, like stopping people from entering a certain area or taking public transport, are widespread whenever the 'wind changes' in the neighborhood. One afternoon for instance, when leaving a bar in the little square behind the market, a young Moroccan known to the police for previous episodes of drug dealing, was stopped by customs officers from the Guardia di Finanza, which often works with the Polizia di Stato, Vigili Urbani and Carabinieri when the square gets militarized. This young man was stopped right in the middle of the square, surrounded by law enforcement personnel and subjected to a very public humiliation. In order to search for illicit substances they made him strip, starting from his tee-shirt. Once in his underwear they made him remove his socks, in front off all the local residents and passers-by. Barefoot on the concrete, when they ascertained that he was not in possession of anything illegal, he was then left alone to get dressed once more, while the officers went on their way and the audience that had formed dispersed.

When people are humiliated social relations in general suffer (cf. Garfinkel 1956). When the context turns reactionary, violence imbues most social relations and the young vendors are as much as part of this escalation as the policemen. The drug addicts are one of the favorite targets. This wide, varied social group also includes many older people, who occupy the square almost permanently. The luckier ones sleep in apartments or garrets in the area, while others sleep rough. This group spends the day spasmodically looking for cash to convert into a fix of heroin consumed in some parts of the neighborhood. The frenetic activity of this world has its own routines and increases constantly into the late evening, the most difficult time, when the last fix of the day is bought before the dealers call it a day. This is why the addicts are all in a rush in the evening, concerned both with getting their hands on some money, and converting goods into cash. The evening market is about this kind of conversion:

> I returned to the square around 10 pm, and there were even fewer people. There were about 15 people there and I knew four of them, plus Sa'id, but my presence was starting to be noticed and talked about. However they were also starting to ignore me. Nearby some pieces of 'hash' were changing hands, and soon after the drug addicts began to arrive.

> They were all over the square, some emaciated, and some older ones who still had a bit of weight on them and were carrying huge

backpacks that looked like they contained the sum total of their possessions. One of them, a thin Italian whose age was impossible to guess, arrived by bike, a brand new mountain bike. He wanted 40 Euros for it and the tormented bargaining got under way. The Moroccans surrounded him, touched the bike, and insinuated that it was nothing special, but were not really interested. The drug addict tried to act like a vendor at first, then went slowly crazy. He was not physically and mentally able to keep pace with the interaction, and began to get mad: 'But you don't even know how much it's worth! Fuck! I'll give it away if that's what you want!'. He had fallen into the trap they had set for him. In turn they made ridiculous offers (it was worth 40 Euros, compared to the 200 it would make in a normal market, and they were offering 20 or 10) and then left. He gave in, but he knew that he couldn't, the dealers were about to leave and he needed that money. He went off, came back two seconds later and tried again with others.

The same scene was played out once more, and at least five more times. He was exhausted, and went to Moustapha to beg for a free sandwich, which he devoured in two seconds flat, while another drug addict, who had wanted to 'have a word with me', probably to sell me something, as I was crossing the square earlier, sidled up to watch the scene. Then a guy I recognized came along. He was young, Moroccan, with a strong Piedmontese accent. He watched the scene, mocked the drug addict then saw me and came over, smirking, 'Did you see that fucking drug addict! We were messing him around – he wants 40 for that bike... too much. I offered him 20 but no deal. What the fuck? He's just a fucking drug addict!'. (fieldnote 16 October 2002)

The conditions of social construction in this market, the forced coexistence with people pursuing criminal careers, the lengthier times involved and the overlapping social approaches give rise to a new, different setup. The market gets illegal on all levels: goods, exchanges and social relations. The goods, even when they are not the product of an illegal production process like narcotics, are sold as if they were. The telephone cards seem more illegal than those sold in the morning. The sellers hide them in their pockets more carefully and check out their potential customers more suspiciously. The exchanges which arise are more tense, and all the pleasantries which framed it as an occasion for multicultural relations in the morning are eliminated by the surrounding tensions. People buy and sell, and they do it fast.

As the general situation deteriorates, several 'degradation ceremonies' (Garfinkel 1956) starts and a precise cooperative team-work appears to set precise traps to the victims of this shift in the marketplace frame: The drug-addicts. These customers, dominated throughout their daily life by the weight of their addiction, become also dominated by the reversal of roles made possible by the changing of the general interaction frame. The informal vendors who become illegal vendors by subjugating their practices to the new frame of the marketplace take their revenge on other social actors, thereby becoming tactically and liminally dominants. This shifting is made possible by different reasons: the formal marketplace isn't there anymore, the great density of interactions that occurs throughout the morning leaves for little focalized interactions, the square becomes a great void ot interactions with a little, single, marketplace of youngmen. All around the environment participate to this scene, a great void square, the nightscape, the silence interrupted by cars passing or by police sirens: the marketplace becomes then radically different.

Conclusions

The overlap between the dimensions which constitute the structure of the exchange – the formal, informal and illegal markets – and the relational approaches which have been described starting from the ethnographic material available, have shown the various rapports between the institutional framework and interaction in public areas. At times it has even approached the idea of a public space, as conjectured by Hannah Arendt, namely a place one enters leaving behind one's most striking differences (1958). In the formal market the dominant frame, created and ruled by public institutions as the municipality, the police, and the legal vendors, enables the various sellers and customers to exploit the traditional potential of a system of interactions such as that offered by a market, comprised of insults and banter, but also customer loyalty and exchanges which generally have positive outcomes.

On the other hand the uncertainties of the informal sale where police, customers and other formal and informal vendors may cooperate or come into conflict gives rise to a set of practices aimed at offering reassurance, taming the encounter and making for a peaceful exchange process. There are more intercultural communications and identity is used in a different way compared to the previous case, that of the formal market.

But the informal market exists because there is a formal market to lean on, to feed off, to offer services to, and to take shelter in its shadow. In the afternoon, evening and night, when 'there's no market' aside from the illegal market, narcotics in particular, the activities which could legitimately be considered informal in the morning become illegal. This is because of how they are viewed by the institutions, and also because the differentiated, multi-faceted exchanges of the morning tend to get more uniform and focus on a single ethnic minority in the evening. 'The market' is thus framed in different, relational ways, often in contradistinction to 'non-' or 'sub-' markets and practices.

The existence of a market that draws together various different exchange contexts along the lines I have attempted to sketch out is in turn linked to the current urban transitions and the new lines of tension being felt on a global level. There are many markets like this in Berlin, Paris, London, Milan or Marseilles. According to Vincenzo Ruggiero and Nigel South, contemporary cities can be viewed as markets, and the 'continuum of regular and irregular markets in cities represents a late-modern bazaar' (1997: 55). According to the two authors the concept of bazaar implies 'the coexistence of legality and illegality and constantly shifting boundaries between the two' (ibid. 63). In the case of Porta Palazzo the boundaries shift according to the operating times of the regular market, even when there are clamp-downs and new boundaries form. Within the formal market you can hide, and seek protection, but when this is absent the situation changes, with significant consequences. The changing of a frame is made possible by a mutual, interactive, process of status shifting, the one that ethnicizes and yet degradates identities as the marketplace of Porta Palazzo, with it's density of plays, representations and even conflicts, leaves the field.

Notes

1. A Moroccan soup traditionally consumed during Ramadan.
2. Research into conflict during the exchange process, which often materializes in the form of insults, as Linda J. Seligmann suggests, shows that these are, 'integrated into the fabric of daily life,' and that they have 'significance in the dynamics of the construction and perpetuation of particular kinds of interethnic relations' (1993: 207).

References

Arendt, H. (1958) *The Human Condition*. Chicago: University of Chicago Press.
Bateson, G. (1972) *Steps to an Ecology of Mind*, Chandler Publishing Company.
Berthoud, A. (1992) 'Marché rencontre et marché mécanique,' *Cahiers d'Economie Politique*, vol. nos. 20–21: pp. 167–86.
Black, R. (2006) *Going to Market: Places of Sociability in Lyon and Turin*, unpublished PhD dissertation, Università degli Studi di Torino, Italy.

Calabi, D. (1993) *Il mercato e la città: piazze, strade, architetture d'Europa in età moderna.* Venezia: Marsilio.

Carter, D. M. (1997) *States of Grace. Senegalese in Italy and the New European Immigration,* Minneapolis, University of Minnesota Press.

de Certeau, M. (1988) *The Practice of Everyday Life,* Berkeley, University of California Press.

de La Pradelle, M. (2006) *Market Day in Provence,* Chicago, University of Chicago Press.

Garfinkel, H. (1956) 'Conditions of Successful Degradation Ceremonies,' *American Journal of Sociology,* vol. no. 61: pp. 420–4.

Geertz, C. (1979) 'Suq: the bazaar economy in Sefrou,' in Geertz Clifford and Geertz Hildred and Rosen Lawrence (eds), *Meaning and Order in Moroccan Society.* Cambridge: Cambridge University Press.

Goffman, E. (1959) *The Presentation of Self in Everyday Life,* New York, Anchor.

Goffman, E. (1969) *Strategic Interaction,* Philadelphia, University of Pennsylvania Press.

Goffman, E. (1974) *Frame Analysis. An Essay on the Organization of Experience,* New York, Harper and Row.

Kapchan, D. (2001) 'Gender on the Market in Moroccan Women's Verbal Art: Performative Sphere of Feminine Authority,' in Seligmann Linda J. (ed.), *Women Traders in Cross-Cultural Perspective: Mediating Identities, Marketing Wares.* Stanford: Stanford University Press.

North, D. (1994) *Institutions, Institutional Change and Economic Performance.* Cambridge: Cambridge University Press.

Portes, A. (1995) 'The Informal Economy and Its Paradoxes,' in Smelser Neil and Swedberg Richard (eds), *The Handbook of Economic Sociology.* Princeton: Princeton University Press and Russell Sage Foundation.

Ruggiero, V. and South, N. (1997) 'The Late–Modern City as a Bazaar: Drug Markets, Illegal Enterprise and the "Barricades",' *The British Journal of Sociology,* vol. no. 48 (issue no. 1): pp. 54–70.

Seligmann, L. J. (1993), 'Between Worlds of Exchange: Ethnicity among Peruvian Market Women,' *Cultural Anthropology,* vol. no. 8 (issue no. 2): pp. 187–213.

Seligmann, L. J. (2000), 'Market Places, Social Spaces in Cuzco, Peru,' *Urban Anthropology,* vol. no. 29 (issue no. 1): pp. 1–68.

Sarnelli, E. (2003) 'Relazioni scherzose. Senegalesi e autoctoni in un mercato di Napoli,' in Gallini Clara (ed.), *Patrie Elettive: I segni dell'appartenenza.* Torino: Bollati Boringhieri.

Semi, G. (2006) 'Il ritorno dell'economia di bazar. Attività commerciali marocchine a Porta Palazzo, Torino' in Decimo Francesca e Sciortino Giuseppe (eds), *Stranieri in Italia: Reti Migranti.* Bologna: Il Mulino.

Wagner-Pacifici, R. E. (2000) *Theorizing the Standoff: Contingency in Action.* Cambridge: Cambridge University Press.

Part IV
Global Patrons, Globalizing Markets

8
Beyond Borders: The Politics and Place of the Global Shop[1]

Kim Humphery
RMIT University

Introduction

Global retail spaces, from the Body Shop and Benetton, to Gap and Ikea, are a common feature now of urban streetscapes and shopping precincts throughout the economically developed and developing world. Together, this group of retail outlets constitute a kind of global 'high street'. Indeed, the global shop, as I will call it, can be understood as a very particular retail space – not one which is spatially or even managerially innovative compared to other retail environments, but which is certainly unique in being defined through its geographical spread, the globally branded merchandize within it, and its involvement in the making of a sense of global place. These environments of consumption and social relations have an everyday prominence in many people's lives, and they are moreover the subject of sometimes intense public debate and political opposition. In this chapter, it is this second element of opposition with which I will be concerned, most especially in relation to exploring the presence of and critical public response to the global shop in Australia.

Let us begin, however, with the recent world-wide consolidation of the global shop itself. By the end of 2005, the top 250 global retailers – involved in everything from supermarkets and fast food outlets to discount and specialty stores – collectively operated in 135 countries and had recorded annual retail sales of US$2.6 *trillion* (million million). Not surprisingly, the North American 'discount warehouse' company Wal-Mart, operating in eleven countries, topped the list of 250 by overall retail sales, while the French company Carrefour, operating supermarkets in over 30 countries, came in second. The icon of globalization, McDonald's, came in at number 49 on the basis of sales figures, and the ubiquitous Ikea, operating in over 34 countries, ranked 50th in terms of sales (Deloitte, 2005). If these figures are something to go on, then the era of the global shop has most certainly arrived.

In face of this arrival, and in no uncertain terms, academic writers and social commentators have generally sounded alarm at the emergence of, to use Benjamin Barber's phrase, a 'McWorld' in which culture becomes homogenized and consumption replaces citizenship (Barber, 2001). On the most obvious level the global shop stands as the talisman *par excellence* of a rampantly neo-liberal globalization, lending itself very easily to readings of contemporary consumption as a terrain of economic colonization and cultural homogenization. This is and remains a powerful public intellectual critique. There has been an unmistakable tendency however for critics of globalization to talk in rather absolute and less than nuanced terms of the outright destruction of local cultures (see for example Ritzer, 2003; Seabrook, 2004). It is thus on an alternative culturalist level that some have written of a global commodity culture as implicated in processes of intense contestation, underscored by the rise of hybridity and difference as much as a global sameness (see Cvetkovich and Kellner, 1997; Jackson, 1999; Rennie Short, 2001). I sympathize with this more dynamic approach. Yet within the broad field of consumption studies this dichotomy between (global) ideological dominance and its (local) popular undoing has become analytically tired and unproductive. In utilizing such categories, scholarly readings of various commodities and consumption spaces have proven adept at rather wild, ethnographically baseless *overstatement* regarding the globally dominating nature of consumer culture, or at naively ambivalent *understatement* regarding the power of trans-national capitalism to reframe our lives.

In this chapter then, recognizing the analytical dead-ends in which an analysis of the global shop might lead, I do not seek to explore the extent to which people are drawn in to its consumptive and homogenizing reaches or alternatively utilize it as agents of transformation and hybridization. Instead, the chapter explores global commercial space in terms of what we might call 'a public discourse of unease', a discourse which is informed by the lived experience of transnational commercial development and the imagined futures it invokes. And in taking this path the chapter is informed and marked by the recent re-emergence of an interest in consumption as a site of avowedly oppositional politics (for a discussion of this see Crewe, 2001).

The global shop – as opposed to global manufacturing and merchandizing or branding – has to date been the subject of only patchy analysis within much of the academic literature on consumption and consumerism, with the notable exception of McDonald's (see, for example, Watson, 1997; Probyn, 1998; Illouz and John, 2003). Indeed, global retail space appears to have been predominantly analysed in terms of the so called McDonaldization thesis (Ritzer, 1993; Alfino, Caputo and Wynyard, 1998; Smart, 1999). To a lesser extent, work has been forthcoming on a range of other global retailers, including The Body Shop, Nike and Starbucks (Kaplan, 1995; Smith, 1996; Lury, 1999; Stabile, 2000; Brabazon, 2001; Scerri, 2003; Goodman and Papson, 2004; Thompson and Arsel, 2004). Much of this work, whatever its theoretical bent, is useful, especially in its analysis of the rationalizing logic of global capital and the labour and trade practices of global retail companies. Yet many writers tend not to 'enter' the global shop itself as a physical space or to focus, as we will do here, on how these concrete commercial operations are construed in terms of a local sensibility.

In the remainder of this chapter I want to begin to explore this latter idea and, in particular, I want to suggest that the global shop can be actively read on a number of publicly articulated levels of unease. These various levels of concern, at least in the Australian context, emanate from a nationalistic/localist sense of the global shop being 'not of us', from a commercial sense of international retailing being monopolistic and from a politically activist sense of global retail space as colonizing and exploitative. But there is another more embodied level as well on which an unease about global retail outlets can be understood. This concerns the ontological insecurity and negative affect they evoke; embedded within their failure (in part through a conflation of global space and local place) to 'hold' us.

In pursuing this analysis I will move in the following section to historically outline the emergence and consolidation of global retailing in Australia, suggesting that the global shop, at least in the antipodes, has a longer history than is sometimes supposed. This historical discussion is followed by a documentary and ethnographic section that explores, albeit briefly, the manner in which global retailing in Australia, particularly the very recent rise of Borders and Starbucks, has been variously opposed and critiqued by small business operators, inner-city residents groups, national commentators and political activists. Even within 'first-world' countries such as Australia, a global western (and particularly American) commercialism can be, and often is, understood as colonization. Indeed, Australia's periphery status as a middle-ranking power geographically distant from the North, has led to a contradictory national desire to both share in a western modernity but retain a vaguely defined 'Australianness.' The latter imperative can be expressed as a parochial cultural nationalism, but also as a much more politically nuanced resistance to a loss of economic and political independence and to cultural imperialism. In the concluding section of the chapter, I shift to a more theoretical mode of discussion, exploring the critical conceptualization of global consumer environments as articulated both inside and outside the academy. This does not constitute a discussion of the sociological and marketing concept of 'third place', but centres instead on the need to understand the global shop as hypercommercial space (rather than simply 'non-place'), and as embedded within an engineering of affect.

Emergence and consolidation

Many, but not all, of the big names in global retailing are here in the major Australian cities, covering all parts of the body and the soul: McDonald's and KFC, The Body Shop and Nike, Ikea and Aldi, Tommy Hilfiger and FCUK, Borders, Starbucks, Gloria Jean's and Delifrance, Toys 'R' Us, Virgin and Krispy Kreme – to name but a few. Historically, Australia – a relatively small nation of 20 million people – has been a fertile ground of consumption. Australians are undoubtedly prodigious consumers with a consistently solid to high household consumption expenditure relative to other western nations (Organization for Economic Cooperation and Development, 2006). Politically, however, Australia also has a strong regulatory and state welfare tradition which, while the subject of an intense neo-liberal, deregulatory attack over the past decade or so, has made for a quite different commercial environment to that of a country such as the United States. These facts have not been lost on multinational retailers. Many, despite having to deal with what they perceive as a restrictive regulatory environment, have been eager to enter the Australian market over the last few decades.

In this context, it seems indisputable that the transforming retail streetscapes of Australian cities is part of a broader process of globalization – that process almost always vaguely defined as the accelerated economic integration of markets, the unsettling of national boundaries and sovereignty and the compression or distantiation, through media and information technologies above all, of world time and space (see Held and McGrew, 2000). Yet as Held and McGrew and others have noted there is a tendency within discussions of globalization to make the present overly novel and to forget history; to forget the uneven cycles through which our world has become transnationalized. This is crucially important in the context of discussing consumption, and is illustrated well by retailing history in Australia.

Australian consumption has long been globalized. Established as a British penal colony in 1788 (and quickly transformed into a killing-field in relation to its displaced Indigenous population), commodities in Australia have always come, either literally or culturally, from elsewhere. In terms of brands, Heinz and Kellogg's, Campbell's and Cadbury, have been Australian household names for a century and a half while, in terms of the nature of retail space, Australia has long been internationalized, or rather 'Americanized'. Australian retailers were quick to simply copy American retail innovations; variety store chains were established in the early 1900s while the 'American style' supermarket emerged during the 1950s (see Humphery, 1998).

The establishment by multinational retailers of global shops in Australia however has followed a somewhat slower path. 1964 was a point of beginning, a year in which the American Safeway company opened its first American designed but Australian-based supermarket. By 1969 there were 21 of these global Safeways operating throughout the Australian state of Victoria. The iconic K Mart (then run by the US Kresge Corporation) also came to the antipodes in 1969, while 7 Eleven stores emerged in Australia in 1977. Inevitably, McDonald's emerged in 1971 while Ikea, the Swedish home furnishings empire, opened its first Australian store in 1975. The British-based Body Shop, too, has long been one of the most recognizable global outlets in Australia since the opening of the first Australian franchise in Melbourne in 1983 (ibid., chs 5 and 7).

Throughout the last two decades this rise of Australian-based global retail space has progressed, though not unproblematically. Indeed, within the financial media, much has recently been made of the fact that certain key global retailers, such as Wal-Mart, Carrefour and Costco, do not have a presence in Australia at all. With its small population and well-established local players in certain market segments, Australia has been far less attractive to some global companies than neighboring South East Asia (Mitchell, 2006). Similarly, the growth of the global shop in Australia cannot be characterized as a commercial take-over, or at least not yet. Most of the 'foreign' retailers operating in Australia hold only a minority share of the markets in which they deal.

Yet market share is not, for most, the measure of the impact of the global retailer. On the contrary, many Australians imagine the impact of global retailing in cultural rather than simply commercial terms. And, as the global shop has become an absolutely visible part of Australian urban landscapes, a sense of unease and of commercial and political opposition has crept into a public discourse of global consumer space. Indeed, there has been a transition in Australia over the last few decades from a sense of the 'foreign store' as representing the coming of a sophisticated modernity, to a sense of the global shop as being, in the early 2000s, a little more problematic. While the Australian public certainly use and indeed welcome the presence of global shops from Ikea to Nike, and while some stores may simply be seen as essentially local or at least 'nationless' (such as 7 Eleven or The Body Shop), there is a certain fragility now in relation to an Australian consumer landscape 'going global'. It is no coincidence that this fragility is related to the rise of both a political ethos of anti-globalization and a more widespread popular concern that globalization itself is responsible for a whole set of social ills from job losses to the 'decline' of a home-grown Australian culture. It is a fragility that can be clearly seen in relation to two of the most recent global arrivals on the Australian consumer scene: Borders and Starbucks.

The book and the beverage

It is interesting to note that when the German discount supermarket chain Aldi entered the Australian market there was little public concern expressed other in terms of the potential commercial impact on local grocery retailers. But other recently arrived global stores have invoked disquiet, particularly those that seemingly touch Australian cultural life rather more so than the mundanity of a cut-price supermarket. In Bourdieu's terms, it might be said that some global retailers come up against a *habitus* with little taste for a bland internationalization of key, and often highly embodied, aspects of Australian everyday life. Two such aspects concern books and beverages.

The North American book giant Borders opened its first Australian superstore in the up-market, Melbourne retail hub of South Yarra in October 1998. Even as it entered the Australian market, the company was clearly aware of a potential commercial *and* cultural opposition given the long articulated concerns within Australian social commentary and national politics about too closely emulating American 'ways and values' – or becoming, as one of Australia's leading intellectuals put it in the 1960s, 'Austerica' (Boyd, 1961). The Borders management thus vigorously insisted that: 'we are not an American bookstore that has been plopped down in the middle of Australia. ... 'It's about taking the best that is here, and the best we can bring from the US and the UK and creating something new' (cited in Finlay, 1998). A further store, sprawled over three levels, was opened within the icon of Australian retailing, Chadstone Shopping Centre, in April 2001, boasting 200,000 book titles in stock.

The global book retailer finally moved into Carlton, Melbourne's oldest café and University precinct, in November 2002. This opening, however, was accompanied by a considerable outcry from local retailers and residents as well as within the mainstream media. It was an outcry that was interesting for its mix of commercial concern at the economic impact on other book retailers present in the area – particularly the large home-grown independent Readings chain – and a vaguely articulated cultural concern about the unholy alliance between the book and the global shop. As Mark Rubbo, the co-owner of Readings, insisted; 'I don't think a business like Borders can champion Australian writing and culture like an Australian business can'. Others voiced similar concerns. One local resident, Lloyd Jones, complained that 'Yet another multinational invades and threatens the harmony of a genuine community', while one Carlton-based writer playfully coined the local residents' group campaign slogan 'Livres sans Frontieres' – books without *borders* (cited in Farouque, 2002).

Such opposition, despite its highly local and rather middle-class flavour, has in some respects reflected a broader reticence in Australia to embrace the Borders phenomenon. In moving into the Australian market Borders has had less than a dream run, attracting far fewer customers than projected. The company did not actually turn a profit on its Australian stores until 2004 (Webb, 2004) and its share of the retail market for books remains considerably eclipsed by Australian-owned chains (Hooper, 2006).

Yet Borders has certainly been part of an increasing corporatization of bookselling nationwide (Smith, 2005) and, in this context, a mixture of commercial and cultural disquiet with the global bookstore, and global retailing generally, has not abated. Far from being simply ensnared in a circumstance of local retailer opposition and isolated bourgeois distaste for global shops, Borders (along with the likes of Ikea, Nike, Starbucks and McDonald's) has become somewhat iconic in Australia of an encroaching globalization undermining of the nation's commercial and cultural independence and integrity. A detailed search of the Australia media over the last five years (undertaken for the much broader project on which this chapter is based) indicates the regularity with which the global shop has become invoked in negative terms. This is evidenced in the context of discussions of 'foreign ownership' (see, for example, Hooper 2006), of the destruction of local community (see, for example, Ketchell, 2003; Maskell 2005), and – in the hands of major columnists and social commentators – of consumerism and cultural and civic decline (see, for example, Freeman-Green, 2001; Souter, 2006). As Souter has rhetorically put it, in Australia (as in North America) 'hunger equals Big Mac, drowsiness equals Starbucks....'

Indeed, as this comment signals, if books have become a cultural and commercial battleground over globalization in Australia, so too has the cup of coffee. Aside from the rise of Borders in Australia it has been the market entry of the Seattle-based Starbucks company that has garnered most attention. Opening its first store in Australia in 2000 in Sydney's Hyde Park, the company expanded its Australian operations rapidly, although breaking into the coffee 'literate' Melbourne market was apparently seen by company executives as a bit of challenge (House, 2001). By late 2001, in one of those fatuous statistical moments so beloved of retailing, the company reported that it had sold its one millionth cup of coffee in Australia, and by the beginning of 2006 the company had opened its 60th Australian store (Starbucks, 2006).

But, once again, the emergence of yet another global retailer, this time peddling an apparently good coffee, has not gone without 'local' opposition – nor has the Starbucks Australian story proved one of easy commercial success. In Sydney's Balmain district in 2002 a petition was launched to stop Starbucks opening an outlet in the fashionable inner-city retail and residential hub of Darling Street (and the slogan STARSUCKS was liberally utilized). Similarly, in Melbourne, news of Starbucks opening (particularly in the major café belts) was greeted with disdain by local café owners and inner-city residents for its efforts to inject a 'global sameness' into the coffee experience (cited in Webb, 2004).

Of course, such sentiments, at least on the part of café proprietors, are self-interested. Starbucks has certainly constituted a commercial threat and this fact has not been lost on the Australian food service industry. Starbucks is well known for its extraordinarily aggressive strategies of commercial expansion, dependent on opening a large number of stores, often in the same retail precinct, and thus blitzing (or as business analysts call it cannibalizing) opposition (Klein, 2001). Yet much of this initial opposition to Starbucks was, once again, not simply commercially motivated, but on the part of local residents seemed to connect with a deep-seated Australian perception of global commercial culture as destructive and depthless; a perception now heightened, as we noted previously, by a quite general view in Australia of 'globalization' as a juggernaut riding rough-shod over jobs, businesses and cultural traditions. For Australian cafes owners and their clientele, as well as for residents of gentrified suburbs, the Starbucks rhetoric of offering a 'third place' of respite and relaxation (beyond work and home) has been seen as simply re-branding an experience already on offer to Australians, and moreover rendering that experience shallow despite the Starbucks pitch of offering more than fast food (Carlin, 2003; see also Scerri, 2003 for an excellent discussion of Starbucks as third place).

This perhaps goes some way to explaining why the rise of Starbucks in Australia, as with Borders, has been somewhat patchy. Australia has proved no prized market for the company compared to Asia (where Starbucks has a large number of stores). Indeed, in Australia the company has had to, against company tradition, launch an advertizing campaign to drum up custom (Shoebridge, 2003). By 2004 the company actually began closing some of its Australian outlets in response to sluggish growth and continued financial loss (Lee, 2004). Yet, as with Borders, this has occurred in the context of an intensified corporatization of the Australian coffee market, an intensification to which Starbucks has been a contributor (Hall, 2003).

Both Borders and Starbucks, then, have at the level of public discourse and in terms of generating customer numbers received a rather circumspect reception in Australia. Unravelling the reasons for this is complex. But we can glean something further by way of explanation through turning to a fourth field of opposition to global retailing beyond the terrain of small business operators, inner-city residents groups, and media commentators.

This chapter is in part informed by a broader study on the politics of anti-consumerism within western countries, a study involving an ethnographic investigation of the activism connected with this politics. One element of this larger study has involved an exploration of how activists and advocates think about and negotiate landscapes of consumption, from shopping malls to farmers markets. In this context, participants in this broader study have readily commented on the presence of the global shop, and in doing so they have often articulated ideas that overlap commercial and cultural concerns in ways very similar to those articulated by local business operators, inner-city residents and mainstream media columnists. A couple of comments will suffice to illustrate this point. As one female interviewee from a large environmentalist organization put it in relation to a question which asked if she utilized global retail outlets:

> Not if I can help it. I've got a cultural issue with them .... Well, I've got an ethical issue with them, maybe that's a better word. For lots of reasons, I'm conscious of the impact of those sorts of chains on

cultures; on making a monoculture, a world monoculture... where everything's the same. It's a consumer culture; it's an American culture, so I'm opposed to that. So, on that principle alone, I'd prefer not to shop there. Yeah, you know, there are lots of reasons [why I don't shop in them]. They take business away from local individual shops and local businesses who need jobs, and profits are sent to America or wherever the chain comes from. It's also mass consumerism, so it's driving unsustainable consumption because it's large-scale, things are cheap so people can buy more. They just do everything I'm opposed to basically.

This dual concern for the cultural and commercial impact of global retailing was reiterated in many other interviews with Australian activists and was almost always voiced in the context of a much wider concern for the environmental impact of consumption and/or the impact of exploitative labour practices globally. The was articulated well in the following response by a male activist involved in regular 'flash' street protests outside Starbucks cafés and other global retailers:

I categorically do not on principle patronise or step foot in Nike, Starbucks, McDonald's, Hungry Jacks, Borders, Bunnings, Ikea, among others, although not including *all* of these types of shops. The reason the above examples come to mind first is because I have, for various reasons and at different times, been made aware of the specific injustices and poor form of their practices and policies. Becoming involved in actions against these corporations usually fortifies my resolve no end. Usually these international shops exist for the primary purpose of making a lot of money for the least cost. This primary aim usually results in exploitation (usually in countries already made poor by the colonial powers from which the companies hail), sometimes of the worst possible kind. Further, many companies like those above, have as a strategy of attack to flood the market with their chosen commodity and push out any competition, destroying "healthy" competition.... Healthy competition works on the principle of equal opportunity for all parties, from a level playing ground. This clearly isn't the case for multinational corporations...

It is, of course, a little ironic that an anti-globalization activism can articulate concerns that are so close to those of the small business retailer; but is also perhaps encouraging of the possibility of shared dialogue between quite different social actors. Indeed, this confluence of perspective illustrates an emergent commonality of public concern in face of the globalization of Australian retailing and of economic life more generally. Politically poles apart on many issues they may be, but small business operators, inner-city resident groups, mainstream commentators and young activists share a sense of opposition to the corporate and particularly global shop (as Thomson and Arsel, 2004 similarly found in their US-based study of Starbucks). There is no suggestion here that this opposition articulates, in a metric of public opinion, a general consensus amongst the Australian population; merely that it stands as a widely recognized and in some respects influential discourse of unease.

What I would suggest is that this discourse is bound up in complex ways with an Australian (and at times parochial and chauvinistic) nationalism, with a commercial opposition to 'unfair' competition, with a desire to preserve and protect a perceived sense of the local and of bounded community, and with an ideological opposition to consumer capitalism. In no uncertain terms this field of opposition is peopled by those who wish to remain outside global retail space – and it is this 'outside', rather than the everyday usage of stores such as Borders and Starbucks, that I have wanted to briefly document in this section. This is to recognize that a politics of consumption always takes place through the modes of both engagement *and* distancing, of participation and 'aloofness' (Humphery, 1998: 211). It would be drawing a rather long bow to suggest that Borders and Starbucks have struggled in Australia simply because of such 'non-user' opposition – and it is likely that they will eventually commercially succeed on a significant level. Yet, it would be rash to downplay the importance of such broad-based public concern in face of the rise of the global store, particularly since it can be seen to be connected to a thoroughly embodied sense of how place should be constituted and experienced. It is to this broader theoretical issue of place that I will turn in concluding this chapter. In doing so, I will both concur with elements of the oppositional perspective documented above but also take issue with these articulations by interrogating the limits of how global retail space is currently conceived by its critics both inside and outside the academy.

In place

There is now a considerable body of work on the relationship between consumption and place, and more broadly on the contribution of human geography to our understanding of consumption itself (see for example Sack, 1992; Urry, 1995; Miller *et al.*, 1998). I do not want to review this work here, a task that has been recently undertaken very ably by Juliana Mansvelt (2005). Rather, in bringing this chapter to a close, I want to explore how recent commentators have specifically dealt with global commercial space.

It was Robert Sack (1992) who importantly noted that consumption is both place-creating and place-altering. Sack recognized places of consumption as terrains of human agency but read modern and postmodern landscapes of (western) consumption as implicated in a severing of connection to the rest of the world and to others – rendering contemporary consumption disorienting and preventing the moral evaluation of our consumer actions in terms of their environmental, social and international impact. It is interesting to note that there has now been a vigorous return to the politics and morality of consumption, at least within the literature on sustainability and anti-consumerism (see Princen *et al.*, 2002). It was, however, Sack's thesis on disorientation and the play between reality and unreality within contemporary consumer landscapes that connected his work to a broader – and very much ongoing – critical tradition within social theory. Of particular note here is the work of writers that have had much to say about the disorienting and fragmenting effects of contemporary consumerism and the places in which it is enacted such as David Harvey (1989), Fredrick Jameson (1991), Marc Augé (1995), Zygmunt Bauman (2005) and others.

Few writers in this tradition have focused specifically on the global shop, but the work of George Ritzer is a notable exception. Indeed, within his most recent work Ritzer designates globalized commercial spaces from McDonald's to Ikea as *non-places* (rather than third places) by virtue of being 'centrally conceived and controlled social forms that are comparatively devoid of distinctive substantive content' (Ritzer, 2003: xi). While Ritzer gives a brief nod to the idea that such retail spaces are socially meaningful to some people and can become understood as local as much as global, he works very much within the orthodox sense of globalization as a force that undermines local cultures and empties social space and relations of a grounded, connected sense of reality and value. In this, Ritzer loosely follows the work of Relph (1976) and particularly Marc Augé (1995) who has, in his now much cited essay on supermodernity, contrasted what he terms 'anthropological place' – or place as geometric, relational, historical and embodied – with the excess of *space* characteristic of the western present. This excess produces non-places – from supermarkets to airports – that invoke in us a sense of solitary individuality and which are characterized by similitude and the ephemeral. Augé gives us a sense of just how globalized these non-places have become, and how connected they are with market exchange, in his reference to what he calls 'world-wide consumption space' (Augé, 1995: 107). I do not, here, want to simply reject this perspective. It is one that very clearly has resonance within many of the comments cited above from small retailers to anti-globalization activists, and it remains a strategically crucial political critique of global capital. Indeed, there is a sense in which much contemporary 'high theory' in relation to global consumption departs little (other than in the complexity of language used) from widely held, publicly articulated and eminently reasonable views about the dangers of a rampant commodity capitalism, particularly when cocktailed with globalization.

But having said this, a conceptualization of the global shop as a non-place, whether proffered through academic analysis or everyday opposition, just won't quite do. Such a formulation lacks theoretical nuance, articulates a classed position of cultural taste as much as political objection, and privileges a structural view of shops and shopping that comes perilously close to an asocial, 'unpeopled' sociology. A formulation of the global shop as non-place, however carefully conceived, effectively dismisses that alternative interpretative stream within the study of consumption that has been informed by ethnographic and phenomenological frameworks and that, quite rightly, insists that consumption places are socially made and culturally dynamic, not *a priori* fragmenting and meaningless. While a de Certeauian cultural studies has been influential here so too has work within material culture studies and human geography. And while such work has been not unfairly taken to task for its blinkered focus on the specificity of social practices to the detriment of structural analysis, its strength has been its deeply anthropological orientation (see for example Miller *et al.*, 1998).

The key insights of this orientation, both in relation to place and questions of the local and the global, are well rehearsed. Place is a social phenomenon, it is not, as discussions of consumer non-places imply, entirely given or precluded by a particular type of building and set of commercial procedures. As the American philosopher Edward S. Casey (1998: 315) has so nicely put it 'place is what a building expands *into*'. Space is made place through use and the giving of meaning, even in the most unlikely of settings; as has been well illustrated, for example, in relation to McDonald's (Bak, 1997; Finklestein, 1999). Similarly, people 'place' themselves not simply in the local understood in a concrete sense, but do so within networks or flows of relations, such that to participate in a world outside, to move beyond local boundaries, is not antithetical to a sense of belonging (on this see Cook and Crang, 1996). As Gaston Bachelard (1994 [1958]: 47) so succinctly put it, 'Inhabited space transcends geometrical space'.

Within more recent guise, these ideas are embodied in the rubric notion of transnationalism, that sense in which the life-world can now only be understood and lived, to a greater or lesser extent, as cross-bordered, as beyond a nostalgically understood 'local'. Recognizing this term as potentially rendered meaningless through the wide variety of ways in which it is utilized, Philip Crang, Claire Dwyer and Peter Jackson (2003) have usefully designated transnationalism as a notion that merely sensitizes us to a 'de- and recoupling of culture and place, through which cultural identities are no longer clearly wedded to particular nation states, and places are rethought not as intrinsically bounded entities but as constellations of connections within those wider cultural circuits'. Such a formulation does not offer support for dubious formulations regarding the concept of third place, but instead unsettles a sense that the local and the global constitute discrete domains.

Where, then, does this discussion leave us in terms of understanding the place of the global shop? It leaves us, as I suggested in the introduction, with the need to move well beyond static dichotomies between a view of global retailing as a contentless, dominating and homogenizing force and a view of it as subject to a 'glocalized' remaking of its meanings and effects through local engagement and use. There is no simple opposition here – either between the local and the global or between place and space. One can insist that we treat the global shop as a socially dynamic *place* that is meaningful to some individuals, but we must equally insist as Augé and others might argue that such retail environments inescapably remain hypercommercial *space* and, as such, highly problematic in terms of the sociality they can offer. Rather than render the global shop a non-place, we thus need to ask (in a reformulation of both academic and popular critique): what possibilities for the making of place and sociality does global, hypercommercial space give rise to and delimit, and what historically and affectively shaped sensibilities of place does it invoke and preclude?

We can begin to answer these questions by drawing on the analysis offered in this chapter. Global shops are clearly places that are used and enjoyed, but their presence (or entry into a national market) can give rise as well to a quite general public discourse of nation, community and commercial practice that is marked, at least in the Australian context, by a sense of great unease. This latter response is driven by notions of unfair competition and/or by a clear political opposition to a perceived globalization. Yet it is informed also by a sense of what place should be, and how it should act on us. While sometimes articulated as a high-haded dismissal of those who find meaning in 'McWorld', this unease is essentially embedded, I would suggest, within a politically crucial sensibility of place that is marked by a deep objection to what Nigel Thrift (2004: 68) has called the engineering of affect; i.e. the creation of an embodied sense of fulfilment, social connection, and pleasure deliberately undertaken by global retailers in order to construct 'regimes of feeling'.

It is in this latter sense that the global shop for some, perhaps many, is simply too hypercommercially stretched-out across world space, simply too engineered, to provide a sense of being 'sincerely held' *in place*. Even for those who do not share this sensibility, it is unlikely that global shops are viewed as being particularly socially rich places to find oneself within; a fact underscored by social surveys and qualitative research in Australia which indicates that people do not generally rank shopping and consumption (of any kind) as a key source of social connection and wellbeing (Humphery, 1998, ch.9; Eckersley, 2004, ch.6). As such, global shops may be understood as terrains that we move through, enact certain events within, have a knowledge and memory of, but they are – even more so than commercial space generally – unable to rival the ontological security of places where an affective sense of connection, community or satisfaction 'happens' rather than is constructed for us. Global retailing will, no doubt, continue its commercial expansion and reap increasing profits. But the extent to which this path may ultimately be checked will be in part dependent on the degree to which populations sense, resent and reject the imposition of corporately engineered limits on the expression of a sociality.

Notes

1. This chapter is based on research generously funded by RMIT University and the Australian Research Council. In undertaking this research I am most grateful to Andy Scerri and Ferne Edwards for research assistance and to my colleague Paul James at the Globalism Institute, RMIT.

References

Augé, M. (1995) *Non-Places: Introduction to an Anthropology of Supermodernity*, London: Verso.
Alfino,M., Caputo J.S. and Wynyard R. (eds) (1998) *McDonaldization Revisited: Critical Essays on Consumer Culture*, Westport: Praeger.
Bachelard, G. (1994) *The Poetics of Space*, Boston: Beacon Press.

Bak, S. (1997) 'McDonald's in Seoul: Food Choices, Identity, and Nationalism', in Watson, J.L. (ed.) *Golden Arches East: McDonald's in East Asia*, Stanford: Stanford University Press, pp. 136–60.

Barber, B.R. (2001) *Jihad vs McWorld*, Ballantine, New York: Ballantine.

Bauman, Z. (2005) *Liquid Life*, Cambridge: Polity Press.

Boyd, R. (1961) *The Australian Ugliness*, Melbourne: Cheshire.

Brabazon, T. (2001) 'Buff Puffing an Empire: The Body Shop and Colonization by Other Means', *Continuum: Journal of Media & Cultural Studies*, 15(2), pp. 187–200.

Carlin, J. (2003) 'Observer Food Monthly', insert in *The Observer*, 13 July.

Casey, E.S. (1998) *The Fate of Place: A Philosophical History*, Berkeley: University of California Press.

Cook, I. and Crang, P. (1996) 'The World on a Plate: Culinary Cultures, Displacement and Geographical Knowledges', *Journal of Material Culture*, 1(July), pp. 131–53.

Crang, P., Dwyer, C. and Jackson, P. (2003) 'Transnationalism and the Spaces of Commodity Culture', *Progress in Human Geography*, 27(4), pp. 438–56.

Cvetkovich, A. and Kellner, D. (1997) 'Introduction: Thinking Global and Local', in Cvetkovich, A. and Kellner, D. (eds), *Articulating the Global and the Local: Globalization and Cultural Studies*, Boulder: Westview Press, pp. 1–30.

Crewe, L. (2001) 'The Besieged Body: Geographies of Retailing and Consumption', *Progress in Human Geography*, 25(4), pp. 629–40.

Deloitte. (2005) '2005 Global Powers of Retailing', report published in *Stores*, January.

Eckersley, R. (2004) *Well & Good: How We Feel and Why it Matters*, Melbourne: Text.

Farouque, F. (2002) 'The War of Words Comes to Lygon Street', *The Age,* 17 August.

Finlay, S. (1998) 'US Book chain Storms our Borders', *The Age*, 22 October.

Finklestein, J. (1999) 'Rich Food: McDonald's and Modern Life', in Smart, B. (ed.), *Revisiting McDonaldization*, London: Sage, pp. 70–82.

Freeman-Greene, S. (2001) 'Counter Culture', *The Age* (Good Weekend supplement), pp. 70–2.

Goodman, R. and Papson, S. (2004) *Nike Culture: The Sign of the Swoosh*, London: Sage.

Hall, J. (2003) 'Brand it Like Starbucks', *Australian Financial Review*, 12 September.

Harvey, D. (1989) *The Condition of Postmodernity*, Oxford: Blackwell.

Held, D. and McGrew, A. (2000) 'The Great Globalization Debate: An Introduction' in Held, D. and McGrew, A. (eds), *The Global Transformations Reader*, Cambridge: Polity, pp. 1–45.

House, K. (2001) 'Starbucks is Tops in Australia', *Australian Financial Review*, 9 July.

Hooper, N. (2006) 'Who Owns Australia?', *Financial Review*, 21 January.

Humphery, K. (1998) *Shelf Life: Supermarkets and the Changing Cultures of Consumption*, Melbourne: Cambridge University Press.

Illouz, E. and John, N. (2003) 'Global Habitus, Local Stratification and Symbolic Struggles over Identity: the case of McDonald's Israel', *American Behavioural Scientist*, 47(2), pp. 201–29.

Jackson, P. (1999) 'Commodity Cultures: The Traffic in Things', *Transactions of the Institute of British Geographers*, NS 24, pp. 95–108.

Jameson, F. (1991) *Postmodernism; or The Cultural Logic of Late Capitalism*, London: Verso.

Kaplan, C. (1995) '"A World Without Boundaries": The Body Shop's Trans/National Geographies', *Social Text*, 13, pp. 45–66.

Ketchell., M. (2003) 'Soul Searching', *The Age*, 11 November.

Klein. (2001) *No Logo*, London: Flamingo.

Lee, J. (2004) 'Starbucks Adds Shop Closures to the Experience', *The Sydney Morning Herald*, 26 August.

Lury, C. (1999) 'Marking Time with Nike: The Illusion of the Durable', *Public Culture*, 11(3), pp. 499–526.

Mansvelt, J. (2005) *Geographies of Consumption*, London: Sage.

Maskell, V. (2005) 'Bookshop's Last Word a Sign of the Times', *The Age*, 12 March.

Miller, D., Jackson, P., Thrift, N., Holbrook, B. and Rowlands, M. (1998) *Shopping, Place and Identity*, London: Routledge.

Mitchell, N. (2006) 'Fortress Australia defies Foreign Stores', *Financial Review*, 24 January.

Organization for Economic Cooperation and Development (2006) *Economic Outlook*, No.79, May (Statistical Annex, Table 3, Real Private Consumption Expenditure) www.oecd.org/dataoecd/6/27/2483806.xls accessed 30/10/06.

Princen, P., Maniates, M. and Conca, K. (eds) (2002) *Confronting Consumption*, Cambridge: MIT Press.

Probyn, E. (1998) 'Mc-Identities: Food and the Familial Citizen', *Theory, Culture & Society*, 15(2), pp. 155–73.

Relph, E. (1976), *Place and Placelessness*, London: Pion.

Rennie Short, J. (2001) *Global Dimensions: Space, Place and the Contemporary World*, London: Reaktion Books.

Ritzer, G. (1993) *The McDonaldization of Society: An Investigation into the Changing Character of Contemporary Social Life*, Thousand Oaks: Pine Forge Press.

Ritzer, G. (2003) *The Globalization of Nothing*, London: Sage.

Sack, R. (1992) *Place, Modernity and the Consumer's World: A Relational Framework for Geographical Analysis*, Baltimore: John Hopkins University Press.

Scerri, A. (2003) 'Triple-Bottom-Line Capitalism and the 3rd Place', *Arena Journal*, (New Series), no. 20, pp. 56–67.

Seabrook, J. (2004) *Consuming Cultures: Globalization and Local Lives*, London: New Internationalist Publications.

Shoebridge. (2003) 'Wake Up and Smell the Starbucks Adds', *Australian Financial Review*, 29 September.

Smart, B. (ed.) (1999) *Revisiting McDonaldization*, London: Sage.

Smith, M.D. (1996) 'The Empire Filters Back: Consumption, Production, and the Politics of Starbucks Coffee', *Urban Geography*, 17(6), pp. 502–24;

Smith, B. (2005) 'Book Industry Plays it Cool as it Shops for Collins', *The Age*, 20 May.

Souter, F. (2006) 'Buy Now, Pay Later', *The Age* (Good Weekend supplement), pp. 37–42.

Stabile, C.A. (2000) 'Nike, Social responsibility, and the Hidden Abode of Production', *Critical Studies in Media Communication*, 1(2), pp. 186–204.

Starbucks. (2006) www.starbucks.com (accessed 31/8/06).

Thompson, C.J. and Arsel, Z. (2004) 'The Starbucks Brandscape and Consumers' (Anticorporate) Experiences of Glocalization', *Journal of Consumer Research*, 31(December), pp. 631–42.

Thrift, N. (2004) 'Intensities of Feeling: Towards a Spatial Politics of Affect', *Geografiska Annaler*, 86(B) pp. 57–78.

Urry, J. (1995) *Consuming Places*, London: Routledge.

Watson, J.L. (ed.) (1994) *Golden Arches East: McDonald's in East Asia*, Stanford: Stanford University Press.

Webb, C. (2001) 'Coffee Wars', *The Age*, 19 April.

Webb, C. (2004) 'Book Chain Crosses Border into Black', *The Age*, 7 July 2004.

9
Framing a Fair Trade Life: Tensions in the Fair Trade Marketplace[1]

Keith Brown
University of Pennsylvania

In October of 2005, over 750 consumers, store owners, and activists attended the first national FT conference, entitled 'Living a Fair Trade Life', in Chicago, IL. Pauline Tiffen, author, activist, and founding member of the North American Fair Trade Alliance, gave the keynote address and explained how 'the market' should be reframed as a place where people come to interact and actively make decisions:

> Conventional wisdom now suggests that 'the market' is a neutral, uncontrollable force, immune to morality or persuasion, and not to be blamed for the harmful impact of certain trade practices. I suggest we all view 'the market' as 'the marketplace' where people come to buy and sell their goods, and where people – not some invisible, unaccountable force – decide what is acceptable and saleable.

Tiffen emphasized that the market is not simply driven by 'uncontrollable' economic forces, but equally influenced by a 'sense of adventure and discovery,' 'burning ideas and innovations,' a 'notion of service,' and an 'appreciation of a culture or a place.' Many sociologists and cultural anthropologists agree with Tiffen and show how economic activity shapes and is shaped by cultural processes (Zelizer, 1981, 1994, 2006; DiMaggio, 1994; Velthuis, 2003; Miller, 2006; Wherry, 2006). These scholars do not view economics and culture as two 'hostile worlds' with distinct modes of operating (the economic as calculating and rational and the cultural as emotive and impulsive) but view culture and economics as mutually interlinked processes (see Zelizer, 2006). This essay contributes to this burgeoning literature by showing how *fair traders* – people who are in some way involved in the FT movement as store owners, managers, volunteers, activists, and even some consumers[2] – maintain their altruistic beliefs in the face of the tensions associated with capitalist free markets.

One of the goals of the FT movement is to change the criteria that consumers use to make purchases. Leaders of the FT movement want consumers to think about what Kopytoff (1986) calls the 'cultural biography' of things, which in this case means: where goods come from, who made them, and how buying certain goods benefits people in developing countries. This is an attempt to create what collective identity theorists call an 'alternative reward structure' around FT products. These theorists 'emphasize ideological, normative, and cultural processes that induce individual participation in collective action and ensure social solidarity' (Roscigno and Danaher, 2001: 24). The extent to which retailers successfully foster this alternative reward structure is dependent upon the iconography of the store, socially responsible labels, narratives accompanying the products, and most importantly, the 'educational' face-to-face interactions between retailers and customers. In these interactions fair traders strive to frame FT as a socially conscious criterion that consumers should use to make decisions in the marketplace. They take pride in consuming socially responsible products, emphasize the moral implications of consumption, and encourage consumers to look at the social relationships surrounding the products they buy.

Fair traders explicitly focus on the economic, social, and environmental benefits of consuming FT in the hope of increasing the perceived value of these items. By telling stories about the cultural biographies of FT products, retailers encourage consumers to look beyond prices. While price is still important, it is the feelings of moral satisfaction and the quest for the most socially responsible products that motivates fair traders to continue buying and selling these products. In this paper, I examine how fair traders who share altruistic ideals confront the tensions associated with free markets. I use the word 'tensions' to signify that the decisions of fair traders are mediated by both economic and cultural criteria. Tensions should not imply that economic or cultural factors structure decisions, but rather that both economic and cultural processes inform the decision making of fair traders. To this end, I utilize interviews and ethnographic data to describe the primary market tensions for consumers, managers, and owners of FT coffee and handicraft stores.

Selecting handicrafts and coffee allows an examination of two distinct retail outlets, and two different kinds of objects. I collected data from a Ten Thousand Villages retail store, part of a large centrally-run non-profit organization selling handicrafts, and the Independents

Coffee Cooperative, a group of independently owned FT coffee shops in Philadelphia, PA. Handicrafts were the first products to be sold under FT criteria and still comprise a large proportion of FT sales. Handicrafts are tangible objects that consumers display in their homes or give as gifts. In both cases handicrafts are a reflection of one's identity and can serve as a way to talk about what 'FT' means to other people. Coffee on the other hand, is responsible for the sharp increase in total FT sales.[3] While FT handicrafts have remained somewhat of a niche market, FT coffee is being sold in mainstream stores such as Starbucks, McDonalds, Dunkin' Donuts, and Wal-Mart. FT coffee exposes people to the missions of the FT movement who otherwise might not be aware of or concerned with socially responsible consumption. It is an ingested commodity that many consumers purchase on a daily basis. I provide a brief overview of the growth of FT followed by a description of the movement and market tensions that 'fair traders' encounter.

Origins of Fair Trade

Products certified as FT are sold in order to improve the social, economic, and environmental living conditions of producers in Central and South America, Africa, and parts of Asia (Littrell and Dickson, 1999; Simpson and Rapone, 2000; Raynolds, 2002; Tarmann, 2002; Frank, 2003; Leclair, 2003; Levi and Linton, 2003; Linton *et al.*, 2004). What we today call FT organizations first appeared after World War II in England, Holland, Germany, Canada, and the United States. In the US, missionaries from the Mennonite church became aware of artisans who were financially struggling; subsequently, church members generated money to sustain these artisans (Littrell and Dickson, 1999). Alternative Trade Organizations (ATOs) such as Ten Thousand Villages (1946) and FT Organisatie (1967) were created to support artisans in developing countries (Littrell and Dickson, 1999; Levi and Linton, 2003). In the 1960s FT began to expand as international travelers became aware of the poor economic situation of artisans around the world (Littrell and Dickson, 1999). Networks between producers and consumers were established to provide wages to artisans who were selling their goods in Western countries. This movement struggled as it competed with more mainstream for-profit organizations that also started to import cultural products from abroad.[4] Throughout the 1990s, the expansion of these ATOs is reflected in the founding of a number of FT non-profit organizations: Global Exchange (1988), FT Federation (1994), TransFair USA (1998), and the FT Resource Network (2001).

Because the origins of this movement are diverse, it is no surprise that various organizations exist to certify products as FT. Organizations such as Ten Thousand Villages, and Equal Exchange (founded 1986) initially certified their own products as fairly produced. FT certification gained more credibility as independent labeling organizations were founded in different countries.[5] As the number of national certifying organizations increased, these organizations recognized a need to create an international standard for FT certifications. In 1997, the 17 different FT organizations founded the FT Labeling Organization-International (FLO). Its standards for FT apply to producers, traders, processors, wholesalers, and retailers. FLO certification requires that FT organizations:

> 'pay a price to producers that covers the costs of sustainable production and living; pay a premium that producers can invest in development; partially pay in advance, when producers ask for it; sign contracts that allow for long-term planning and sustainable production practices' (FLO, 2006).

The FLO definition suggests a fixed set of criteria governing what FT means, but understandings of FT are much more fluid and contextually contingent than this definition suggests. As one store manager told me, 'there is no FT sound-bite,' by which she means that there is no catchphrase or simple definition of FT. Rather, the meanings of FT often emerge in face-to-face interactions. My research shows that few people who sell or consume FT products have the same understanding of what FT means. FT encompasses a broad range of issues and retailers often seek the stories about products that best resonate with consumers.

Research design

Most FT retail shops are located in college towns or urban areas, so Philadelphia provides a convenient and fairly generalizable space to conduct most of this research. I collected both interview and ethnographic data from a Ten Thousand Villages store and from a cooperative of FT coffee shops called 'Independents.'[6] There are over 160 Ten Thousand Villages retail stores in the US and Canada making the organization the largest retailer of FT handicrafts in North America. Independents, on the other hand, is a small for-profit cooperative formed in order to better advertise member coffee shops and to buy coffee and other items in bulk at lower prices. Members of the FT coffee cooperative chose the name 'Independents' to stress that they are all independently owned stores.

The name also plays off Philadelphia's historical connections with the Declaration of Independence.

For 18 months I visited FT handicraft and coffee shops throughout Philadelphia. I volunteered at a Ten Thousand Villages store, and gathered ethnographic data at the four original Independents coffee shops. I worked as a retail clerk at Ten Thousand Villages in order to see what the best selling products are, how FT products are framed to attract consumers, and how meanings of FT emerge through face-to-face interactions with consumers.[7] At coffee shops I took note of how retailers discussed FT to consumers. I also attended the Independents cooperative meetings where they chose the cooperative's logo, discussed how to advertise the cooperative, and planned how to minimize costs by buying in bulk. These meetings provided insight into the framing strategies utilized to advertise and promote a socially responsible organization. Framing is an 'interpretative schema that simplifies and condenses the "world out there" by selectively punctuating and encoding objects, situations, events, experiences, and sequences of action' (Snow and Benford, 1988: 137). Framing strategies are used by store owners to mobilize consumers to purchase FT and other socially responsible products. I also conducted 95 interviews with consumers, owners, activists, and managers who are involved with FT.[8] Many people in the world of FT wear multiple hats, but in this group 45 identified primarily as consumers; 25 as owners, managers, or volunteers; and 25 as activists or NGO employees working primarily on FT campaigns.

In addition to collecting data locally, I attended the aforementioned *Living a Fair Trade Life* conference, a Ten Thousand Villages Annual Workshop, and a 'reality tour'[9] with Global Exchange to a FT coffee cooperative in Nicaragua. The FT conference was created to provide further education about what FT means and to help determine the future direction for the movement. Consumers, activists, owners, and managers in the FT movement attended the conference from 35 states and 17 countries. The Ten Thousand Villages Workshop updated employees on the current state and future direction of Ten Thousand Villages. The workshop promoted interactions between store staff and the artisans from developing countries who make products for the organization. These interactions with artisans help employees tell more detailed (and seemingly more authentic) stories about the products sold in each store. Finally, I traveled to Nicaragua with fourteen activists to see how FT coffee is produced. This trip provided activists with a sense of how labor intensive coffee production is and how FT is affecting rural communities in Nicaragua.

Who are 'Fair Traders?'

The FT store owners and managers I interviewed ranged in age from their late twenties to their early fifties, but most are in their early to mid-30s. Almost all are white and come from solidly middle class backgrounds. They are interested in a wide range of global issues, but are also concerned with local social justice issues. Most traveled internationally and derived more pleasure from their excursions to developing countries than in more mundane trips to Europe or the Caribbean. Ten of the owners/managers are women and ten are men. Women comprise a high percentage of handicraft retail store managers in Ten Thousand Villages and this is reflected in my sample, as 6 out of my 9 interviews with handicraft managers were with women.

Members of Independents look to other socially responsible companies for business advice while managers at Ten Thousand Villages receive assistance from the main office in central Pennsylvania. Most of the Independents store owners are members of the Sustainable Business Network, which provides strategies for small businesses that support a triple bottom line of people, profit, and planet. Managers of Ten Thousand Villages have the advantage of being supported by a large centrally run office. The central office sends out merchandising consultants to help display the handicrafts, and they disseminate marketing strategies that were used successfully in other stores. Both Independents and Ten Thousand Villages stores have a network of socially responsible retail stores from which they can seek advice, technical assistance, and marketing strategies.

The national leaders within the FT movement and some local store owners/managers identify as members of a social movement, but I found that consumers usually do not think of themselves as part of a broader FT movement. Many consumers did not know about FT until they began shopping at a Ten Thousand Villages or until they frequented an Independents coffee shop. Others learned about FT after being exposed to the anti-sweatshop movement, or through their consumption of organic certified food. The great majority of consumers are not familiar with FT logos or certification organizations such as TransFair USA. Nevertheless, most consumers choose to trust that 'Fair Trade' means producers are getting a 'fair' deal.

Coffee consumers are closely split between men and women, and handicraft consumers are overwhelmingly women. Many of the consumers at Ten Thousand Villages are shopping for gifts or for decorative products for their own homes. Many FT customers are highly educated,[10] have traveled internationally, and take pride in consuming in a more socially responsible manner than other consumers. Many of the respondents who identified as socially conscious said their travel experiences greatly impacted their consumption patterns. Maura,[11] a 26 year old Independents customer explained:

> When I came back (from Romania) I was not only really broke, I was really disgusted even with my own things ... You feel horrible for having all this stuff. And I had been told by the people I lived with in Romania 'don't go home and get rid of everything....Wait a few months and see how you feel about it and then start cleaning out.' And so when I went home, I said I really don't want gifts this year for Christmas because I really don't feel comfortable. I couldn't go in a mall for months; it just made me so uncomfortable and disgusted.

Maura's story is typical among fair traders who have traveled outside of the US and Western Europe. A handful of respondents told me similar stories about returning home from abroad and cleaning out their closets. More than half of the interviewees do not consider themselves to be big shoppers and claim they shop only 'out of necessity.' Many expressed guilt over their own consumption patterns, especially when they shopped at stores that they did not consider to be socially conscious. In a confessional tone, many mentioned that they enjoy an occasional Starbucks coffee and often shop at Target.

Most FT consumers believe that change can take place through everyday actions and that their consumption patterns have an effect on producers' lives. Many said they are willing to make sacrifices in their own lifestyle to help improve the lives of people in developing countries. Almost every consumer said they try not to shop at Wal-Mart because of the way their workers are treated. The most steadfast fair traders claimed they have never been to a Wal-Mart or recited how many years it has been since they last entered the store. Upon asking probing questions a few others confided that they had been to Wal-Mart recently and recounted the guilt they felt over their last purchase at the store. Most said they do not like to shop in large chain stores, and strive to purchase organic and locally produced goods.

Four economic and cultural tensions: market demands and the Fair Trade movement

Grimes and Milgram (2000) explain that many FT retailers opened their stores because they wanted to support producers in the Global South.

Most retailers I encountered were guided by altruistic beliefs, but soon faced a number of tensions: (1) they need to 'educate' customers about what FT means without 'preaching' to them, (2) deal with customers who are not necessarily activists, and (3) create and maintain a market niche as a socially responsible alternative to more profit-driven stores. All of these tensions are influenced by an overarching market tension within the FT movement which requires retailers to (4) maintain a viable business and sell competitively priced products while adhering to socially responsible beliefs. These tensions are reflected by and inflected in the everyday actions of store owners, managers, activists, and even consumers. These tensions are not mutually exclusive, but I describe them as such for analytical clarity.

Educate, but don't preach: social interactions and the infusion of moral value

FT products only retain their value as 'socially responsible' when they are purchased by or given as gifts to people who know what FT means. Within these networks of shared meaning FT products are highly valued, but outside of these networks the commodities have the same value as other handicrafts or cups of coffee. Using an interactionist model, Collins (2004) emphasizes the 'situations' in which money and commodities are exchanged, thus pointing to the importance of social interactions in influencing the meanings behind economic transactions. The exchange of socially responsible goods such as FT products, free-range meats, organic fruits and vegetables, and sweat-shop free clothes (to name just a few) is only viewed as morally valuable among select networks of activists, store owners, and customers. Within these networks the meaning of FT is not static but is negotiated in social interactions. Forging shared understandings of FT serves to direct the meaning of FT commodities and thereby enhances their moral and social value.

Commodities do not have value in and of themselves (Douglas and Isherwood, 1996). Rather their value is created and sustained through narratives, social interactions, and the ways the commodities are exchanged. The FT movement is relatively new and many consumers are unaware of what it means or how it can help producers. As a result, the point where retail staff discusses FT with consumers is essential for increasing the moral value of these goods. Retailers frame FT as the socially responsible alternative to products that are sold in more conventional profit-driven markets. They encourage people to act in ways that economists would consider to be irrational- i.e. to consider the 'cultural biographies' of objects rather than just the objects' utility or price.

Upon entering Ten Thousand Villages customers are often greeted by a store employee asking if they are familiar with the mission of the organization. If they are not familiar, the retail worker provides a quick overview that stresses how purchasing FT products directly benefits the artisans. Oftentimes the retail workers emphasize the non-profit status of Ten Thousand Villages, other times they stress the economic or environmental benefits to producers, and still other times they mention particular groups of people that benefit from FT, often women and children. Unlike the increasing number of routinized interactions between service workers and customers described by Leidner (1993), workers at Ten Thousand Villages can pick and choose the FT narrative that will best enhance the value of the products being sold.

When I began volunteering, I found the challenge of explaining what FT means to be more difficult than I expected. I knew the fine details of FT certification, but I found it hard to find a clear and concise narrative that explains what FT means. As a volunteer, I eventually realized that emphasizing the non-profit status of Ten Thousand Villages and the economic benefits to producers seemed to interest many customers who were unfamiliar with FT. I also learned that customers who already knew what FT means often wanted more detailed stories about the artisans making the products. FT is a complicated and multi-issue movement and as such retailers frame the social benefits of FT consumption in a number of different ways to attract consumers.

The interaction with customers is the single most important way to generate more interest in FT products and to enhance the value of what is being sold. Nancy, a current employee and long-time volunteer of Ten Thousand Villages, explains how she describes FT to customers as they enter the store:

> I start with the concept of the product being made by an artisan from a developing country, and I like to mention the country by name. And then I talk about how they are given some money up front for buying the raw materials and they are paid in full as soon as the product is finished. They can depend on the income because of the way that we work with them. And that whole groups of women particularly and some handicapped groups are able to support themselves that never were able to before. And by that time those people look at me and say "oh isn't that wonderful" and start to look around (*begins to laugh*).

Nancy laughs towards the end of this story because she realizes that her description almost never takes place in reality. It is a rare instance where a retailer can tell a long story about what FT means in one interaction. Some customers do not like being approached and will often not make eye contact with retail workers. Others are initially very skeptical about what FT certification can do to help artisans. Unless a particular theme resonates with consumers, most quickly become disinterested. Nancy continues:

> ... a lot of people are truly impressed but they only want so much information ... different people are at different places and you can usually tell by your first couple sentences if somebody perks up and wants to know more.

By emphasizing the social justice issues surrounding the production and consumption of these products, fair traders add a moral dimension to consumption and increase the perceived value of FT products.

Retailers realize that the shift in consumers' views about FT and consumption does not ordinarily occur through one interaction. The marketing department of Ten Thousand Villages sees raising the consciousness of consumers as a process where customers will eventually consider the impact of all their purchases on the lives of producers. My research supports this view, as coffee and handicraft consumers repeatedly told me that it took a long time for them to really grasp how FT benefits artisans and farmers. Before understanding what FT means, consumers returned to the store for the large number of unique products and the interesting stories about the products. The short-term goal of retailers is to educate consumers without overwhelming them; the more ambitious long-term goal is to change the basis on which consumers make decisions about consumption.

In addition to the initial greeting, FT retailers use other strategies to promote the moral aspects of consumption in their stores. Prominent signs throughout Ten Thousand Villages stress the benefits of purchasing FT handicrafts. One sign quotes two producers from El Salvador: 'With each product you buy, there is one more tortilla for our families.' Here the consumer is taught that it is morally necessary to purchase products from this store. Another sign quotes an artisan from India: 'Not by charity or by sympathy but through hard work and integrity we shall strive for our dignity.' Here the emphasis is placed on work. The message implies that the artisans at Ten Thousand Villages are all hard workers and do not need charity from consumers. Producers want to be thought of just like any other hard worker; ironically, this sign suggests that the producers from India are not thought of like other workers, but are framed as people in need.

The emphasis on social responsibility is also seen in the short, written narratives that accompany products when they are sold. The narratives, which are printed on a small card, frame the key issues of the FT movement and focus on the cultural biographies of the products. They emphasize how the product was made, who made it, and how purchasing the product will benefit the community in which it was produced. Almost every consumer who said they gave a FT product as a gift made sure to include a narrative of the product.[12] Most narratives describe the artisan or group that produced the product and emphasize the gender or ethnicity of the producing group. This narrative of a children's puzzle is characteristic of many:

> Artisans at Gospel House turn local materials into colorful puzzles. Young men with little education or financial means learn new skills working with wood. Talented women carefully add the details using lead free paint, and in turn pass on their expertise to others.

> Albezia wood is a fast growing, renewable soft wood that is often used to provide windbreaks on tea plantations in Sri Lanka. It is ideal for wood carving.

This narrative emphasizes how men and women with 'little education' use their talents and expertise to produce these puzzles. The fact that the wood is renewable provides a little extra value for consumers concerned about the environment. This narrative goes on to describe how the artisans who make these puzzles were affected by the tsunami of December 2004. Oftentimes emphasis is placed on artisans who were particularly hard hit by prominent natural disasters such as hurricanes, tsunamis, or earthquakes. The goal of FT retailers is to 'put a face' on the people who make the products consumers buy. Emphasizing a widely publicized natural disaster provides a strong connection between consumers in the North and producers who are often in the Global South. The initial interaction with retail staff, the signs within the store, and the accompanying narrative with the product are all tactics of an overall strategy designed to frame FT as a practical solution to reducing global inequalities and as a way to increase consumers' willingness to buy FT commodities.

Coffee store retailers also vary their selected FT narratives in order to find a theme that resonates with customers. Store owners often say they want to 'educate' their customers about the benefits of FT, but don't want to come off as 'too preachy.' Given that many customers enter the store every day- or at least a couple times a week- the retail staff is not encouraged to tell everyone about FT. Nevertheless, over time discussions about FT often emerge. These discussions are sometimes prompted by the FT advertisements that are found throughout each of the Independents coffee shops. Other times store customers or store owners initiate the conversations. Just like at Ten Thousand Villages, retailers seek the narrative that best resonates with consumers. The stories used to describe FT vary both within and across FT coffee stores.

Customers, not activists

The first FT coffee and handicraft consumers were very concerned with supporting artisans and farmers in developing countries. FT handicrafts were originally sold outside churches or within thrift stores controlled by the Mennonite Central Committee. In 1995 'SELFHELP Crafts of the World' changed its name to Ten Thousand Villages with the goal of targeting more mainstream consumers (Littrell and Dickson, 1999). FT coffee is also shifting from somewhat of a niche market to a more mainstream type of specialty coffee. The founders of Equal Exchange, the first FT coffee importer in the US, began importing coffee from Nicaragua in 1986 as an act of solidarity with Nicaraguan coffee farmers.[13] The organization had a hard time selling the products in mainstream stores, but gained a niche by targeting small food cooperatives. To better help coffee farmers (and reach more mainstream markets) Equal Exchange emphasized the high quality of their arabica coffee beans. Equal Exchange and Ten Thousand Villages both realized that to best help producers and grow their own organizations they had to target more mainstream consumers.

Most consumers at Independents and Ten Thousand Villages do not identify as activists. Many search for independently owned stores where they can buy unique, high quality, competitively priced products, and thus they are initially and centrally oriented to products and not production and distribution processes. By framing products as 'socially responsible,' FT shops create a market niche, even as they compete in a larger economic field with mainstream stores such as Starbucks and Pier One Imports. If shoppers were simply activists, FT retailers would not have to focus so much on importing high quality coffee beans or aesthetically pleasing handicrafts. But, shoppers tend to be consumers first and activists second as exemplified by Lisa, a 27-year-old Ten Thousand Villages customer:

> I like what they are doing as a company. They are sort of socially responsible and are helping people sell their goods and products in a fair and equitable way. I like their stuff. I wouldn't just buy it because it's fair and equitable if I didn't like it – to be honest. So, I like their stuff!

The Ten Thousand Villages in upscale Chestnut Hill emphasizes the FT aspect of their products to almost every customer who enters the store. They attempt to target consumers who identify as 'socially conscious' and also seek consumers with little or no interest in FT. Like other successful retail stores, much effort goes into creating displays that are aesthetically pleasing and will lead to increased sales. In all Ten Thousand Villages stores[14] products are displayed by color rather than by the function of the product, the area where it was produced, or by the total benefits to producer groups. Members of the Visual Merchandising department from the central office visit each store more than four times each year to re-organize the products and create displays designed to increase sales.

Store employees occasionally emphasize handicraft aesthetics and functionality in their discussions with customers. Some of the best selling products from Ten Thousand Villages include functional items such as cookbooks, planters, and picture frames. Many fair traders do not identify as 'big shoppers,' so finding functional products may allow these consumers to alleviate their guilt over buying products they say they do not necessarily need. Retailers also emphasize the aesthetic properties of handicrafts in order to encourage customers to buy more products (see Postrel, 2003 on importance of aesthetics). One store manager told me her store has been successful because of the FT aspect of all the products, but also because 'people like pretty stuff.' Since FT handicrafts and coffee are priced competitively with imported handicrafts and specialty coffees, FT certification provides a form of 'value added' to otherwise similar commodities.

FT coffee retailers are especially sensitive to the fact that their customers often just want a cup of good coffee and don't necessarily care too much about FT. Instead of framing FT coffee as a socially responsible alternative to each and every customer, FT retailers are more likely to note that they only sell high quality coffee. In interviews most owners mentioned that they used blind taste testing of FT and non-FT coffees to find the best quality coffee beans. They tended to emphasize how labor intensive coffee production is, and how the cooperatives they buy from grow some of the best coffee beans in the world. Levi and Linton's (2003: 420) interviews with FT coffee consumers shows that 'for many – perhaps most – quality trumps "doing the right thing."' Initially FT was an expression of political solidarity with impoverished coffee farmers, but the expansion into mainstream markets has forced retailers to focus on coffee quality. By emphasizing the high quality of the coffee beans, retailers avoid being labeled as simply a charitable organization.

Entrepreneur, but not a capitalist: establishing and maintaining a market niche

FT retailers do not want their stores to be thought of like conventional retail outlets. They position their stores as socially conscious alternatives to corporate outlets like Pier 1 Imports or Starbucks. Ten Thousand Villages, which is a large chain, benefits by selling products that are thought of as unique, socially responsible, and unlike typical commodities found in malls or other retail outlets. Members of the Independents Coffee Cooperative express great pride in being independently owned and often position themselves as an alternative to chain stores. Both Independents and Ten Thousand Villages have benefited greatly by the anti-sweatshop movements of the late 1990s and the widespread critiques of chain stores described by Naomi Klein in her book *No Logo* (2001).

Customers of Ten Thousand Villages often say they like the store because they find products that 'can't be found anywhere else.' Some customers shop at Ten Thousand Villages because they can buy products symbolizing their ethnic heritage. Others like to buy gifts that were made in places they once visited. Consumers often mention that they like the fact that the products are all hand-made and that each is unique. Many of the products come with a short description saying that any irregularities in the product are a function of the individualistic nature of the production process. Artisans of the Craft Resource Center in Calcutta India include a short message with many of the products they produce for Ten Thousand Villages:

> Any irregularities or unevenness in the product is not always a manufacturing defect but an assurity that this is a genuine hand made product. It creates a beauty unmatched by any mass produced material.

Rather than viewed as defective, as might be the case in a more conventional store, products with irregularities are reframed as possessing positive attributes of the handmade production process. By framing the product as 'authentically' made-by-hand these narratives serve to distinguish handicrafts from mass-produced commodities (see Benjamin, 1968).

Interviews with coffee shop owners reveal that many designed their shops in contrast to chain stores like Starbucks. One owner states:

> I was very much against, from a visual point, doing the whole 'cozy-café look.' In my opinion this is a continuation of the whole Starbucks design motif ... you get the preferred oranges (referring

to wall color) ... you know, look, I want to do something different from that.

This owner serves his coffee and teas in ceramic cups to provide a formal atmosphere evoking images from his experiences in European coffee shops. This formality provides a contrast to the informal, disposable cups given out at Starbucks. This desire to differentiate FT coffee shops from places like Starbucks also is manifested in advertising campaigns and in discussions with customers. Another coffee shop owner tells many of his regular customers how much is salary differs from that of Howard Schultz, the CEO of Starbucks.

Independents coffee shop owners want to maintain their market niche as a socially responsible organization, but often get stuck debating both what 'social responsibility' entails and whether it is worth paying extra for. In an email exchange to other cooperative members, one coffee store owner questions what kind of cups to purchase:

> I suspect that if compostable cups go to the landfill it's not much different than plastic cups sitting in the landfill. I don't think the corn cups are recyclable...I wonder if producing cups from corn rather than petroleum is superior for the environment or if it takes less energy.... Geez, trying to do the right thing starts to get a little complicated, eh? I guess we have to decide if it's worth an extra $5/case and the hassle of switching suppliers.

Determining what is the most socially responsible product requires retailers to consider economic factors (price) and cultural criteria (are we doing what we believe is best for the environment). Maintaining a niche as 'socially responsible' can be difficult, as one prominent store that is outside the scope of this study demonstrated. The store uses wind power for its electricity, buys organic meats, uses locally grown vegetables, and says it provides a living wage for its workers. However, this stores' image was damaged in the eyes of some of the fair traders I interviewed when a local newspaper described how the owner prevented the workers from unionizing.

Sarah, a co-owner of an Independents coffee shop, explained that her store's mission is to remain profitable while helping farmers in developing countries. She does not like to consider herself a capitalist, but realizes that on an everyday basis she has to make decisions that have major financial implications for herself and her store. When she first opened her coffee shop Sarah overheard her father talking to another family member, 'oh you know she (referring to Sarah) went from like doing all this non-profit work to being a capitalist. Now she is just like the rest of us.' Sarah said she 'just kind of looked at him,' but she admitted that:

> ultimately we do have to be a profitable business if we are going to survive. And that is not just for Cindy (other co-owner) and I to make more money. It has nothing to do with that. But if we want to help these farmers from other countries we have to sell more coffee. Like when Cindy was there (in Nicaragua) she asked the farmers point blank "what can we do for you" and they said "sell more coffee." ... The more FT coffee we can sell, the better their lives will be.

Sarah acknowledges that her overall goal must be that of maintaining a profitable business, the same as any entrepreneur. However, she deflects attention away from how much money she is able to make, eschewing profit as the singular goal of her endeavors, citing instead the 'alternative reward' of helping small farmers as the motivation for her hard work.

Giuseppe also does not like to be thought of as a profit-driven capitalist. He opened the first FT coffee shop in Philadelphia and frames his store as a place where buying a cup of coffee can make a difference in the world. Giuseppe's store is located in a commercial district next to a theater that recently closed for much of the year. The theatre used to provide Giuseppe with a good deal of business. As his five year lease was expiring Giuseppe began to question why he continued to work 80 to 100 hours a week when he was not making much money and could not afford health insurance. Giuseppe confided in me that he was debating selling the store. Soon after this conversation he traveled with Equal Exchange to Nicaragua in order to live with some of the FT farmers that he buys his coffee from. He came back from the trip rejuvenated and soon re-signed his lease for another three years. He told me that 'part of what made me keep the store open was the trip to Nicaragua.' Once Giuseppe saw how his work directly benefited farmers (alternative rewards) he realized that his own financial struggles paled in comparison to these farmers. Like Sarah and many other fair traders, Giuseppe claims that his motivation to continue supporting FT is not based on profits, but on the satisfaction he receives for providing material benefits to coffee farmers.

Altruistic, but still profitable: an overarching tension

Maybe the most obvious and important tension for FT organizations is that they must remain economically viable while still adhering to 'socially responsible' beliefs. This tension is inter-related to each of the above three tensions. In order to remain profitable, FT retail stores must successfully convey what FT means, sell to customers rather than activists, and maintain a market niche as a socially responsible organization. The ability to make money is a bit easier for Ten Thousand Villages as they are a non-profit organization and rely heavily on volunteers to keep their labor costs down (Littrell and Dickson, 1999).

Store employees take pride that Ten Thousand Villages helps some of the most impoverished artisans in the world, yet acknowledge the larger, competitive context of the handicraft market. When customers come into the store and ask why no products are being sold from Brazil or China, one employee responds by saying that Ten Thousand Villages maintains long-term trade relationships with artisans from only the 'poorest countries in the world.' However, this is not entirely true. Ten Thousand Villages wants to create trading relationships with artisans in central Africa, but high transportation costs restrict trade in this region. Ten Thousand Villages is hesitant to trade with artisans in central Africa until the transportation costs can be lowered enabling competitive pricing of the goods.

Members of Independents face a different set of tensions associated with remaining profitable. The owners strongly encourage consumers to recycle products in the store and often use environmentally friendly and locally produced products. In a recent flurry of emails, the members of Independents expressed pride in being able to pay their employees a few dollars above minimum wage, and for giving raises to employees after a short trial period. Still, all the Independents owners are not able to provide health benefits for their full-time employees.

With more and more organic, FT, and locally produced products available, store owners constantly debate how much social responsibility is worth paying extra for Sarah explains:

> We just started looking at prices to get organic milk ... Like for us to make the shift to organic milk – it's twice as much money. As committed as we are to the issue, that is ... an example of where there might be a tension where we have to make a decision that speaks more on the financial picture versus what is the right thing to do. I don't feel like we are wrong but I would love to say that all of our milk and dairy products are organic. But, I don't know that people would continue to come in and buy a small latte for four or five dollars.

Sarah's quote demonstrates that price remains a factor in each of the purchases she makes for the store. If the customers were all activists who were motivated strongly by the social-political efforts of FT, she may have been willing to pay extra for the milk.

About a year after my initial interview with Sarah, her store began selling locally produced milk from Lancaster County. The milk is not certified as organic but is produced from 'hormone free' and 'pastured cows.' Sarah and Cindy decided that they would pay a bit more money[15] for the milk saying that 'right now we can justify the additional cost.' Sarah and Cindy put a story about their locally produced milk on their website and Sarah told me, 'We feel like it is our responsibility to educate our customers.' They tell their customers that the milk is from a local farm and that their hormone-free milk is healthier than conventional milk. Sarah and Cindy's emphasis on the cultural biographies of the stuff they sell demonstrates the merger of cultural and economic factors in the consumption process. Their concern over how much to pay for milk is influenced by the cultural biography of the milk itself.

Fair trade retailers are correct in recognizing that consumers are often price-sensitive. National surveys show that consumers say they are willing to pay more for products not made in sweatshops (Kimeldorf *et al.*, 2006). Of course, what people say and what they actually do are often at odds. Kimeldorf *et al.* (2006) set out to explore consumers' willingness to pay more for 'Good Working Condition' socks as opposed to socks made in conventional sweatshops. Their preliminary findings suggest that 'the market for conscientious consumption in the real world of American shoppers is close to that reported in the national surveys' (27). While it seems Americans are willing to pay a little extra to remedy some inequalities, this should not suggest that Americans (or even socially responsible consumers) are not concerned about price. One regular at Ten Thousand Villages told me she loves this store because the prices are 'realistic.' She knows that the products support artisans but implies that there is a price threshold she would not cross. Many other consumers that I interviewed agreed saying that they were willing to pay a little extra for socially responsible products, but that it was still important to them that the products were priced 'reasonably.'

Some fair traders who are very concerned about the conditions of producers express frustration about an over-emphasis on price. Bill Harris, a founder of Cooperative Coffees, which represents 21 roasters in the US and Canada, said 'I am tired of the argument that we are priced out (too high). ... We hear this too much. If you are worried too much about the price, why are you selling FT?' Bill is more concerned with making sure coffee farmers are treated 'fairly' than in increasing the total sales of FT coffee. Bill believes that by focusing on the stories associated with coffee production, consumers will see a greater value in the products themselves. While Bill is right to emphasize that product narratives can increase the perceived value of FT products, the expansion of FT products into more mainstream markets means FT retailers will have to continue to price their products competitively.

Both Bill's concern with telling better stories and the Ten Thousand Villages consumers' emphasis on 'realistic' prices demonstrate the ways cultural and economic criterions are combined in the FT marketplace. Retailers highlight the cultural biographies of FT coffee and handicrafts to add a moral dimension to consumption and motivate FT consumers to continue to buy goods that support small-scale producers.

Discussion

The first two of the tensions described above (explaining the meaning of FT and selling to consumers rather than activists) point to the importance of social interactions for explaining how the meanings of FT emerge and are sustained. FT has grown in a different way than early mass society theorists of consumption would have predicted. Adorno and Horkheimer constructed consumers as passive and easily manipulated by mass-marketing strategies (Adorno and Horkheimer, 1977; Adorno, 1991). However, the growth of FT is not dependent on mass-advertising campaigns, but relies on face-to-face interactions for spreading the meaning of FT. In fact, the rapid growth of the FT movement has occurred without much advertising and without a catchy sound-bite explaining what FT means.

The first two tensions are evident in micro-level interactions between retailers and customers while the third and fourth tensions (maintaining a market niche and a profitable business) are more structural issues faced by a wide range of retailers selling socially responsible goods. As large companies begin to sell more socially responsible products, consumers often question the goals of these companies. Are these companies 'in it for the money?' Or are they actually concerned about improving the lives of artisans and farmers in developing countries?

Consumers rely on a wide range of certifications and labels to determine if a product is socially just: FT, organic, union-made, free-range, locally grown, and made in the USA are a few prominent examples. While these certifications are extremely helpful, the most knowledgeable consumers know that all FT products are not the same. These consumers are in search of the most authentically socially just products possible and employ a 'sliding scale of authenticity' to evaluate the degree to which these products are produced in a socially responsible manner (see Grazian, 2003). They do not view products as either authentic or not, but view authenticity on a continuum. Consumers' search for social responsibility is a never-ending process where they differentiate themselves from others and create meaning through their consumption patterns.

The introduction of large corporations into niche-markets can also lead to the re-definition of what social responsibility entails. Products that were once considered socially responsible may not be thought of in the same way today. As the market for FT and organic products expands, FT shop owners have a more difficult time maintaining a niche as 'independent,' 'unique,' and 'socially responsible.' One customer of Ten Thousand Villages said she was very disappointed to find out that the store is a large chain. She said the fact that Ten Thousand Villages is a chain made her a bit more hesitant to shop at the store.

New markets are created when store owners closely look at their competition to see what they are producing (White, 2002). Understanding the competition allows insight into what types of products can successfully be sold in a new market. The owners of Independents all told me they extensively researched other local and chain coffee shops to help them see how they could design their own shops. Owners distinguished their stores from Starbucks by being independently owned, and emphasized their social responsibility to provide distinction from other locally owned shops. As large corporations encroach on their market niches, it will be interesting to see how organizations like Independents and Ten Thousand Villages redefine what social responsibility entails.

The final tension, maintaining a profitable business, is a common issue associated with organizations competing in capitalist markets (see for example Fine, 1992; Miller, 2006). Fine (1992: 1292) describes the conflict nicely when referring to culinary chefs who face market constraints: 'No matter how idealistic the goals of the worker, ultimately these goals are embedded in the negotiated compromises of work.' While fair traders share many altruistic goals, their livelihood is dependent upon maintaining a profitable business.

There is one caveat regarding this final tension that is worth discussing. The evidence that I describe in support of this tension shows conflicts between prices (economic criteria) and adherence to social responsibility (cultural criteria). During the *Living a Fair Trade Life* conference a few presenters argued that there is no tension between being socially responsible and maintaining a viable business. Rather, they claimed that social responsibility is an asset or a form of value added that serves to increase the amount of money consumers are willing to pay. Throughout the conference this became a very controversial issue. Many small business owners said that profitability and social responsibility should not be in conflict with each other, but on an everyday basis they have to decide how much social responsibility 'is worth paying extra for.' As the demand for FT and other socially responsible products increases I expect there will be less of a tension between profitability and social responsibility. Currently, however, retailers at both Independents and Ten Thousand Villages must constantly navigate between economic and cultural criteria when deciding how best to maintain successful businesses.

I suspect that there are other tensions imposed on fair traders who are outside of the scope of this project. My sample of interviewees only permit an examination of fair traders who have some idea of what FT means and who (at least occasionally) shop at FT retail stores. Other tensions intrinsic to the wider world of FT include *time* – it takes a significant amount of time to locate and learn about 'socially responsible' products, and *space* – which can be a factor for consumers who do not live close to FT retail stores and who don't feel comfortable shopping over, or do not have access to, the internet. These issues are likely to be more germane for consumers who do not live in metropolitan areas or college towns where FT retail stores are more commonly found.

The rapid increase in the number of FT, organic, sweatshop free, and other socially conscious products is beginning to catch the attention of critics, journalists, and social scientists looking to understand how meaning and social boundaries develop through consumption. This paper contributes to our understanding of this social phenomenon by conceptualizing FT as a movement embedded within the confines of capitalist free markets. In Pauline Tiffen's opening quote she explicitly reframes markets as a site where cultural and economic processes interlink to inform our decisions in the marketplace. Tiffen could easily have been addressing sociologists, anthropologists, and economists who continue to theorize economics and culture as two distinct spheres, or 'hostile worlds' as Zelizer (2006) calls them. Rather than viewing consumption as comprised of two 'hostile worlds,' fair traders self-consciously struggle to frame markets as a combination of the two. It is in this framing and reframing of socially conscious consumption that fair traders differentiate themselves from other consumers and create meaning in their patterns of consumption.

Notes

1. This chapter benefited greatly from the thoughtful comments and critiques on earlier drafts by Dan Cook, Robin Leidner, Stefan Klusemann, and Kathleen O'Malley. I would also like to thank Bill Bielby, Joe Cesa, Randall

Collins, Adair Crosley, Jill Fink, David Grazian, Bryant Simon, and Fred Wherry for their advice and assistance throughout this project. I gratefully acknowledge financial support for the collection of these data from the Pollak Summer Research Fellowship at the University of Pennsylvania.

2. The consumers I interviewed generally do not identify as part of a broader social movement. There is, however, a small group of consumers who identify as conscientious consumers. These consumers explicitly look for products certified as socially responsible and will be referred alongside store owners, managers, and volunteers as 'fair traders.'

3. In 1998, approximately 76,000 lbs of coffee was certified as FT in the US, but by 2006 over 100 million pounds of coffee was certified (Chettero, 2006).

4. For example, Pier 1 Imports was founded in 1962 and imported ethnic handicrafts from around the world.

5. Max Havelaar is the first Independent Labeling Organization and began certifying coffee in Holland as FT in 1988.

6. When Independents was founded in 2003 it was comprised of four coffee shops: The Greenline Café in west Philadelphia, Joe Coffee Bar in center city, Mugshots in the art museum area, and Infusion in Mt. Airy. The cooperative has expanded, but I collected the bulk of my data from these four shops.

7. I volunteered as a retail clerk for about 4 hours each week. Volunteering gave me the opportunity to recruit consumers for in-depth interviews. At Ten Thousand Villages and Independents I targeted interviewees who are regular customers of the stores.

8. I was hired by the FT Resource Network to interview national leaders of the FT movement. Two other interviewers and I conducted 25 interviews over the phone. These interviews are provided insight into the major conflicts in the FT movement. The remaining interviews were conducted face-to-face with customers, managers, volunteers, and FT store owners. Most interviews lasted between one and two hours and each was tape recorded.

9. These reality tours are designed to bring FT activists in contact with producers and to better educate activists about the merits of FT. Participants on the Global Exchange trip lived in the homes of farmers in a Nicaraguan FT coffee cooperative.

10. Ten Thousand Villages' market research found that many of their best consumers are highly educated and often possess a master's degree. Almost all of the consumers I interviewed have a college degree and about half have at least some post-bachelor education.

11. All respondents were given a pseudonym.

12. I have no way of knowing how many people actually read the narratives, but a few people said that they learned about FT after receiving a gift.

13. Equal Exchange provides most of the FT certified coffee to both Ten Thousand Villages and Independents. In the mid-1980s there was a ban in the US against imports from Nicaragua. Equal Exchange got around the ban by importing the coffee to Canada and roasting it there. Roasting the coffee significantly altered the content of the beans and this allowed the coffee to be imported into the United States.

14. The Ten Thousand Villages where I volunteer is a 'company store' meaning that the central office in Akron PA makes decisions about how products are displayed. 'Contract stores' share the Ten Thousand Villages name but are

individually owned and operated. Both contract and company stores receive consulting assistance from the Visual Merchandising department.
15. The price of locally produced milk is 19% higher than conventional milk and the certified organic milk is still over double the price of conventional milk.

References

Adorno, T. (1991) *The Culture Industry: Selected Essays on Mass Culture*. New York: Routledge.

Adorno, T. and Horkheimer, M. (1977) 'The Culture Industry: Enlightenment as Mass Deception,' in Curran, J., Gurevitch, M., and Woolacott (eds) *Mass Communication and Society*, pp. 349–83. Beverly Hills, CA: Sage.

Benjamin, W. (1968) *Illuminations: Essays and Reflections*, Arendt, H. (ed.). New York: Harcourt Brace Jovanovich, Inc.

Chettero, N. (2006) 'TransFair USA Certifies Over 100 Million Pounds of Fair Trade Coffee,' *TransFair USA Press Release* (consulted December 2006): http://www.transfairusa.org/content/about/pr_060407.php

Cohen, L. (2003) *A Consumer's Republic: The Politics of Mass Consumption in Postwar America*. New York: Vintage Books.

Collins, R. (1992) 'Women and the Production of Status Cultures', in M. Lamont and M. Fournier (eds), *Cultivating Differences: Symbolic Boundaries and the Making of Inequality*. Chicago: University of Chicago Press.

Collins, R. (2004) *Interaction Ritual Chains*. Princeton: Princeton University Press.

DiMaggio, P. (1994) 'Culture and Economy', in N. Smelser and R. Swedberg (eds), *The Handbook of Economic Sociology*. Princeton: Princeton University Press.

Douglas, M. and Isherwood, B. (1996) *The World of Goods: Towards an Anthropology of Consumption*. New York: Routledge.

Fine, G. A. (1992) 'The Culture of Production: Aesthetic Choices and Constraints in Culinary Work,' *American Journal of Sociology* 97 (5): 1268–94.

FLO website (2006) 'Trade Standards,' *Fair Trade Labeling Organization – International* (consulted December 2006): http://www.fairtrade.net/trade_standards.html

Frank, D. (2003) 'Where are the Workers in Consumer-Worker Alliances?: 'Class Dynamics and the History of Consumer-Labor Campaigns,' *Politics and Society* 31 (3): 363–79.

Grazian, D. (2003) *Blue Chicago: The Search for Authenticity in Urban Blues Clubs*. Chicago: University of Chicago Press.

Grimes, K. M. and Lynne Milgram, B. (ed.) (2000). *Artisans and Cooperatives: Developing Alternative Trade for the Global Economy*. Tucson: University of Arizona Press.

Kimeldorf, H., Meyer, R., Prasad, M., and Robinson, I. (2006). 'Consumers with a Conscience: Will they pay more?,' *Contexts* 5 (1): 24–9.

Klein, N. (2001). *No Logo*. London: Flamingo.

Kopytoff, I. (1986) 'The Cultural Biography of Things: Commoditization as Process', in A. Appadurai (ed.), *The Social Life of Things: Commodities in Cultural Perspective*, pp. 64–91. Cambridge: Cambridge University Press.

Leclair, M. (2003) 'Fighting Back: The Growth of Alternative Trade', *Development* 46 (1): 66–73.

Leidner, R. (1993) *Fast Food, Fast Talk: Service Work and the Routinization of Everyday Life*. Berkeley: University of California Press.

Levi, M. and Linton, A. (2003) 'Fair Trade: A Cup at a Time?,' *Politics and Society* 31 (3): 407–32.

Linton, A., Liou, C., and Shaw, K. (2004) 'A Taste of Trade Justice: Marketing Global Responsibility via Fair Trade Coffee,' *Globalizations* 1 (2): 223–46.

Littrell, M. A., and Dickson, M. (1999) *Social Responsibility in the Global Market: Fair Trade of Cultural Products*. Thousand Oaks, CA: Sage Publications.

Miller, L. (2006) *Reluctant Capitalists: Bookselling and the Culture of Consumption*. Chicago: University of Chicago Press.

Postrel, V. (2003) *The Substance of Style: How the Rise of Aesthetic Value Is Remaking Commerce, Culture, and Consciousness*. New York: Perennial.

Raynolds, L. (2002) 'Poverty Alleviation Through Participation in Fair Trade Coffee Networks: Existing Research and Critical Issues,' *Community and Resource Development Program*, The Ford Foundation.

Roscigno, V. J., and Danaher, W. (2001) 'Media and Mobilization: The Case of Radio and Southern Textile Worker Insurgency, 1929–1934,' *American Sociological Review 66* (February): 21–48.

Simpson, C., and Rapone, A. (2000) 'Community Development from the Ground Up: Social Justice Coffee,' *Human Ecology Review* 7 (1): 46–57.

Snow, D., and Benford, R. (1988) 'Ideology, Frame Resonance, and Participant Mobilization,' *International Social Movement Research* 1: 197–218.

Tarmann, K. (2002) 'The Fair Trade Coffee Movement: Norm Change or Niche Marketing?,' University of Virginia (dissertation).

Velthuis, O. (2003) 'Symbolic Meanings of Prices: Constructing the Value of Contemporary Art in Amsterdam and New York Galleries,' *Theory and Society* 32: 181–215.

Wherry, F. (2006) 'The Social Sources of Authenticity in Global Handicraft Markets: Evidence from Northern Thailand,' *Journal of Consumer Culture* 6 (1): 5–32.

White, H. (2002) *Markets from Networks: Socioeconomic Models of Production*. Princeton: Princeton University Press.

Zelizer, V. (1981) 'The Price and Value of Children: The Case of Children's Insurance,' *American Journal of Sociology* 86 (5): 1036–56.

Zelizer, V. (1994) *The Social Meaning of Money*. New York: Basic Books.

Zelizer, V. (2006) 'Do Markets Poison Intimacy?' *Contexts* 5 (2): 33–8.

10
The Mall and the Street: Practices of Public Consumption in Mumbai[1]

Jonathan Shapiro Anjaria
University of California

Practices of consumption are at the center of diverse debates surrounding the changing landscape of post-industrial Mumbai, India. For many, the city's glittering new supermarkets and shopping malls and the consumption possibilities offered within them herald Mumbai's membership into an elite group of 'world class cities.' Malls have also produced a euphoria among business and political elites, as well as some journalists, who see them as signaling a city-wide revolution in consumption practices in which localized retail formats – such as street markets and *kinara* stores (the ubiquitous small, family-run shops) – are gradually replaced by 'global' retail environments. With regularity, newspaper articles with titles such as 'From mills to malls, the sky's the limit' and 'Mall mania' announce the arrival of a new kind of consumption that will irrevocably alter the city's social and physical landscape by 'supplant[ing] the riotous urban Indian street market' (Johnson and Merchant, 2005). By contrast, others more critical of the mode of urban development of which the shopping malls are a part see malls as representing a capitulation to the forces of global capital, and as symbolic of the government's skewed development priorities. Yet for these critics as well, the elite forms of consumption found within the mall fundamentally contradicts previous practices of consumption, and thus are seen as radically changing the experience of daily life in Mumbai.

That the political economy of Mumbai has changed in recent years is without question; since the late 1990s, the city has witnessed an unprecedented growth in large-scale organized retail sites, many of which were designed by multi-national firms. And in localized instances, these businesses have successfully managed to alter the visual aesthetic of markets and the practice of consumption. However, investigating the meaning and function of the new retail environments from the perspective of everyday practice reveals a more complex picture.[2] Rather than simply representing structural rupture of experience, new and old retail environments exist in crosscurrents of meaning and signification that cannot be reduced to narratives of radical transformation. This suggests, for one, that the narratives of radical change activated by those on both ends of the political spectrum to explain the everyday life of the city have the potential to overlook other narratives, generated from the immediate sites of consumption, which call the former into question.

To this end, this chapter is divided into three main sections, each of which provides a snapshot of a space of consumption: the street, the space outside the mall, and the mall itself. As is apparent from these categories, these spaces of consumption do not exist in discrete social spheres; rather, when put together, they convey the continuity of everyday experience between the street and the mall. By way of introducing these spaces of consumption, I show how, despite shifts in urban development policy and elite, NGO-led campaigns to 'clean' the city, the street continues to be central to the consumptive sphere, the economy, everyday life and the imagination of Mumbai. Then I proceed to explore the lived experiences of consumption on the street and in the mall. First, I discuss how changing market aesthetics and various conceptions of the morality of public space inform interactions between buyers and sellers on the street. Second, I discuss the way in which the street market functions when infused by a palpable sense of looming shopping mall culture, in order to show how malls' existence does not simply negate buyer-seller interactions on the street, but informs the consumption and trade practices found at these sites. And finally, I discuss the practices that take place *within* the mall. Despite the fact that shopping malls are ostensibly for the large-scale sale of goods, as Meaghan Morris writes, 'we cannot derive commentary on their function, people's responses to them, or their own cultural production of "place" in and around them, from this economic rationale' (Morris, 1988: 195, also quoted in Miller *et al.*, 1998: 27). In this section, I show how for most Mumbai residents, the appeal of the mall lies in the visual spectacle and the promise of participation in global modernity it offers, not in the practice – that of consumption – for which it was designed. By showing how these retail spaces do not herald a revolution in consumer practices, but have instead been incorporated into existing practices of consumption, I also hope to interrogate assumed correspondences between a changing political economy and changing experiences of everyday life in the city.

This chapter, which is part of a larger project on contestations over the reconfiguration of open space in Mumbai, draws on long-term fieldwork in the city, conducted between June 2005 and May 2006, and intermittently in 2003 and 2004. Participant observation with street vendors for months at a time, during which I literally sat on the side of the road, enabled me to investigate firsthand the everyday interactions among street vendors, customers, and nearby residents. In addition, long-term participant observation in the city's major shopping malls enabled a thorough exploration of the totality of the dynamics of public space and new retail environments in Mumbai.

Geography of street consumption

A wide variety of goods are available for purchase on Mumbai's streets. They include, but are not limited to, prepared foods, fruits, vegetables, flowers, *paan*, cigarettes, juices, household items, beauty accessories, clothes, sandals, pirated VCDs, religious articles and books. Street vendors display these items on small handcarts, metal frame tables, wooden boxes, baskets or plastic tarps spread on the pavement. While a few of the city's 200,000[3] vendors (Bhowmik, 2000) operate in areas marked 'hawking zones' scattered throughout the city, in the absence of strict enforcement of street vending regulations, the vast majority (nearly 90 per cent) of street vendors operate in unauthorized areas (Tata Institute of Social Sciences and YUVA, 1998). In this way, dense, and officially illegal, street trade takes place on the open spaces and lanes emanating from commuter train stations, hospitals, religious institutions and municipal markets, as well as in the bylanes of residential neighborhoods or in busy commercial zones. Moreover, in setting up business in the nooks between buildings, on the vacant spaces between structures, at the interstitial spaces between a road and an empty lot, under pedestrian bridges, or adjacent to a crumbling wall, street vendors have transformed otherwise useless spaces throughout the city – most no larger than a square meter – into productive sites for the marketing and consumption of goods.

One of the most significant ways vendors assert their claim to the city's marginal spaces is through a process of 'quiet encroachment' (Bayat, 2000: 545–9), in which they slowly normalize their presence into what might otherwise be a hostile terrain. This requires *continuous* and long-term occupation of a particular space (it is not uncommon, for instance, for street vendors to work on one spot for decades, and to be physically present on the same space on the side of the road for over twelve hours a day, seven days a week) and the establishment of habitual – if not always personal – relationships with women, men and children who live, work and shop in the area. In this way, vendors' long-term presence enables them to gather intimate details about the people around them. As I discuss below, this long-term contact with customers deeply informs the practice of consumption on the street.

By setting up small businesses in the sundry nooks and crannies of the built environment, street vendors, and the practices of consumption they are associated with, are inextricably linked with the city's geography and popular imaginary. To many people, street vendors symbolically represent Mumbai's vibrancy, dynamism and culture of enterprise. Vendors of foods such as the *vada pao*, sidewalk booksellers, clothes vendors and *paan*-sellers are considered to count among the city's landmarks. In this way, despite the seemingly non-modern visuality of this mode of exchange, street vendors and consumption are not quaint relics of an urban past that have persisted into the contemporary age, as some scholars have suggested,[4] but are in many ways markers of the city's unique modernity. However poor, vendors are independent entrepreneurs (indeed, they describe their own work as *danda*, or business) who also happen to regularly assert decidedly modern, rights-based claims to urban space. Moreover, street vendors are deeply interconnected with complex national and transnational flows of goods. Street vendors sell clothing, shoes and beauty accessories that have been produced for export, but have since found their way onto the street due to surplus production or manufacturing design errors. Once on the street, these items are consumed by a broad spectrum of the population, from slum residents with meager incomes to trend-conscious, rich youth. The street is also the primary site of the enormous daily trade in fruits and vegetables. Nearly 1000 metric tonnes of vegetables are purchased for household consumption daily from street vendors.[5]

The continued centrality of street vending in the economy and everyday life of Mumbai contradicts the urban teleology in which traditional markets are inevitably replaced by western-style shopping malls. For instance, Hannigan writes, in reference to east Asia, 'Jettisoning the traditional Asian department stores, street-level retail and night markets, Asian consumers are embracing western retail formats, specialty boutiques, [and] entertainment concepts.... Shopping malls, for example, have sprouted up everywhere, both in city enters and in the new suburbs' (1998: 178–9). In Mumbai, in spite of the explosion of shopping malls and other western-style retail sites in recent years, the street remains central to the city's consumptive sphere. In fact, if one goes by the claims of some residents and business associations, there has been an *increase* in the number of street vendors (and thus an increase in street consumption) since the late 1990s, when 'westernized' retail environments first arrived. The centrality of the street market in the everyday life of city residents is also evinced by the failed attempts by NGOs and residents' associations to 'educate' the public not to shop from informal street markets. Much to the frustration of these powerful groups, the public has failed to obey their desperate pleas to maintain a orderly city; for all but the most elite residents (who would nevertheless send their servants to shop on the street), the street continues to be a central site for the consumption of goods.

The continued centrality of the street market is further evinced in the areas close to the very malls whose presence was purported to transform the street consumption. For instance, in contrast to the empty stores and bored shop assistants at Inorbit Mall – Mumbai's largest – the hawker-lined street leading to the commuter train station nearest the mall throbs with life. On a lane barely wider than the width of a car, hundreds of women and men can be seen hovering over hawkers squatting on the ground, inspecting goods, bargaining and making large purchases. Repeated municipality raids and continuous police harassment of these vendors have failed to dislodge them from this area, attesting to their deep imbrication in the lives of nearby residents and commuters. The continued co-existence of two irreconcilable forms of consumption questions the assumption that prior forms of exchange are inevitably subsumed by exchange associated with global capital, thus urging a reconsideration of the relationship of everyday practice to large-scale changes in political economy.

On the street

Iqbal sells sandals and women's beauty accessories near a commuter train station in northwestern Mumbai. He is in his mid-thirties, clean-cut, and dresses in the same style (simple button-down shirt and trousers) as the male clerks and shop assistants who work in the area. For the past ten years he has hawked goods from display tables precariously perched between the slow crawl of exhaust-spewing cars and trucks and the rush of pedestrians. Having initially sold Indian-made goods, he has since switched to better-selling items that have recently started coming from China. The cheap imports from China have proven to be quite popular. At five rupees a piece (roughly US 10 cents), Iqbal's hairclips are affordable to most passersby. Potential customers, mostly young women, stop by his table throughout the day, casually inspect the items for sale, engage in small banter over the price, and if satisfied, purchase the goods. Between sales, nearby residents, passing commuters, shopowners, city workers, and even policemen stop by and make small talk.

Although located in a bustling commercial area through which tens of thousands of people pass daily, the interactions Iqbal has with customers are marked by an intimacy acquired over daily contact. After working at the same spot daily for nearly a decade, he is keenly aware, for instance, of the financial limitations of his customers, most of whom are working-class and, like him, live in humble one-room shanties in nearby slums. He also knows intimate details of the customers' personal lives: their consumption habits, family histories, and relations.

After customers walk out of earshot, these bits of information – gleaned from overheard cell phone conversations, unusual purchases, new clothing, or surprising companions – are later used to piece together stories peppered with wild speculation which, in turn, inform future encounters. For instance, once, after a customer departed from earshot, Iqbal turned to me and explained how he figured out, from overheard telephone conversations, that the woman had been purchasing large quantities of his hairclips to send to distant relatives in the United States.

The familiarity of the transactions, the extremely low pressure sales tactics and casual conversations reveal a level of intimacy that exceeds a social world defined solely by the exchange of goods. Moreover, street vendors such as Iqbal exhibit a sense of responsibility to the space in which they work, and to the women and men poorer than them who use this space to go to work, shop, or simply roam about. And thus it is with great pride that street vendors offer a certain amount of respect to people who might otherwise feel intimidated by upscale, air-conditioned, retail environments characterized by English-speaking sales clerks, exorbitant prices and unfamiliar styles.

Likewise, customers often know about, and gather information on, personal details about the street vendors' lives. It is common for customers to inquire about housing issues, family health, the latest trip to the native village, or an unexplained absence from the street. Because vendors' children often spend after-school time with their parents on the street, customers are also familiar with the vendors' children, and inquire about their education and health. Moreover, customers and other passersby regularly inquire about the general goings-on in the neighborhood, as vendors are known to be reliable sources on events such as thefts, car accidents and government development plans for the area.

Says Iqbal, explaining the social significance of his small stall, 'Everyone comes here; they can't afford to shop in a store. This is a real public space [*Yeh to ekdum public space hai*].'⁶ This comment is in part addressed at the new form of upper class activism in Mumbai, consisting of neighborhood associations and city-wide NGOs such as CitiSpace (all locally referred to as 'citizens' groups'), that seek to 'take back' the city's open spaces from the encroaching poor. While activists in these organizations claim to be against all forms of encroachment, their efforts, and their palpable rage, is overwhelmingly directed at street vendors such as Iqbal. By saying this is a 'real public space', Iqbal links the everyday practice of street consumption to a larger politics of space and urban development. For, while these organizations, concerned with the disorderly condition of Mumbai's streets and sidewalks employ the term 'public space' to denote a space restricted to the bourgeois public, and often inimical to the working poor, Iqbal's 'public space' refers to an urban space open to street vendors and their slum-dwelling customers. In this way, street consumption as well is reconfigured as a lens through which democratic visions for the city can be envisioned.

Iqbal's idea of a 'public space' inclusive of both street vendors and working-class consumers is self-consciously opposed to elite claims that public consumption on the street constitutes a 'nuisance.' For the elite NGOs who claim to clean up Mumbai's public spaces by eradicating street vendors, the street market is imagined in terms of the stereotypical *bazaar*, a space of ambiguity, chaos, lawlessness and potential danger (Chakrabarty, 2002). In turn, street vendors are aware of the stereotypes of the street market, and actively distance themselves from them. Says one vendor, 'Hawkers must do business with respect. I don't call out to customers, or harass them.' Tilting his head in pantomime of a dishonest-looking vendor, he mimics: 'Come here, it's cheap.' He continues, back to seriousness: 'We don't like to haggle; we know the customers and they know us. It's not good to say certain things.' In explicitly parodying the well-worn stereotypes of the chaotic *bazaar*, this vendor distances himself from it, and in doing so establishes a positive image of street markets that fits in with claims of an orderly, rather than chaotic, city.

Indeed, the fact that elite discourses of an orderly city have relied upon the exclusion of street vendors has not precluded vendors' own desires for an orderly space of consumption. At times, this desire for order informs their encounters with customers and other people in the marketplace. For instance, vendors often reprimand careless customers for littering and educate people to keep the surrounding area clean. Their ideas of an orderly urban space are also demonstrated in comments they make regarding the inappropriate public conduct of aggressive or, in their mind, unworthy, beggars, as well as the behavior of city officials and, most importantly, other vendors. Indeed, long-term street vendors lament the lack of responsibility newcomers have toward the spaces in which they work and the other people who occupy them. Says one vendor, 'Hawkers who have worked for years sit next to the building, away from the road and the footpath, while the others set up their business in the middle of the road, creating obstructions for people.' Moreover, vendors of pirated VCDs and semi-pornographic films are seen by older vendors such as Iqbal as irresponsible youth who sacrifice their responsibility towards public space in favor of quick profits. In this way, vendors see the street as a moral space which informs how they relate to discourses of the city more powerful than their own, as well as to other vendors whom they see as 'disordering' the marketplace. Indeed, as I discuss below, the street market as moral space is the most powerful trope through which vendors understand the new retail formats entering the city.

In the mall's shadow

One of the city's largest 'informal' (in that it is not officially recognized by the state) vegetable markets is located on a busy road emanating from the Kandivali commuter station, in northwestern Mumbai. This market, consisting of one hundred and fifty unlicensed vendors who sit adjacent to the street, services tens of thousands of people, most of whom live in the nearby slums and squatter settlements. A wide variety of people shop here, ranging from homemakers, procurers for small restaurants, informal shop owners, independent caterers and other, smaller-scale, mobile vendors who hawk their goods in poorer areas.

In 2005, a massive western-style supermarket called Big Bazaar opened on this road, on the site of a closed-down factory. In its imposing visuality, Big Bazaar stands for the new aesthetic of consumption representative of the 'global' economy; it is a place that displays the fruits, vegetables and household items usually sold on the street (albeit at greater cost and lesser quality, as street vendors are proud to say) within a hushed, clean and air-conditioned environment. Big Bazaar also represents the new form of consumption that is marked by anonymous interactions between buyer and seller. This is a space structured around cosmopolitan aspirations, which eschews all that is associated with the street, such as bargaining, banter and informal arrangements between buyer and seller. In its place are the trappings of the rationalized international supermarket experience, such as the open display of items, English-language announcements of sales, bright signs announcing reduced prices and minimal interaction between employees and customers. In this way, consumption is reconfigured, at least on the surface, from a social act to something marked by the aura of comfort, efficiency and sophistication.

According to street vendors and street vendor union leaders in the area, shortly after the 2005 opening of this supermarket, the police and municipality conducted a series of violent actions against street vendors in the market's proximity. The repeated demolitions and confiscations of vendors' goods led to the street markets' total closure for three months, sparking well-founded rumors that the owners of Big Bazaar had paid the police and the municipality large bribes to carry out the demolitions. Since then, street vendors have returned to the area, although the fifteen people who had worked in the space immediately in front of the site were permanently evicted. Put in their place were ten, large concrete planters, guarded over by a bevy of private security guards.

Ramesh is one of the street vendors who works in the shadow of this new retail outlet. He has worked on this street for twelve years, and witnessed firsthand the violent actions taken against other vendors after Big Bazaar was built. Like other street vendors, his encounters with customers and other passersby are textured by a familiarity developed through daily interactions over many years. Ramesh's rich exchanges with customers include biting sarcasm, the use of a litany of kinship terms, ingenious word play, good-natured heckling, physical contact and, of course, bargaining. Like most vendors, Ramesh treats regular customers, most of whom are self-employed women, with great respect, providing discounts and other services. He also gives away large amounts of vegetables for free, an act he describes as 'public service' ['public *seva*']. In turn, these women trust Ramesh enough to leave their heavy purchases with him while they walk down the road to other vendors. Customers and other passersby linger at his stall, chat, and discuss business. Much to his discomfort, they even joke about representing the police or municipality, asking for bribes, and mimicking the speech and body language of a corrupt official.

One afternoon, two young women dressed in expensive looking clothing began to vigorously bargain with Ramesh over the price of green onions. They continued the argument for over five minutes. Explaining that the market price at that time of the year was already quite low, Ramesh nevertheless relented, offering what he felt was a generous discount. Yet the two women refused the offer rudely and turned away, expecting him to call out after them with an even lower offer. Just as they turned around, Ramesh shouted out, with bitter sarcasm, 'Go to Big Bazaar, you'll get it cheaper there!'

Although Ramesh had never been inside Big Bazaar, the store symbol- ically looms large in his, and other street vendors', imagination. As his comment shows, Ramesh knows that the store stands for a different prac- tice of consumption; at Big Bazaar, there is no need to understand the social rules of a bargaining exchange – indeed, there is no need to respect any social obligation at all. It is in this vein too that street vendors good- naturedly heckle their regular customers who happen to carry Big Bazaar plastic bags. On various occasions, on seeing the Big Bazaar logo, ven- dors say, 'What, you went to Big Bazaar?' subtley hinting at the potential affront this may cause. They often pass this comment on occasions when they know very well that the customer *did not* go to Big Bazaar, but that, as is often the case, she is using the bag to carry vegetables purchased from street vendors observing a city-wide ban on plastic bags.

These articulations of the larger social meaning of Big Bazaar are informed by street vendors' awareness of alternative ways in which veg- etables are sold, often expressed through the English word 'showroom.' For vegetable vendors, the 'showroom' signifies a sterile store in which, as one street vendor explained, 'stale, refrigerated, vegetables are sold by a man sitting behind a computer,' and represents the way vegetables are sold in places like Singapore or the United States. In one sense, the idea of the showroom represents street vendors' internalization of a hierarchy of marketplaces that places street vending 'behind' supermarket-based vending. However, at the same time, although the financial and polit- ical power of these big stores is well known, vendors nevertheless refer to the 'showroom' as an example of a failed venture, the idea being that few people would want to buy vegetables from a man sitting behind a computer.[7] In these rich moments of interaction, we can see how the different market environments of the 'showroom,' the supermarket and the shopping mall do not simply negate the practices of exchange and consumption on the street but, in part, infuse them with new meanings.

In the mall

The 'showroom' of the street vendors' imagination stands for the new retail world of supermarkets and shopping malls, both relative new- comers to Mumbai's consumptive sphere. The popularity of these retail environments – characterized by an aesthetic radically different from that of the street market – has been read by some as signaling the ascen- dancy of 'new urban aesthetics' (Fernandes, 2004: 2420) for the city as a whole, which is resulting in the marginalization of the street as a site of consumption (Rajagopal, 2001). However, attention to the uses to which the malls are put, and to the particular attractions of the mall space to visitors, contradicts the assumption that the mall heralds a fundamental transformation of consumption practices for Mumbai residents.

The 1999 opening of Crossroads, Mumbai's first American-style shopping mall, was met with euphoric predictions of the future transformation of consumption practices, which were based in part on the huge volume of mall visitors. Initial crowds were so large that mall operators instituted a door policy that restricted entry to only those carrying a credit card or a mobile phone. However, it soon became clear that even those brandishing money or cell phones visited the mall primarily in order to witness the novelty of the space – the large atrium, central air-conditioning, cosmopolitan atmosphere, unique sense of order, and shops full of previously hard-to-obtain foreign brands – rather than to purchase goods. Over time, the mall lost its appeal to many of its early visitors, with some attributing the thin crowds to the clean-up of a nearby park.[8] In retrospect, it appears that middle- and upper-class south Mumbai residents, eager for an open space to congregate, initially appropriated the mall as a public space, but only until an alternative was made available. Needless to say, Crossroads has since discontinued its redundant door policy and, in 2006, widely considered a disappointment, the mall was sold to a company with plans for a new project on the site (*Times of India*, 10 April, 2006).

The history of Crossroads reveals how the function of shopping malls exceeds the plans of architects and the rhetoric of mall operators. While both proponents and critics of malls see this new retail environment primarily as a site defined by the exchange of goods, this is not the primary way mall visitors see and use the space. As a number of scholars have shown, despite being designed for maximum consumption, and equipped with rigorous surveillance to that effect, shopping malls still do not 'succeed in "managing" either the total spectacle (which includes what people do with what they [the malls] provide) or the responses it provokes (and may include)' (Morris, 1988: 195–6).[9] The diversity of ways people make meaning and derive pleasure from malls complicate the assumption that these new spaces of consumption will necessarily revolutionize consumption practices.

In India, the significance of shopping malls is inseparable from recent changes in the meaning of consumption. Before economic liberalization in the early 1990s, socialist-inspired, post-colonial development policies which favored domestic production over imports meant that, even for those with the means, consumption possibilities were highly restricted. As purported 'palaces' of consumption, shopping malls, supermarkets, and large showrooms with their impressive plate-glass facades (Phadke, 2005a) are thus representative of a larger reconfiguration of the meaning of consumption from a 'notion of guilt' to a practice 'sanctified' as 'an index to [national] progress' (Varma, 1998: 175). In this way, the contemporary euphoria over shopping malls is in part a product of the psychic scars pre-liberalization economic policies left on the urban middle-class, who are now offered the 'promise of the dream of immediate gratification' (Mazzarella, 2003: 91).

However, much to the growing concern of mall developers and operators, people appear content to merely consume the spectacle of the malls, rather than the objects for sale.[10] For most people who visit the malls, their attraction does not lie in the items for sale – most of which, as many people would point out, can be found on the street for much cheaper – but for the other pleasures the space offers. Instead of consuming economically, most people 'consume' the place visually and spatially – often preferring to come to sit in the open, clean and air-conditioned expanses of the atria, to walk around the multiple levels of shops, and to ride up and down the escalators. Whatever few purchases are made take place in the food court, by far the malls' most vibrant space of consumption.

The mall also represents a novel 'public' space, albeit to the privileged few. For the small percentage of the city's population with the cultural capital, or courage, to enter its rarified environs, the mall is a 'safe free "public" social space – a way to meet and interact with others' (Jacobs, 1984: 16), albeit within strict parameters laid out by the mall management (see also Miller *et al.*, 1998). For instance, in recent years Mumbai's malls and other new retail environments have 'approximate[d] a "new" private space for [high class] women' (Phadke, 2005a: 47–8), thus enlarging the possibilities for 'going out' in the city (see also Miller *et al.*, 1998: 26). Moreover, while it is an unabashedly elite space of consumption that 'masquerade[s] as a public space' (Phadke, 2005a: 50), the mall does allow for the possibility of appropriation by a non-consuming public. Because the cosmopolitan built environment of the mall is seen to allow a different morality of public space,[11] Mumbai's malls are considered safe spaces for young couples to cuddle, hold hands and kiss – activities not possible in other public spaces in the city.

For young people and even for the poor, the social life of the mall exceeds its role as a site of consumption. Scholars of US shopping malls have noted how youth, often in circumvention of mall operators, derive tremendous pleasure from the space that is not derived from consumption. Despite the fact that in the US, as in India, '[s]hoppers, especially young ones, are tightly regulated in terms of what they may or may not do' (Hannigan, 1998: 82), researchers have documented how young people nevertheless engage in a diversity of activities for which malls were not designed. As Elizabeth Chin notes in her study of preteen, African–American girls in New Haven, Connecticut:

> This was *their* mall: a large, open, interesting, exciting space, full of cute boys, though dotted with inconvenient security guards and disapproving grownups ... They were not there only or even primarily to shop, but to explore, to go 'boy huntin' as Natalia said and to generate a safe yet thrilling excitement (Chin, 2001: 109)

In Mumbai, as in the New Haven malls of Chin's study, the carnivalesque space of the mall can also, at least momentarily, allow for the 'play' of identity and subjectivity not available elsewhere. Whereas the mall environment is alienating to large sections of Mumbai's poor – most of whom would feel too intimidated to even walk through the front entrance – it does not mean that the poor do not enter its rarified premises to avail of the pleasures offered within. According to one report, slum residents constitute a significant percentage of mall visitors, for whom the malls are a 'place to just stand and gape, a dazzling place filled with moving staircases, smoking girls, comical lingerie and truly entertaining price tags' (Ganesan, 2005). As one newspaper writes,

> Nineteen-year-old Yousuf M, a resident of Sonapur slums in Bhandup, waits for friends outside R Mall in Mulund. They are regular visitors, but have never shopped there. "We don't have that much money," says Yusuf [sic], "Every weekend, we just take a bus to R Mall or walk it to Nirmal Lifestyle ... We hang around for two-three hours. It's absolutely free" (Purohit, 2006).

And finally, the space of the mall offers the promise of cosmopolitanism. As discussed above, the postcolonial history of consumption and the legacy of memories of denied gratification it left (cf. Varma, 1998 and Mazzarella, 2003) informs the meanings associated with dazzling retail environments such as shopping malls. To many, the mall also offers the hope of participation in a global modernity that they felt had been long denied as a possibility *within* India. As a slum resident and frequent visitor to one of Mumbai's largest malls says, bringing his visiting relatives from a rural area to the mall was essential because '[now] we've shown them Dubai' (Ganesan, 2005). Indeed, mall visitors often say that they come to malls because their 'international' feel reminds them of relatives' stories of Singapore and Gulf countries, whose shopping paradises have, by now, achieved mythic status in the eyes of many Mumbai residents. While scholars have dismissed such affective responses to shopping malls as a product of a strategically planned landscape in which 'designers manufacture the illusion that something else other than mere shopping in [*sic*] is going on' (Goss, 1993: 19), it is this very 'illusion' which informs the reality of people's experiences of the spaces, which in turn has very much to do with the reality of the way shopping malls function within the consumptive sphere of the city at large.

As these examples show, the ways in which people inhabit built environments such as shopping malls are far more complex than what is seemingly embedded in their physical design, calling into question theoretical models that infer larger social meaning from the ideologies embedded in built spaces. The point here is that people come to the mall to participate in and be a part of the new spectacle it offers, but not to actually participate in the form of consumption it supposedly represents. Like the appropriation of Crossroads as a much needed open space by the middle classes, the use of the mall as a means of participating in a much yearned-for global modernity rather than of shopping far exceeds the intentions of its designers, and most importantly, calls into question the revolutionizing potential of these sites of consumption. Indeed, rather than triggering a revolution in consumption practices in the city, it appears that at the moment, the malls have been incorporated into other ways of enjoying spectacle and, in a way, into the already existing social practices of consumption and leisure in the city.

The incorporation of shopping malls into other practices of consumption is no more apparent than on the streets, sidewalks and lanes emanating from the malls. While mall operators have considerable power to remove unlicensed street vendors from their immediate surroundings, street vendors of food and other items nevertheless continue to do a brisk business outside malls, where they service visitors and mall staff alike. Street vendors selling snacks outside Crossroads, for instance, have created a vibrant market environment that is absent within the mall's premises. In fact, some street vendors claim that their business was greatest when Crossroads mall was at its *most* popular. As one street vendor is quoted as saying, 'When this mall opened five-six years back, people would come just to see it. The crowd outside was more than inside . . . this curiosity lasted for around three-four years. Then our boom ended' (Purohit, 2006).

Conclusion

Due, in part, to the successful lobbying efforts of business groups and transnational consultancy firms, shopping malls have come to represent in Mumbai what it means to be a 'world class' city along the lines of Shanghai or Singapore. Despite the fact that from a planning standpoint malls are myopic endeavors that represent skewed development priorities, their mark of globality gives them a certain sense of legitimacy. This, in turn, enables mall developers to assert influence on the city, which includes, in certain instances, the reconfiguring of its visual aesthetic and of practices of everyday consumption.

The question remains, however, of how to understand the effect of the changing political economy, of which malls are a part, on the everyday experiences and social practices of the city, without drawing a one-to-one relationship between the two. The experience of malls in Mumbai has shown that they are hardly the 'bridgeheads of an all-conquering capitalism' (Miller *et al.*, 1998: 24) that both their proponents and critics make them out to be; there is little evidence that the street is being abandoned for the mall. As I have tried to show in this chapter, as in Britain (and unlike in the US), few people in Mumbai use the mall as a regular place to shop, and those who do, do so irregularly (Miller *et al.*, 1998: 29). We should be wary of assuming that the mere existence of shopping malls and other retail spaces 'carefully contrived to differentiate [themselves] from the perceived ills of the contemporary city and the alleged disorder of its fearful streets' (Jackson, 1998: 178) will, for instance, correspond to an end to such disorder and the remaking of the streets in the image of the mall.

Indeed, an understanding of the effects of a changing political economy on public consumption practices best emerges out of an investigation of the continuities between apparently radically different market environments, requiring a focused examination of the lives and meanings of those who inhabit them. Perhaps surprisingly for scholars interested in discrete sites of consumption, an understanding of the meaning and function of the shopping mall necessitates a study of other sites of consumption as well – here, of consumption on the *street*, the mall's purported Other. A methodology interested in large-scale change in consumption practices would therefore necessitate a multi-sited approach that questions, rather than assumes, the revolutionizing capabilities of shopping malls in the very design of its study, and remains open to the possibility that changes in markets' visual aesthetics do not necessarily correspond with changes in practices of consumption. As we have seen, the mall is less a metonymy for larger social changes than it is a rich site of practices that have emerged from the larger urban landscape of which it is a part.

Acknowledgements

I thank Dan Cook for his generous comments on this chapter. This chapter is based on research made possible with the support of the American Institute of Indian Studies.

Notes

1. In this chapter I refer to the city as 'Mumbai' simply because it is the official name of the city. In everyday speech, however, the city is commonly referred to as 'Bombay'.
2. For instance, Morris (1988), Miller *et al.* (1998) and Chin (1999) have demonstrated a complex understanding of the relationship between new retail environments and changing social practices. The work of Shilpa Phadke (2005a, b) is notable for its sensitivity to the complex relationships between built form, social meaning and everyday practice in Mumbai. Moreover, Kaviraj (1997) and Chakrabarty (2002) provide thorough historical and sociological analyses of everyday life on the street in urban India.
3. There is no comprehensive survey of the number of street vendors in Mumbai. Current estimates of the number of street vendors vary from 200,000 to 300,000.
4. For instance, Arjun Appadurai describes Mumbai's street markets as 'a late industrial repetition of the sort of medieval European markets described by Fernand Braudel' (2000: 642).
5. Abhinash Patel, Deputy Secretary of APMC (Agricultural Produce Marketing Committee), Vashi, New Mumbai, (personal communication, 2005).
6. I also discuss the significance of this comment in the larger politics of public space in Mumbai in Anjaria (2006).
7. In fact, for the most part, they are correct. Large, well-financed, corporations have failed to successfully sell produce in large-scale formats in Mumbai, and elsewhere in India. For instance, as a result of its inability to compete with street vendors, Big Bazaar has been forced to keep vegetables and other food items usually found on the street at only 30 per cent of the total goods for sale, in comparison to 70 per cent typical in other countries (Joshi, 2004).
8. I thank Ashwini Kamath, Ruchitra Hemani and Apeksha Gupta – undergraduate students at Kamla Raheja Vidyanidhi Institute for Architecture, Mumbai – for their insightful observations on Crossroads mall.
9. By contrast, many readings of malls stress the ideology embedded in their design. For instance, Goss writes, '[t]he contemporary flaneur cannot escape the imperative to consume: she or he cannot loiter in the mall unless implicitly invited to do so, and this generally only applies to the elderly' (1993: 35). According to Miller *et al.*, such readings tend to see malls as 'an instrumental

landscape, designed by the "captains of consciousness" to bend consumers to its will' (1998: 26).
10. According to a manager of Inorbit Mall at most 20% of all visitors make a purchase while inside (personal communication, 2006).
11. Similarly, in reference to the city's new international style chain-coffee shops, Shilpa Phadke (2005a: 51) writes that these spaces are read by customers to contain a different morality. The cafe's 'cosmopolitan' style, and the cuddling couples found within, are seen to indicate that 'these are global spaces with global rules, where one can leave behind the city and its parochial cultural contexts'.

References

Anjaria, J. (2006) 'Street Hawkers and Public Space in Mumbai,' *Economic and Political Weekly* 41(21): 2140–6.

Appadurai, A. (2000) 'Spectral Housing and Urban Cleansing: Notes on Millennial Mumbai,' *Public Culture* 12(3): 627–51.

Bayat, A. (2000) 'From "Dangerous Classes" to "Quiet Rebels": Politics of the Urban Subaltern in the Global South,' *International Sociology* 15(3): 533–57.

Bhowmik, S. (2000) 'A Raw Deal?,' *Seminar* 491, July.

Chakrabarty, D. (2002) 'Of Garbage, Modernity, and the Citizen's Gaze.' In D. Chakrabarty (ed.), *Habitations of Modernity: Essays in the Wake of Subaltern Studies*, pp. 65–79. Chicago: University of Chicago Press.

Chin, E. (2001) *Purchasing Power: Black Kids and American Consumer Culture.* Minneapolis: University of Minnesota Press.

Doshi, A. (2004) 'Mall mania,' *Business India*, 1 January.

Fernandes, L. (2004) 'The Politics of Forgetting: Class politics, State Power and the Restructuring of Urban Space in India,' *Urban Studies* 41(12): 2415–30.

Ganesan, S. (2005) 'Look Who's in the Mall', *Times of India*, 6 November.

Goss, J. (1993) 'The Magic of the Mall: An Analysis of Form, Function, and Meaning in the Contemporary Retail Built Environment,' *Annals of the Association of American Geographers* 83(1): 18–47.

Hannigan, J. (1998) *Fantasy City: Pleasure and Profit in the Postmodern Metropolis.* London: Routledge.

Jackson, P. (1998) 'Domesticating the Street: The Contested Spaces of the High Street and the Mall,' in N. Fyfe (ed.), *Images of the Street: Planning, Identity and Control in Public Space*, pp. 176–91. London: Routledge.

Jacobs, J. (1984) *The Mall: An Attempted Escape from Everyday Life.* Prospect Heights, IL: Waveland Press.

Johnson, J. and Merchant, K. (2005) 'India opens its doors to the west's supermarkets,' *Financial Times*, 10 July.

Joshi, S. (2004) 'The Issue of Retail Formats,' *The Hindu Business Line.* 28 October.

Kaviraj, Sudipta. 1997 'Filth and the Public Sphere: Concepts and practices about space in Calcutta,' *In Public Culture* 10(1): 83–113.

Mazzarella, W. (2003) *Shoveling Smoke: Advertising and Globalization in Contemporary India.* New Delhi: Oxford University Press.

Miller, D., Jackson, P., Thrift, N., Holbrook, B. and Rowlands, M. (1998) *Shopping, Place and Identity.* London: Routledge.

Morris, M. (1988) 'Things To Do with Shopping Malls,' in S. Sheridan (ed.), *Grafts: Feminist Cultural Criticism*, pp. 193–226. London: Verso.

Phadke, S. (2005a) 'Gender Maps: Glass Barriers,' *Architecture: Time, Space & People* (December): 50–1.

——. (2005b) '"You can be lonely in a crowd": The production of safety in Mumbai', *Indian Journal of Gender Studies*. 12(1): 41–62.

Purohit, J. (2006) 'Malls and their ripple effect,' *Mid Day*, 9 April.

Rajagopal, A. (2001) 'The Violence of Commodity Aesthetics: Hawkers, demolition raids, and a new regime of consumption,' *Social Text* 19(3), 91–113.

Times of India. (2003) 'From Mills to Malls, the Sky Is the Limit,' 24 November.

Times of India. (2006) 'Pantaloon buys India's 1st mall for Rs. 260 cr,' 10 April.

Varma, P. (1998) *The Great Indian Middle Class*. New Delhi: Penguin.

Tata Institute of Social Sciences and YUVA, *Census Survey of Hawkers on BMC Lands*, 1998.

11

'They Come, and They Are Happy': A Gender Topography of Consumer Space in Dubai

Anette Baldauf
University of Applied Arts Vienna

In 2004, several US-American newspapers published articles praising Saudi Arabia for a step towards women's liberation. In Riyadh, a shopping center had dedicated an entire floor to women's-only usage; women could take off their veils and shop without fear of interruption by male intruders. The *Los Angeles Times*, the *Washington Post* and the *Seattle Times* were unanimous in their approval of the Lady's Kingdom shopping center. According to their accounts, it was a 'liberated zone' in the midst of a land, 'where women are kept under wraps by packs of cane-wielding religious police.' The *Los Angeles Times* article quoted the manager of a Giorgio Armani store, who reported that women storm the place, 'they come, they take their "abayas" off, and they're happy' (Stack, 2004).

Judging from such writing, these US newspapers interpreted the women's-only shopping area as a foreign and highly exotic phenomenon. The reports were able to combine two widespread clusters of social categorizations – that of a consumption-oriented, materialist woman and that of an oppressive, patriarchal Arabic society. As a subtle thesis underlying these constructions, they also recited popular ideas about the market's liberating power, suggesting that women's participation in the consumer market enhances women's participation in society, and hence, their happiness.

Contrary to these accounts, women's-only consumer spaces are not unusual on the Arabic peninsula, but their success is often limited. Five years before the introduction of Lady's Kingdom in Riyadh, a women's-only shopping center was introduced in Abu Dhabi, the capital of the United Arabic Emirates. A local development firm introduced the space as a prototype for additional centers. If the project succeeded, they announced, thirteen additional centers in various Emirate cities would follow (Khalili, 1999). The She Zone in Abu Dhabi comprised 33 stores, a mosque, a business center, coffee shops, a beauty and health center, a cinema and a children's party space. The administration excluded males older than ten from the center. Shop assistants and security guards were all female and no surveillance cameras were allowed inside the center. Under these conditions, the center was able to provide women with the privacy and freedom to remove their black abaya robes and scarves without violating the tradition of covering one's entire body, when leaving the private home. As the president of She Zone developer Mark Link Property Management explained to the *Middle East* newspaper, 'Even in the US ... you have women's gyms and even cigar clubs. It's all about specialization' (Thomas, 2000: 27–8).

In Western history, the discursive association of consumerism and femininity has a long and resilient tradition. A wide range of voices, from popular market analysts to social scientists, have insisted on an innate link between these two concepts. As early as in the mid nineteenth century, when the first department stores were introduced, the public debate on consumerism focused on the danger as well as the potential of this relationship (Bowlby, 1985; McRobbie, 1997; Nava, 1997). According to popular accounts of the time, the hormonal turbulence which middle class women experienced on a regular basis caused an overall malleability and irrationality in the female mind, and destabilized her mental health, as well as her shopping habits (Abelson, 1989). In the late nineteenth century, social scientists also argued that women's affinity for consumption was stimulated by middle class women's duty to represent, or embody, the status of the family. In 1902, Thorstein Veblen (1953) defined women's conspicuous consumption less as an issue of individual irrationality than one of collective labor.

Today, many of the popular arguments about women's consumerism build on these two trajectories and assert the impact of manipulation and representation. At the same time, feminist studies associate women's consumptive practices with processes of identification and signification. They are interested in reconstructing the cycles of production and consumption in everyday life. While these approaches also guided the 2004 US newspaper reports on the women's shopping spaces in the Middle East, processes of othering and orientalism added another layer onto the already complex discursive convolute: that is, these reports attributed a uniqueness in constellation to a geographic environment which was then signed by a radical otherness. In the postcolonial world, the constructed difference between the West and the Rest is often projected onto women's bodies. In this context, women have become powerful symbols of identity, as well as embodiments of visions of society and the nation; the status of women is considered an indication of a nation's position between modernism and traditionalism. According to Lila Abu-Lughod and Deniz Kandiyoti, this is why the negotiation of women's issues is part of an ideological terrain 'where broader notions of cultural authenticity and integrity are debated and where women's appropriate place and conduct may be made to serve as boundary marker' (Kandiyoti, 1992: 246; Abu-Lughod, 1998: 3).

Inside the women's center

In July 2003, conceptual artist Dorit Margreiter and I flew to United Arabic Emirates to visit the She Zone. In contrast to the impression conveyed by the media's celebration of women's-only spaces, finding it turned out to be quite difficult. No sign identified the center, and none of the male passers-by had heard of it. Eventually a young woman pointed out a generic high-rise building, with a polished glass facade. At the building's north end, a gaudy entrance broke the complex' generic surface. The words 'All Women's Center' and 'Not Allowed for Men' were written

Figure 11.1 Entrance to the She Zone, Abu Dhabi [photo by Anette Baldauf 2003]

in English and Arabic letters above the doors. Perhaps as an attempt to indicate 'womanhood' by alluding to a sea of roses, the ostentatiously large doors were painted pink and purple. The building's only functional entrance was located at the back of the complex, where a pair of swinging glass doors, a white triangular roof, and two prominent Greek columns invited female visitors into this temple of consumerism.

Inside, a narrow passageway furnished with glass showcases led into a circular, brightly lit atrium of niches, corners and counters. The conventional hardware of a shopping center was in place – escalators, shop-windows, fitting rooms, cashier's kiosks. But something about the center's software was strange and confusing – it was uncannily empty. There were no female crowds shopping either contentedly or intensely. In fact, half of the stores were closed and cleared. Most of them looked like abandoned exhibition spaces. With no goods on display, what remained was the bare technology of presentation – empty shrines, shelves, vitrines, cabinets, mirrors.

Some of the abandoned stores seemed to have been transformed from sacred markets into profane living spaces. At the bridal store, a wedding dress was still on display next to a rack of wet laundry. In the basement playground area, a carousel was still spinning, filling the air with light melodies, long after the departure of the last mother and child. On the first floor, next to the entrance, the window of one jewelry store was filled with featureless, unadorned mannequin heads. One frustrated saleswoman we spoke to claimed that bad management was to blame for the neglected state of the She Zone. The owner, she argued, had no experience managing a place like this; the center was too expensive, not attractive enough and the anticipated crowd of female shoppers just never arrived. When we inquired at the management office on the top floor of the center, a female manager shrugged her shoulders and told us that the She Zone would be closed the next day, due to a lack of business. 'Women don't want to shop in women's-only places,' she explained, before rushing off to welcome a group of investors who were eager to inspect the property as a redevelopment prospect.

Imaginary elsewheres

The failure of the She Zone raises questions about the relationship between gender and shopping, as well as the status of women's-only places in the context of contemporary global economies. It also provides a unique vantage point from which to consider the city of Dubai: Situated midway between the Far East and Europe on the east-west trading

Figure 11.2 Sahara Center in Sharjah, Food Court [photo by Anette Baldauf 2003]

routes and between Africa and the former Soviet Union on the north-south axis, Dubai has become the Arabian Gulf's main trading center and one of the major re-export centers of the world. The city is now regarded as a significant node in the networks of the global economy; it is championed as a laboratory for urban formations and a showplace of future retail spaces (Ali Parsa and Ramin Keivani, 2002).

In 2004, Dubai's 27 upscale shopping malls created a commercial infrastructure that attracted locals and tourists from the region and abroad. Nearly all of the shopping malls displayed an affinity for theming and scenography: The Wafi Center was located in three glass pyramids; the Hyatt's Galleria shopping mall was organized around an ice skating ring; Lamcy Plaza displayed a replica of the Tower Of London; Hamarain Centre was presented as a French mall, and Mercato as a Venetian market. All of these places are the product of an idiosyncratic space-making strategy: In a first phase, they are dissociated from their immediate spatial and cultural environment; a geographic rupture or break is asserted. Building upon this initial de-territorialization, references to architecture and design traditions of foreign, mostly exoticized, places are introduced; they now assert the place's relationship to an imaginary setting.

Culturally pessimistic sociologists, architects and urban planners have often read Dubai's themed shopping malls as the apotheosis of the erosion of place in the context of neoliberal globalization. According to this argument, Dubai's shopping malls resemble a textbook manifestation of what Rem Koolhaas (2002) calls junkspace: 'If space-junk is the human debris that litters the universe, junk-space is the residue mankind leaves on the planet.' Junkspace, he argues in a percussive accumulation of metaphors, is 'additive, layered and lightweight, not articulated in different parts but subdivided, quartered the way a carcass is torn apart – individual chunks severed from a universal condition.' The composition of chunks, Koolhaas stresses, signals a provisional existence; it asserts the space's temporary nature, an expectance of demolition, due any time now. In contrast to architecture which consists of a megastructure and various subsystems, which creates an overall cohesion, junkspace, Koolhaas asserts, consists of 'subsystems only, without superstructure, orphaned particles in search of framework or pattern' (Koolhaas, 2002: 175–90). According to his critique, 'modernization's fall-out' is ugly, ephemeral, and eventually, meaningless. Identifying with this lament, Frederic Jameson suggests that Koolhaas' concept of junkspace and his own theory on the end of history derive from a shared theoretical premise. They both, he claims, define commodity fetishism as the major transitional force and source of transformations. 'The virus ascribed to junkspace is in fact the virus of shopping itself; which, like Disneyfication, gradually spreads like a toxic moss across the known universe,' concludes Jameson, in an essay entitled 'Future City' (Jameson, 2003: 65–79).

Gille Deleuze's writing on contemporary space departs from similar observations, but it reaches a fundamentally different conclusion. Investigating the features of space produced in cinema, Deleuze tries to grasp vacant and disconnected spatial formations, which have been put forth by non-rational links, and which can no longer be understood according to the principles of a particular determined space. In his analysis of these spatial formations, Deleuze uses the term 'any-space-whatever,' a phrase that was introduced by the anthropologist Pascal Augé (1995) in his description of places like subway station waiting rooms and airport terminals. In Augé's writing, the term designates anonymous and deeply de-personalized space, places which may be thought of as homogeneous and de-singularized, i.e. places much like those Koolhaas calls junkspace. Deleuze makes use of Augé's term in order to further elaborate on the spatial qualities of these transitional places, but in contrast to Augé, his concept of any-space-whatever asserts not the isolative but the connective quality of this space. In his writing, any-space-whatever is a mediating space in the transition between other spaces, or between chaos and order. It is composed of parts but this composition does not follow one determining order. The spatial composition can be broken down into its components and then reassembled in a new way, but the basic spatial constituency stays the same. Therefore, spatial variations are radically contingent. But while Koolhaas and Jameson dismiss this condition as ephemeral, and continue to mourn the loss of cohesion, Deleuze emphasizes the potential of this condition: 'It is a space of virtual conjunction, grasped as the pure locus of the possible,' Deleuze writes. 'What in fact manifests the instability, the heterogeneity, the absence of link of such space, is a richness in potentials or singularities which are, as it were, prior conditions of all actualisation, all determination' (Deleuze, 1988: 109).

You belong in the city

If the consumer landscape in Dubai is analyzed through Koolhaas' lens, which, from a god-like position, proclaims the death of modern architecture, then the city can only be seen as the zenith of junkspace. From such a vantage point, the provisional quality of the Dubai mallspaces tempts one to regard the city as architectural litter, and eventually, to dismiss it, both aesthetically and morally. In contrast, an analysis departing from Deleuze's premise supports an open-ended investigation into the various ways in which this spatial condition is actualized, and how it does or does not allow for transitions and transgressions. With such an approach, a central quality of Dubai's shopping malls becomes intelligible: The contingent composition of these spaces and the incomplete process of spatial and temporal separation allows visitors to gain some distance from the constraints of everyday life, and to formulate their own order in this partial, ever changing cosmos. Because of what Koolhaas calls the incoherent nature of the space, users are able to develop a dual state of mind, which Margaret Morse (1998), albeit in a different context, called 'distraction.' Under such conditions, Dubai's shopping spaces satisfy both the need to control women, and the shopper's desire to escape. In these simulated environments of Dubai, women and men find their own way to an imaginary elsewhere.

The delicate nature of such maneuvers is illustrated by one of Dubai's most popular malls, the Deira City Center. In contrast to other malls in Dubai, the theme of this mixed-use environment is subtle as well as daring: It aims, literally and symbolically, to represent the city's center. In fact, when tourists board the buses which read 'City Center,' they often expect to visit Dubai's historic city center, only to be discarded in front of the bright, gaudy entrance of this entertainment center: 'You Belong in the City' is written on the white walls of the passage leading into the mall. With more than 300 stores, restaurants and entertainment facilities, as well as an adjoining hotel, Deira City Center relies on a traditional mall layout; it is a generic, two-story big box complex with a bright atrium and two extended wings. According to the mall's press department, more than 60,000 people visit every day; and even though it opened in 1995 – an ancient era in the ever-booming city of Dubai – it continues to be one of the most popular places in the Emirates (Deira City Center website, 2006).

At the center's food court, three young women meet regularly for lunch. They're all in their mid-twenties, and during the week, they come to Deira because they work in or near the mall; on the weekends, the young women in their twenties come to shop and entertain themselves. 'We meet here every day,' the women laugh. 'Deira City Center is Dubai's city center,' explains Jana, who was born in Dubai to parents of Indian decent, while eating chicken curry: 'If you want to get to know Dubai, Deira City Center is the place to go.' Jana is wearing tight blue jeans with a yellow, long-sleeve t-shirt and sneakers, and she confesses that she likes to buy things – small things, she argues, because of her earnings as a sales person at one of the local retail stores. Meeting her friends here in the food court allows Jana to combine necessity with fun: She can eat lunch, meet friends and then shop here and there. At Deira, Jana says, 'you can spend hours people watching – men, women and children, locals and immigrants, young and old, everybody comes here. I love it.' Sipping on their Cokes, the women gaze at the people passing by; they talk about their own lives as much as they speculate about strangers. They watch guys. When I ask them if they use the mall to meet men, they all laugh, and nod. 'There is a lot of flirtation going on, from both sides,' says Jana. The girlfriends appreciate the mall for what might be described as an urban condition; they assert the center's diversity, density and social integration. 'Everybody meets here at the center,' they say. At the Deira City Center, in other words, everybody belongs to the city.

While Jana and her girlfriends eat lunch, a few doors away, two Emirate women who work at a tourist information center are enjoying a late breakfast at Starbucks. I introduce myself to Nada and Aisha, who are also in their early twenties, and ask if we can talk about their relationship to the mall. Both women nod politely. As they make room for me and ask if I would like to eat or drink something, I feel like I am visiting two young women in their living room. Deira City Center is not their favorite mall, they say. For them, Deira ranks far below places like the Wafi Center, where tasteful boutiques enrich the space with the aura of distinction. Too many different kinds of people shop at the City Center, and the presence of a supermarket adds a bad fish smell, they explain. Nonetheless, Nada and Aisha like Starbucks' convenience and cleanliness; it takes them to a generic elsewhere, a place without attributes.

In this place of utter indifference, Nada and Aisha lounge in oversized chairs, drink a cup of Moccachino, eat a pain au chocolat and discuss Nada's new Channel watch. Wearing a black abaya that covers most of her body, non-tinted sunglasses and a black and white Channel headscarf casually wrapped around her head, Nada confesses her weakness for the Channel brand. 'I was waiting for this watch to arrive in store for over six months ... And then, when I bought it I was wearing it to go to sleep as well. I was wearing sleeveless shirts just to show my watch,' remembers Nada. For her, Channel is fashionable without being trendy. It is inconspicuous and classic; in other words, it is French.

This 'Frenchness' has little to do with France – which they visited but didn't like it much; it is an imaginary landscape composed of images of fashion shows, magazines, and various furnishings of good taste. Along with the meaning of 'Frenchness,' Nada and Aisha discuss the positioning of the abaya's sleeves: it should allow a look at Nada's new watch, yet convey a respectable appearance. As the backdrop for this conversation poised between consumerism and tradition, The so-called third place of Starbucks allows Nada and Aisha to negotiate the semiotics of particular places and the appropriateness of gender behavior (Bhabha, 1994; Soja, 1996; Scerri, 2002: 56–67). Neither of them have heart of She Zone; when I explain, and ask if they would be interested in shopping at such a place, Nada stresses, 'I don't think that women would like to go there.'

From nineteenth-century arcades to contemporary shopping malls

When listening to the voices from Deira City Center, it can be argued that one of the central attractions of the shopping mall lies in its simulation of urban space (Crawford, 1992; Sorkin, 1992; Zukin, 1995; Soja, 2000). This experience includes watching an anonymous crowd passing by, strolling along through aisles and up escalators, merging into the crowd, being absorbed into a flow of strangers. In many respect, these experiences recall Walter Benjamin's writing about the nineteenth

Figure 11.3   Deira City Center in Dubai, Abaya store [photo by Anette Baldauf 2003]

century arcades in Paris, in which he muses upon life's intensified com-modification. In his analysis of these original temples of commodity capitalism, Benjamin introduces the figure of the flâneur, as a liter-ary motif as well as the embodiment of a particular urban experience. The figure allows him to further reflect upon the ambivalent pleasures of the modern city, modernity's visual regime, and the art of walk-ing and watching: 'An intoxication overcomes the person who tramps through the city streets for a long time without goal. With every step the going gains in force; the seduction of the stores, the bistros, the smiling women, grow ever narrower, ever more irresistible grows the magnetism of the next street-corner, a distant mass of foliage, a street-name,' wrote Benjamin in *The Arcades Project* (Benjamin, 1999: 417)

For Benjamin, the flâneur is undoubtedly a male character; in his writing women are the objects of consumption. 'Feminine fauna of the arcades: prostitutes, grisettes, old-hag shopkeepers, female street ven-dors, gloverfs, demoiselle. – This last was the name, around 1830, for incendiaries disguised as women,' he states, reflecting upon the whores' distinct attraction (Benjamin, 1999: 494). Like so many of his contempo-raries, Benjamin was fascinated by the 'asocial' woman – the women he considered a constitutive part of the commodity arrangement of the street and the arcade: 'Love for the prostitute is the apotheosis of empathy with the commodity,' he wrote, as he reasserted his ambivalent approach towards modernity (Benjamin, 1999: 511). But Benjamin's appraisal of the street girl was not shared, at least not officially, by most city officials.

In the nineteenth century, in many European cities, the mere presence of women in the streets was considered a threat to the dominant patriarchal order. Some cities tried to arrest moral decay by introducing curfews, which were meant to keep women from roaming the streets at night. But even though it endangered their reputations, women often chose to experience what Susanne Frank called the 'Abend-teuer Stadt' – or the 'adventures of the night' (Frank, 2003: 89–116). So what drove this undisguised attempt to make women disappear from the streets? Feminists like Elisabeth Wilson argue that the fear of the 'new woman,' who worked in a factory and enjoyed an independent, urban lifestyle, stimulated an eagerness to put women in their place (Wilson, 1991: 146–60).

That 'public women' were discredited and measurements of patriarchal installed, while an expanding consumer culture aggressively addressed middle class women in the city, is according to Wilson one of the big paradoxes of the nineteenth century (Wilson, 1991: 149). After the introduction of the department store in cities like Paris (1852) and New York (1857) bourgeois women visited stores without male company; they pursued their own, independent shopping experiences. With conveniences like childcare, custom tailoring or music centers, the department store dangled signs of luxury in the customer's proximity, and embedded the goods on display in collective imaginaries and popular narratives of longing and despair. According to Benjamin, the department store was the 'flâneur's final coup;' flanerie became a commodity, and the flâneur a paid bureaucrat, producing news, literature and advertisement for the state (Benjamin, 1983: 36). And out of the ashes of the flâneur arose, at least according to Anne Friedberg, the flaneuse, who, strolling along the aisles of the department store, enjoyed the intoxicating, visual resonance of the surroundings (Friedberg, 1993: 37).

But these new liberties came with a certain price. According to Andreas Huyssen (1986), the prevalent association of women with mass culture and, therefore, with manipulation, conformity and contamination that was established after the introduction of the department store also served a political purpose: At the beginning of the twentieth century, socialist and feminist movements rattled the doors of high culture, demanding cultural as well as political participation. Defining women as easy targets of consumer manipulation obviously contradicted the quest for rational and responsible citizens.

Nearly a century later, the introduction of the shopping mall once again refined the relationship between women and consumer spaces. According to Victor Gruen, who was a central protagonist in the development of shopping centers and malls, the shopping mall was designed with a female user in mind. In the mall, Gruen argued repeatedly, 'our little Mrs. Shopper' finds tranquility and comfort in a secure compound (Radio Reports, 1953). Gruen meant to build a place for women, whom he felt were confined to the suburbs without access to cars or public transportation and who felt, according to Gruen, that 'there was nothing to do in the suburbs' (NBC, 1955). Hence, Gruen took advantage of women's social and spatial isolation as well as the potentials of a non-referential modernism; during his lifetime he built 15 million square meters of consumer space that served as gigantic imaginary mobilization machines and transported visitors to other places, other times.

In-between realities and imaginary mobilization

Benjamin defined the arcade as a space in-between that connected the noisy street with the spectacular interior; these so called dream-houses of the collective, he argued, staged the art of phantasmagoria with its ostentatious presentation of light, glass and steel, was most seductively. The shopping mall continues to serve this function; it claims the space in-between realness and fantasy, here and there, now and then. In one of the first books written about shopping malls, William Severini Kowinski argued that malls were set apart from the rest of the world: 'It's meant to be its own special world with its own rules and realities' (Kowinski, 1985: 69). This marked de-territorialization allows for the making of a displaced and derealized space, a kind of elsewhere that is abstracted from the material surroundings and open to the wish images and fantastic projections of visitors. In conjunction with new technologies of control and surveillance, this ostentatiously different place makes it possible for the shoppers to transfer themselves into a different stage of mind, and this is the process, which Morse identifies as 'distraction.' In her analysis of non-spaces like freeways, malls and television, Morse defines distraction as 'related to the expression of two planes of languages represented simultaneously or alternately, the plan of the subject in a here-and-how, or *discourse*, and the plane of an absent or non-present or nonperson in another time, elsewhere, or story' (Morse, 1998: 100). In these episodes of distraction, shoppers explore new territory as much as they negotiate the conventional concepts of femininity and masculinity, local and global, space and place.

These insights allow for the formulation of a thesis on why the She Zone failed. In addition to the bad management addressed by some of the salespeople, the problems at the center may have been caused by the particularity of its place-making strategy and 'theming.' Judging from the accounts of the young female shoppers at the Deira City Center, the gender-specific assignment of the She Zone may have contradicted the needs of local mall shoppers – specifically the need to consume signs of urbanity, diversity and inclusion which, in turn, allow for the negotiation of meaningful themes and topoi. In the context of a study of a popular shopping street in Jiddah, Lisa Wynn describes how young Saudi women and men use consumer space to negate cultural norms imposed by religion, family and the state. In a society where unsupervised, private meetings among the sexes are forbidden and dangerous, Wynn argues, a shopping street can provide young people with opportunities to resist in small ways the older generation's control over courtship. While religious authorities, funded and sanctioned by the state but operated by semi-independent religious organizations, patrol the street, young men find creative ways to pursue young women in cars and follow them into the mall; they pass cards to women and urge them to call. Sometimes, Wynn argues, flirtations follow, occasionally leading to romantic involvements (Wynn, 1997: 30–1). Although in Dubai women's mobility is far less restricted than in Saudi Arabia, Ahmed Kanna suggests that Imarati youth use the shopping mall to negotiate strict family codes of dating and to escape the constraints of everyday life (Kanna, unpublished). Accordingly, the She Zone may have failed because its exclusive modus operandi negated what is more typically the shopping mall's most valuable feature: The simulation of a space that arouses the shopper's imagination, so that he or she may begin to negotiate issues that, outside the mall, seem all too familiar, and written in stone.

Social composition of the City of Dubai

The mall's ability to stimulate imaginary mobilization might be particularly precious in Dubai. Since the discovery of oil here in 1969, and then the introduction of the world's fifth largest Trade Free Zone in 1986, the Dubai Emirate has experienced unprecedented population growth. According to the 2003 census, 180,000 Imarati, or United Arab Emirate nationals, and 640,000 immigrants live in Dubai (Data Dubai, 2006). Just three years later, it is estimated that of the 1.5 million residents, as many

Figure 11.4   Entrance to the Trade Free Zone, Jebel Ali [photo by Anette Baldauf 2003]

as one million are immigrants, many of them unskilled workers and engineers from India, Pakistan, Sri Lanka and Bangladesh (Henderson and Clawson, 2006). *UAE Interact*, an Emirate news website, cites statistics that in 2005, one sixth of the people migrating from developing countries to industrialized states immigrated to the Emirates, making the UAE the world's most popular migration destination after the US, Italy and Spain (UAE Interact, 2006).

The Emirate provides these workers with a tax-exempt status and annual free flights to their home countries. In exchange, unions and politics are taboo, work contracts are temporary and naturalization is not an option. Overall, conditions for the workers are extremely harsh. On the occasion of the World Bank and IMF meeting in Dubai in 2003, *Human Rights News* (2003) reported on recurrent abuses of migrant workers in the UAE, including extended non-payment of wages, denial of proper medical care and terrible living conditions. Two years later, the publication reported that eight major workers' strikes had taken place in Dubai between May and December 2005 (Human Rights News, 2006). In Dubai immigrant jobs are often arranged by contractors, who sustain the workers' dependency upon them through loans provided for worker travel. In effect, the passports and residency permits of many construction workers, nannies and maids are confiscated upon arrival. (Fattah, 2006; Sabban, unpublished working paper). The design of this labor market, as Mike Davis writes, reminds us of the old system brought to the city of Dubai by its former colonial master, Great Britain (Davis, 2005).

In 2001, Dubai's GDP per capita income was estimated at approximately Dhs 69,000 (€15,000). This figure includes all social strata; immigrant worker are expected to earn an average of €120 per month (Mackenzie, 2003). The Emirate's immigration policy states that only workers whose salaries exceed €890 per month may bring their families to the Emirate. This regulation mainly applies to the approximately 50,000 Europeans and US-Americans living in the Emirate; the majority of male workers visit their families abroad only once a year. This immigration policy inscribes a distinct mark upon the city of Dubai. It is a city of guest workers, and an overwhelmingly male one: Since the majority of the workers recruited from India and Pakistan are male, Dubai's ratio of men to women is 3:1 (Data, Dubai 2006).

In short, Dubai is a She Zone, signed by rigid gender division and insurmountable social polarization. Accordingly, the shopping mall is expected to provide a landscape of integration and inclusion. With no other significant public space to enable collective assembly, Dubai residents meet to experience the city's diverse social diorama in the shopping mall. The failure of the She Zone suggests that shoppers expect consumer spaces to signal signs of inclusion and integration, while, at the same time, the spaces of production continue to uninhibitedly exhibit signs of exclusion and segregation. In Dubai's distinct manifestation of extreme capitalism, goods, finances and technologies circulate at high speed in and out of the Emirate's free zone, and tourists and business people cross international borders effortlessly. At the same time, rigid immigration laws regulate the local ethnoscape according to gender and nationality, creating a highly polarized social demography with an adjacent set of social interactions.

On a global scale, Dubai's immigration policy corresponds with the making of distinct she zones in the immigrants' homelands. While men from the Far East and Southeast Asia move to Dubai to work in the cities' trade free zone, their women stay behind, trying to finance their survival in Export Processing Zones. In the 1980s the government of India, the first home of more than thirty percent of Dubai's migrant workers, introduced a five-year tax cut for foreign investors to facilitate industrialization and the investment of foreign capital. Critics like Andrew Ross argue that this plan was a first step toward a refined global trading of goods, laborers and capital (Ross, 1997: 10–37). Since then, corporations operating in India and many developing nations have not only received generous tax cuts but have also taken advantage of a young female work force, who are cut off from family ties and often willing to sign gender specific contracts that are limited to a maximum of five years and prohibit marriage. This short-term female proletariat engages in manual labor six days a week, fourteen hours a day: wages are far below what is needed to cover living expenses; the work is tedious and monotonous (Klein, 1999: 195–230, Rosa-Luxemburg Stiftung, 2000).

Gender topography and globalization

The general basis of Orientalist thought, Edward Said wrote already in 1980, is 'an imaginative geography dividing the word into two unequal parts, the larger and 'different' one called the Orient, the other, also known as *our* world, called the Occident or the West' (Said, 1980: 488–92). It is just this Orientalist notion of the Middle East, which guides both the belief that the dominant relationship between the sexes is signed by

Figure 11.5 Inside the Trade Free Zone, Jebel Ali [photo by Anette Baldauf]

oppression and sexisms and the perception that under such conditions, a women's-only shopping mall is a liberating institution. A gender topography of Dubai's spaces of consumption and production suggests that in fact in this city it is the neoliberal orthodoxy, which inspires and supports the making of gender-segregated spaces. This insight casts a shadow across the fundamental premise of neoliberal ideologies: it questions the equation of the free market with liberal democracy, and it exposes some of the fundamentalist forces that drive the expansion of turbo-capitalism.

In his analysis of the relationship between globalism and tribalism, Benjamin Barber (1996) asserts that the regime of global capitalism operates with the same principles as fundamentalism. In an ultimately problematic reassertion of a dual geography, Benjamin argues that, like the ideology of Jihad, that of the so-called McWorld is based upon the dogma of global expansion, and an aim to erode the sovereignty of the nation state, citizenship and, finally, democracy. David Harvey presents a related, more complex argument: He defines neoliberalism as a concept of flexible accumulation through dispossession, and is thereby able to make intelligible the cannibalistic, predatory and fraudulent practices inherent to this incarnation of capitalism (Harvey, 2003: 148).

The city of Dubai, and particularly its consumer and production spaces, affirms the uneven development described by Harvey and a host of other critical geographers, all of whom are interested in the 'actually existing neo-liberalism' (Brenner and Theodore, 2002: 356–86). But Dubai also illustrates the deficiency of such gender-blind perspectives. The global division of labor, the transnationalization of jobs and human trafficking, and the rigorous expulsion of reproductive labor from the official labor market all correspond with rigid concepts of femininity and masculinity as well as gender geographies. In effect, feminist research has demonstrated how profoundly the regime of neoliberal capitalism, in spite of rhetoric claiming the contrary, depends upon a strict definition of women's bodies and their assignment to a limited array of places. Historically, Western spaces of consumption have always been associated with concepts of femininity; they have been related with imaginary mobilization as well as with manipulation, irrationality, even political exclusion. Perhaps it isn't surprising that Western perceptions of and projections upon the women's-only malls of the Middle East sought refuge in universalizing discourses about patriarchy, Islam and oppression. But in order to counter this tendency in media and research, it is essential to concretize, as Lila Abu-Lughod (1998: 22) advises: 'to specify, to particularize, and to ground in practice, place, class and time, the experiences of women and the dynamic of gender.'

References

Abelson E. S. (1989), *When Ladies Go A-Thieving. Middle-Class Shoplifters in the Victorian Department Store*. New York/Oxford: Oxford University Press.

Abu-Lughod L. (ed.) (1998), *Re-Making Women. Feminism and Modernity in the Middle East*. Princeton University Press: Princeton.

Augé M. (1995), *Non-Places: Introduction to an Anthropology of Supermodernity*. London & New York: Verso Books.

Barber B. (1996), *Jihad vs. McWorld: How Globalism and Tribalism Are Reshaping the World*. New York: Ballentine Books: New York.

Benjamin W. (1989), *Charles Baudelaire: A Lyric Poet in the Era of High Capitalism*. New York: Verso.

Benjamin W. (1999), *The Arcades Project* (Trans. Howard Eiland and Kevin McLaughlin). Harvard University Press: Cambridge.

Bhabha H. K. (1994), *The Location of Culture*. Routledge: London and New York.

Bowlby R. (1985), *Just Looking: Consumer Culture in Dreiser, Gissing, Zola*. London: Methuen.

Brenner N. and Theodore N. (2002), 'Cities and the geographies of "actually existing neoliberalism,"' *Antipode*, vol. 34, no. 3, 356–86.

Crawford M. (1992), 'The World in a Shopping Mall,' Sorkin M. (ed.), *Variations on a Theme Park. The New American City and the End of Public Space*. New York: Hill and Wang, 3–30.

Data Dubai (2007), The Ultimate Dubai Resource, 'Men Outnumber Women 3–1 in Dubai, Survey shows' (*Golf News*, 6 October, 2000), URL (consulted 18 January): http://www.datadubai.com/ratio.htm (10.10.2006).

Davis M. (2005), 'Sinister Paradise,' *TomDisplatch.com* (14 July 2005), URL (consulted 18 January 2007): http://www.tomdispatch.com/index.mhtml?pid= 5807

Deira City Center website (2006), @ http://www.deiracitycentre.com/dcc/default. asp (18 January 2007).

Deleuze G. (1988), *Cinema 2: The Time-Image*. Minneapolis: University of Minnesota Press.

Fattah H. M. (2006), 'Migrants' dreams dry up in Dubai desert,' *The New York Times* (26 March), URL (consulted 18 January 2007): http://www.iht.com/articles/ 2006/03/26/news/dubai.php

Frank S. (2003), *Stadtplanung im Geschlechterkampf. Stadt und Geschlecht in der Großstadtentwicklung des 19. und 20. Jahrhunderts*. Leske und Budrich: Opladen.

Friedberg A. (1993), *Window Shopping. Cinema and the Postmodern*. University of California Press: Berkeley.

Harvey D. (2003), *The New Imperialism*. Oxford University Press: Oxford.

Henderson S. and Clawson P. (2006), 'Gulf Elections: Small Steps and Mixed Results,' *The Washington Institute for Near East Policy*, 'PolicyWatch # 1175', URL (consulted 18 January 2007): http://www.thewashingtoninstitute.org/ templateC05.php?CID=2544

Human Rights Watch (2003), 'Dubai: Migrant Workers at Risk,' *Human Rights News*, 19 September, URL (18 January 2007): http://hrw.org/english/docs/2003/ 09/19/uae6388.htm

Human Rights News (2006), 'UEA: Address Abuse of Migrant Workers,' *Human Rights News*, 30 March URL (consulted 18 January 2007): http://hrw. org/english/docs/2006/03/28/uae13090.htm

Huyssen A. (1986), *After the Great Divide: Modernism, Mass Culture, Postmodernism (Theories of Representation and Difference)*. Indiana: Indiana University Press.

Jameson F. (2003), 'Future City,' *New Left Review* 21 (May/June), 65–79.

Kandiyoti D. (1992), 'Women, Islam, and the State: A Comparative Approach,' Juan R.I Cole (wd.), *Comparing Muslim Societies: Knowledge and the State in a World Civilization*, Ann Arbor: University of Michigan Press.

Kanna A. (2004), 'The "State Philosophical" in the "Land Without Philosophy": Shopping Malls, Interior Cities, and the Image of Utopia in Dubai' (unpublished presentation at the IASTE conference, Dubai).

Khalili L. (1999), ' "She Zone" shopping mall,' *The Iranian Times*, 12 May, (webversion), URL (consulted 18 January 2007): http://www.iranian.com/Times/1999/Mayb/Marvdasht/724front.html

Klein N. (1999), *No Logo. Taking Aim at the Brand Bullies*. New York: Picador.

Koolhaas R. (2002), 'Junkspace,' *October* 100 (Spring), 175–90.

Kowinski, William Severini (1985) *The Malling of America: An Inside Look at the Great Consumer Paradise*. New York: William Morrow.

Mackenzie Alistair (2003), *Dubai Explorer 2003*. Explorer Publishing: Dubai, UAE.

McRobbie A. (1997), 'Bridging the Gap: Feminism, Fashion and Consumption,' *Feminist Review* No. 55 (Spring), 73–89.

Morse M. (1998), *Virtualities. Television, Media Art and Cyberculture*. Indiana University Press: Bloomington.

Nava M. (1997), 'Modernity's Disavowal: Women, the City and the Department Store,' Pasi Falk, Colin Campbell (eds), *The Shopping Experience*. London: Sage, 56–91.

NBC (1955), Show October 9, Channel 4. Library of Congress Papers Victor Gruen, box 81.

Parsa A. and Keivani R. (2002), 'The Hormuz Corridor: Building a Cross-Border Region Between Iran and the UAE,' Sassen Saskia (ed.), *Global Networks. Linked Cities*. Routledge: New York, 183–208.

Radio Reports Inc. (1953), 'Victor Gruen Shows Model Shopping Center of the Future,' 25 January. Library of Congress Papers Victor Gruen box 71, Folder 2.

Rosa-Luxemburg Stiftung (ed.) (2000), *Globalisierung und Geschlecht. Anforderungen an feministische Perspektiven und Strategien* (Werkgespräch Berlin 21.722. Jänner 2000). Karl Dietz Verlag: Berlin.

Ross A. (1997), *No Sweat: Fashion, Free Trade, and the Rights of Garment Workers*. New York: Verso.

Sabban R. (n.d.), 'United Arab Emirates Migrant women in the United Arab Emirates. The case of female domestic workers,' *Gender Promotion Program*, Working Paper # 10. International Labor Office Geneva, URL (consulted 18 January 2007) http://www.ilo.org/public/english/employment/gems/download/ swmuae.pdf

Said E. (1980), 'Islam Through Western Eyes,' *The Nation*, vol. 16, no. 230 (26 April), 488–92.

Scerri A. (2002) 'Triple-Bottom-Line Capitalism and the 3rd Place,' *Arena Journal*, (New Series), no. 20, 56–67.

Soja E. (2000), *Postmetropolis. Critical Studies of Cities and Regions*. Oxford: Blackwell.

Soja E. (1996), *Third Space: Journeys to Los Angeles and Other Real-And-Imagined Spaces*. Oxford: Blackwell.

Sorkin M. (1992) (ed.), *Variations on a Theme Park*. New York: Hill and Wang.

Stack M. K. (2004), 'Saudi shopping mall offers women a bit of liberation,' *Los Angeles Times*, 15 June, 30.

Thomas K. (2000), 'Entering the She Zone,' *Middle East* 298 (February) (webversion), URL (consulted 18 January 2007): http://www.africasia.co.uk/archive/me/00_02/mebf0202.htm

UAE (2006), 'UAE is among top migrant destinations,' *UAE Interact*, 19 August, URL (consulted 18 January 2007): http://uaeinteract.com/news/default.asp?ID=205

Veblen T. (1953), *The Theory of the Leisure Class: An Economic Study of Institutions*. New York: Mentor Books.

Wilson E. (1995), 'The Rhetoric of Urban Space,' *New Left Review* 209, 146–60.

Wynn L. (1997), 'The Romance of Tahliyya Street: Youth Culture, Commodities and the Use of Public Space in Jiddah,' *Middle East Report* 204 (Winter), 30–1.

Zukin S. (1995), *The Cultures of Cities*. Blackwell: New York.

Index